JAMES G. FORLONG SERIES, NO. [illegible]

A CORPUS OF EARLY TIBETAN INSCRIPTIONS

H. E. RICHARDSON

ROYAL ASIATIC SOCIETY
1985

ISBN 0 94759300/4

Printed in England by
Stephen Austin and Sons Ltd, Hertford

CONTENTS

LIST OF PLATES

INTRODUCTION

The principal inscriptions in this collection can be dated between the years 764 and 840 A.D. They are arranged in groups, one for each of the three reigns to which they relate. They have all been published separately over a period of thirty years but by bringing them together in one volume a convenient source of reference will be provided for these important documents which illuminate many facets of early Tibetan history, society and language.

In order to round off the epigraphical material previous to the Manchu era which I was able to collect, some fragments of uncertain date, one inscription of the 11th century, and one of the 15th have been included in an additional section.

The purpose of the major inscriptions of the royal period is to proclaim the circumstances and contents of a *gtsigs* i.e. a sworn edict or undertaking by the *btsan-po*, usually together with his ministers. Those at Bsam-yas and Skar-cung, regarding the maintenance of the Buddhist faith, and the Treaty Inscription at Lhasa are of national significance: the others, except for that at Lcang-bu, are in effect charters guaranteeing privileges to meritorious persons and their families. The Lcang-bu inscription is the account, by royal command, of the building and endowment of a Buddhist temple by a maternal relation of the *btsan-po.*

No single word quite conveys the meaning of *gtsigs* which I have translated in different contexts as edict, charter, agreement. The original sense seems to have become obscured in later Tibetan. In the *Rgyal-po bka'-thang,* probably of the 14th century but drawing on earlier material, *gtsigs* has been replaced by *rtsis*—e.g. *rtsis kyi rdo rings* (f.48a) where it appears to mean "important". That is the primary explanation in Tibetan dictionaries from Csoma de Körös to Dagyab; but a hint of the earlier meaning can be seen in Jaeschke's dictionary in the secondary explanation "subdue, force, compel"; and in the Tibetan-Mongolian dictionary of Sumatiratna *gtsigs bzung* is interpreted as *bka's blangs* (promise, undertake) and as *dam bca'* (sworn agreement).

The texts of the inscriptions are in the main those of my earlier editions but I have here shown the original punctuation as nearly as possible; and some speculative suggestions for restoring partially effaced words have been omitted. Lines have been numbered for ease of reference. Critical apparatus and notes have been kept to a minimum. A Tibetan vocabulary, with some references to other documents of the period, and an index of names in the texts have been provided.

The calligraphy is by Mr Ngawang Thondup Narkyid for whose meticulous care and fine penmanship I am most grateful.

In addition to those scholars from whose published works I have benefited I am indebted for valuable advice on various points to Lopon Tenzin Namdak, Mr Samten Karmay, Professor Hisashi Sato, Tsipon W. D. Shakabpa, Mr Y. Imaeda, the late Zurkhang Shappe, Professor David Snellgrove and Mr Philip Denwood, and doubly grateful to Mr Nicholas Lowick for his expert care and his patience in seeing this work through the press.

Although it is hoped that the texts may be regarded as definitive, no such claim is made for the translations. There are several changes from earlier versions and further improvements should be possible through study of the manuscripts from Tun-huang of which a generous selection has been published in excellent photographic reproduction by the Bibliothèque Nationale in the two volumes of Choix de Documents Tibétains edited by A. Macdonald (Spanien) and Y. Imaeda.

REIGN OF KHRI SRONG-LDE-BRTSAN 755–*c.* 794 A.D.

The Lhasa Zhol *rdo-rings*

[Plates 1–3]

The three connected inscriptions on the east, south, and north faces of the tall and graceful stone pillar standing on the south side of the road that runs past the village of Zhol at the foot of the Potala are the earliest surviving from the time of the kings. It is surprising that this most impressive of the early stone pillars commemorates not some royal personage but a minister, Ngan-lam Stag-sgra klu-khong, a parvenu, possibly of foreign origin, and one who is not exceptionally prominent in contemporary records.

The campaign in the direction of Khar-tsan in which he took part must be that towards Khar-tsan Leng-cu mentioned in the Tun-huang Annals for the year 758 (DTH 57/64). Leng-cu is probably Liang-chou, a fortress city and important trading centre where Hsuan Tsang noted the presence of Tibetan merchants as early as 629 A.D. In *Tibetan Literary Texts and Documents* II by F. W. Thomas (TLTD) on p. 49 there is a reference to Khrom ched-po'i 'dun-sa Leng-cu, and on p. 95 to Mkhar-tsan Khrom-chen-po. Professor Geza Uray in a paper read at Oxford in July 1979 showed clearly that Khrom, Khrom chen-po, denotes the headquarters of a Tibetan military administrative district. He also considers that (m)Khar-tsan Khrom-chen-po was Liang-chou; and further suggested verbally that the name Khar-tsan is the same as Ku-chān in the Hudūd al 'Alam, the Persian geographical work written *c.* 982 A.D. But that identification is not certain—see Minorsky's edition of 1970, p. 230. Moreover the Tibetans in the 8th century applied the name Khar-tsan to places other than Leng-cu- viz. *Khar-tsan Ba-mgo dang Ke'u shan gnyis* (DTH 65). Bacot may be right in his translation of a passage in DTH p. 115 l. 3 . . . *Dba's Btsan-bzher mdo-lod la-stsogs-pas mkhar-tsan yan chad du drangste* as "Dba's etc poussèrent jusqu'à la ligne des forts" (DTH p. 153); but I disagree with his translation of the next sentence . . . *mkhar cu pa brgyad phab nas* as "et, démantelant huit forts sur les dix" which I take to mean "captured eight fortified *chou*". The line of forts may refer to the strong cities along the trade route to Central Asia and the line of the Great Wall built by the Han dynasty which had fallen into dilapidation except for its western extension between Su-chou and Sha-chou by the time of the T'ang. Perhaps Liang-chou, which fell to the Tibetans in 764, came to be known particularly as Khar-tsan Khrom-chen-po from its strategic position.

Stag-sgra klu-khong's activities against the 'A-zha belonging to China, and in Dbyar-mo-thang and Tsong-ka to the south and east of the Kokonor must relate to the events of 759 A.D. in the Tun-huang Annals. In 670 the Tibetans had virtually annihilated the 'A-zha (Tu-yu-hun) and had occupied their country and subjected the people, apart from a section which the Chinese moved into settlements between Shan-chou and Ling-chou.

Although Stag-sgra Klu-khong's part in those campaigns is not mentioned in the Tun-huang Annals he is named as the second general in the campaign of 763 when the Chinese capital at Keng-shi (Ch'ang-an) was captured. The privileges conferred on him and his family may have been a reward for that success.

REIGN OF KHRI SRONG-LDE-BRTSAN 755–*c.* 794 A.D.

In the edict of Khri Srong-lde-brtsan about the maintenance of Buddhism recorded in the *Chos-byung* of Dpa'-bo Gtsug-lag phreng-ba (*ja* ff. 108b–110a) he figures as one of the Great Ministers next after Mchims-rgyal Rgyal-zigs shu-theng, the Chief Minister, whom according to the Tun-Huang Chronicle he succeeded in that post, which may have been for a brief period in 783 A.D. Possibly he was the Sinolo mentioned in the T'ang Annals as visiting China in 781 to discuss the terms of a treaty.

After Stag-sgra klu-khong the Ngan-lam family appears to have lost importance. No member of it is named in the long list of officials in an edict of Khri Lde-srong-brtsan which can be dated between 800 and 810 A.D. (PT *ja* ff. 128b–130b) nor is there any among the witnesses to the Sino-Tibetan treaty of 821–822 A.D. (pp. 128-135). Later history stigmatizes Stag-sgra klu-khong (Ta-ra klu-gong) as a leading opponent of Buddhism at the time of the death of Khri Lde-gtsug-brtsan. In one version he was banished before the building of Bsam-yas (779 A.D. see p. 27) but another part of tradition names him as the builder of the black *mchod-rten* there. In view of his survival in power until about 783 A.D. the story needs further examination. If there is any historical basis for the tradition of his banishment, that might have been in connection with renewed opposition to Buddhism early in the reign of Khri Lde-srong-brtsan (p. 73) or to the dissension at that time which is mentioned in the first of the inscriptions from Zhwa'i Lha-khang (pp. 44, 47).

The date of the Zhol inscriptions may be surmised from internal evidence. The events described in the south inscription fall between the years 755 and 763 A.D. Nowhere in the series is Stag-sgra klu-khong described by a higher rank than *nang-blon chen-po* which is lower than that of Great Minister which he appears to have attained in 783. The inscriptions are a recital by Stag-sgra klu-khong of his own achievements rather than an edict in the name of the king. Nowhere in them is the *btsan-po* accorded the usual honorific title of *'Phrul-gyi-lha* or *Lha-sras.* That seemingly casual attitude suggests a time quite early in the reign of Khri Srong-lde-brtsan before he had asserted himself against the ministers who dominated his youthful years. I suggest, therefore, a date around 764 A.D. or only a little later.

Although the pillar with its proud words stood conspicuously in sight of passers-by for nearly a thousand years, the only indication that any Tibetan historian took notice of its contents is in the *Rgya-bod yig-tshang* (1434) f. 121 *zhang rje rgyal gzigs dang stag sgra klu gong gis phyi'i dgra brtul rgya bkra shis sgo phab pa las sogs lo rgyus sri'i rdo rings la bris yod do:* "an account of how Zhang Rje-rgyal-gzigs and Stag-sgra klu-gong defeated external enemies and captured the Chinese Bkra-shis-sgo is written on the Sri'i rdo-rings". Tibetans nowadays do not know the pillar by that name which is perhaps due to a misreading of *srid* which can be seen twice in the last few lines of the inscriptions on the north and south faces.

The texts below are based on copies made for Sir Charles Bell and photographs taken by him in 1921 and on copies and photographs taken by me between 1946 and 1950 and checked on frequent examination of the pillar. I have also compared the rather unsatisfactory eye-copies made by L. A. Waddell in 1904 and published by him in *JRAS* 1909. In a few instances letters that can be seen on Bell's photographs had been effaced in the years before my visit.

In my edition of the inscriptions in the Prize Publication Fund series of the Royal Asiatic Society vol. xix 1952 the punctuation was rendered, for convenience, according to current practice; but as these are possibly the earliest documents in Tibetan and as the punctuation differs from all later examples, it has been reproduced here as closely as possible.

Most of the lines are preceded by a double *tsheg*, the remainder by a single *tsheg*. Where the sign has been effaced I have supplied the double form. This feature is not found in the other inscriptions and in few of those manuscripts from Tun-huang of which I have seen photo-copies. Division of syllables is predominantly by a double *tsheg* but a single *tsheg* is also found. It may signify a stylistic development or it may simply be the personal preference of different stone-carvers that in the short east inscription there is no example of the single *tsheg* while on the south face it is used occasionally but not consistently after *nga, ta, da,* and *na,* and often after *ra.* Single, double and triple *shad* are used to mark the end of a clause or paragraph. There is quite frequent use of a *tsheg* before a *shad* after letters other than *nga.*

In the Tun-huang documents the double *tsheg* as a divider between words is occasionally found; and the triple *shad* more rarely. Whether any conclusion about the date of a document can be drawn from its pattern of punctuation needs further study but it may be noted that the double *tsheg* between words is found in the Bsam-yas inscription which also dates from the reign of Khri Srong-lde-brtsan (pp. 28, 30) but in none of the inscriptions of later reigns.

The letter *wa* here as in other inscriptions and in the Tun-huang *mss* is written as *a-chung* with a subscribed *ba* and not in its present form.

The few changes of substance in these texts from those in my earlier edition are mentioned in notes; and there are some minor corrections which escaped proof-reading in the 1952 texts.

East Inscription

1 ཀ།:།ཀློན:སྟག:སྒྲ:ཀླུ:

2 :ཁོང:། ནང:བློན:ཆེན:

3 :པོ:དང:ཡོ:གལ: x x x[1]

4 :པ:ཆེན:པོར:བཀ x[2]

5 :སྐུལད:ཀྱིས:ཀྱུང:།

6 :བཀའ:ལུང:དང:འདྲ:

7 :བར:།རྗེ:བླས:དཀ x[3]

8 :དགུ:ཉམསུ:བླངས:

9 :ཏེ:ཕྱི:ནང:གཉིས:ཀྱི:

10 :ཆབ:སྲིད:ཁབ:སོ: x[4]

11 :དཔེནད:པ:དང:ཆེ:

12 :རྒྱུང:གཉིས:ལ:དྲ x[5]

13 :ཞིང:སློམས:ཏེ། བོད:

14 :མགོ་ནག་པོའི:སྲིད:

15 :ལ:ཕན:བ:ལེགས:།།

16 :དགུ:བྱས:སོ།།།

[1] འཆོས:

[2] བཀའ:

[3] དཀའ:

[4] ལས:

[5] དྲང:

THE LHASA ZHOL *RDO-RINGS*

Translation

East Inscription

The minister Stag-sgra klu-khong was appointed Great Inner Minister and Great *Yo-gal 'chos-pa.*[1] Undertaking, as commanded, the difficult duty of *rje-blas*[2] he was of good service to the officers[3] of both the inner and outer administration; and acting with upright impartiality to both great and small alike he conferred many excellent benefits on the kingdom of the black-headed Tibetans.

Notes to Translation

1. The *Chos-byung* of Dpa'-bo gtsug-lag phreng-ba (PT) vol. *ja* f. 112b. mentions the *Yo-gal 'chos-pa. Yo-gal* was explained by the late Zurkhang Shappé as "enmity, dissension"; and Mr Samten Karmay has told me that there is a ritual called *stong-gsum yo-gal 'khrugs bcos* for pacifying discord between the *lha* and the *gnyan.* I also understand that the expression *yo-gal 'chos-pa* or *bcos-pa* is used in Khams meaning the reconciling of adversaries.
2. My earlier, tentative, translation of *rje-blas* as "royal work" derived from Bell's adviser, the Tshenshap. Another Lama suggested the meaning *rje'i 'khor,* "royal retinue" (blas = slas?). F. W. Thomas citing 3rd to 5th century Prakrit parallels, connects it with *rje-ba* "to change" and translates "successor, succession in a post" (TLTD III pp. 5 and 133) or "next vacancy" (AFL p. 166). The references listed in the Vocabulary show that it was a privileged and responsible position in the administration. Pending further enlightenment I have left the term untranslated.
3. *khab so*, mentioned also in Rkong-po inscription (pp. 68, 69) and Lhasa Treaty N. (p. 132), were apparently revenue officials, see V. A. Bogoslovskij, *Histoire du Peuple Tibétain*, pp. 136, 138.

South Inscription

1 ༄།།བཙན་པོ:ཁྲི:ལྡེ:གཙུག:

2 :རྩན:གྱི:རིང:ལའ། །

3 ༄།།ངན:ལམ:ཀླུ:ཁོང:གིས།།

4 :སྒོ:བ:ཉེ:བའི:རྗེ:བླས:བྲེས:པ:

5 །།འབལ:ལྡོང་ཙབ:དང། ལང་

6 :མྱེས:ཟིགས། བློན:པོ:ཆེན:པོ:

7 :བྱེད:བྱེད:པ:ལས། སྒོ:བ:རིནྡ།

8 :ནས།།།བཙན:པོ:ཡབ:ཁྲི:ལྡེ།

9 :གཙུག:རྩན་གྱི:སྐུ:ལ:དརད་ཏེ།

10 :དགུང:དུ:གཤེགས:སོ། ། །

11 :བཙན:པོ:སྲས:ཁྲི:སྲོང་ལྡེ:བརྩན:

12 :གྱི:སྐུ:ལ:ཡི:དརད:དུ:ཏེ། །བོད:

13 :མགོ:ནག:པོའི:སྲིད་ཞི:འཕྲུག:དུ་

14 :བྱེད་པ:ལས།ཀླུ:ཁོང:གིས།འབླ:

15 :དང། ལང:གློ:བ:རིངས:པའི:གདུ་

16 :གཅིགས། །བཙན:པོ:སྲས:ཁྲི:སྲོྔ།

THE LHASA ZHOL *RDO-RINGS*

Translation

South Inscription

In the time of the *btsan-po* Khri Lde-gtsug-rtsan,[1] Ngan-lam klu-khong loyally carried out the duty of *rje-blas.*

'Bal Ldong-tsab and Lang Myes-zigs[2] although they were Great Ministers became disloyal[3] and did injury[4] to the person of the *btsan-po*, the father, Khri Lde-gtsug-rtsan so that he went to heaven. They nearly did injury also to the person of the *btsan-po*, the son, Khri Srong-lde-brtsan. The kingdom of the black-headed Tibetans

Notes to Translation

1. Khri Lde-gtsug-rtsan (brtsan), reigned 706–755 A.D.
2. 'Bal and Lang, see DTH 56/62 and 102/ 132. 'Bal Skye-bzang ldong-tsab who had been active since 729 A.D. succeeded 'Bro Cung-bzang 'or-mang some time after 747, as Chief Minister. In Pt *ja* f. 75 Mang and 'Bal are described as pro-Buddhist ministers who were victimized after the death of Khri Lde-gtsug-brtsan. The origin of both may have been in N.E. Tibet. Stein, *Tribus Anciennes* p. 69 suggests a location for 'Bal or Sbal between Kan-tcheou and the river of Si-ning; and Lang-myi is placed by Thomas TLTD III p. 77 in N.E. Tibet. cf. also the name Lang-'gro associated with Kan-chou TLTD II p. 86.
3. *glo-ba rings* "disloyal", cf. *glo-ba 'dring* DTH 110, 111, 112. the opposite of *glo-ba nye.*
4. *dard*, explained to Bell as an obsolete equivalent of *bdo-ba.*

South Inscription

17 :ལྡེ:བརྩན:གྱི:སྐན:དུ་གསོལད་ནས

18 :འབལ:དང་། ཡང་གློ:བ:རིངས:།

19 :བདེན་པར:གྱུརད:ཏེ། ཁོང་ཏ:ཞི:

20 :བཀྱོན:ཕབ:སྟེ། །ཀླུ:ཁོང:གློ:བ:ཉེའོ:

21 ༄།:།བཙན:པོ:ཁྲི:སྲོང་ལྡེ:བརྩན:གྱི:རྗེ་

22 :ལ། ། །ངན:ལམ:ཀླུ:ཁོང:གློ:བ:ཉེ:ལ:

23 :བཀའ:གྲོས:ཆེ:ནས། ཐུགས:བརྟན:

24 :ཏེ། །ནང:བློན:བཀའ:ལ:གཏོགས:

25 :པར:བཅུག:ནས། །རྒྱལི:སྲིད:གྱི:ཉམ:

26 :ཉོད:རྟོག:ཅིང་། ཁར:ཙན:ཕྱོགས:སུ:

27 :ཕྱོག:མ:དྲངས:པའོ། དམག:དཔོན:

28 :དུ། བཀའ:སྩལད་གྱིས:ཀྱང་། དགྱའ:

29 :ཐབས:མཁས:ལ:གྲོས:གྱིས:སོད:དེ།

30 :རྒྱལི:ཁམས:སུ:གཏོགས:པའི:འོ:ན:

31 x[1]ང:པོ:བསྡུས། རྒྱུ:ལས:མནངས:ཕལ

[1] མང:

Translation

having been thrown into commotion Klu-khong brought to the notice of the *btsan-po*, the son, Khri Srong-lde-brtsan the facts of the disloyalty of 'Bal and Lang and on it being proved that 'Bal and Lang were disloyal they were condemned. Klu-khong was received into allegiance.

In the time of the *btsan-po* Khri Srong-lde-brtsan, Ngan-lam klu-khong in his loyalty was great in counsel; and being steadfast of mind he was appointed Inner Minister of the royal council.[5] Considering

Notes to Translation (continued)

5. *bka'-la gtogs-pa*, Li Fang-kuei in his article of the Treaty Inscription of 821–822 A.D. (TP 1956 p. 72) shows this to be the equivalent of the Chinese *t'ung p'ing chang shih* "participating in the deliberation of state affairs.

South Inscription

32 ×[1]ཆེ་བཙད་པས། རྒྱ་སྤྱ་གོང་སྟེ། །རྒྱའི།

33 × × × × × ×ོགས་ [2]པ་དབྱར་མོ་ཐང་།

34 × × × × × × × ན་དང་ཅོང་ཀ་ཕྱོགས་

35 × × × × × × ×[3]ར་དང་ནས་ལས་སྣོགས་

36 × × × × × × × × ང་ཕོ་གཙལད་། སྤྲུ་

37 × ×[4] × × × × × × × × འཁྲུགས་པའི་དགྲ

38 × × × × × × × × བ་[5]སྲིད་ཆེན་པོ་× ×[6]

39 × × × × × × × ×[7]གྲོས་ཆེན་པོ་གསོལྡུ་

40 × × × × ×[8]བ་ཏེ་ཞིང་ཆབ་སྲིད་ལ་དཔེནུ་

41 × ×[9]× × × དཀའ་བ་བྲུསོ།།། བཙན་

42 × × × ×[10]ལྡེ་བརྟན་ཐུགས་སྐམ་ལའ་།

43 × × ×[11]གྲོས་གྱི་རྒྱ་ཆེ་བས་ཆབ་སྲིད་གར་

44 ་མཛོད་དེ་ཅོག་དུའང་ལེགས་སྟེ། རྒྱའི་ཁམས་

45 ་སྤུ་གདོགས་པའི་ཡུལ་དང་མཁར་མང་པོ་

[1] པོ་ [2] ཁམས་སྤུ་གདོགས་ [3] སྣང་ [4] ཆོང་ཞིས་ [5] ཆབ་

[6] མཛད་ [7] བཀའ་ [8] སྒོ་ [9] པའི་སེམས་ [10] ཕོ་ཁྲི་སྲོང་ [11] བཀའ་

Translation

the state of affairs in China he was commissioned as general to make an attack first in the direction of Khar-tsan. Prospering[6] by his skilled advice in the art of war he brought into subjection the 'A-zha who belonged to China. China was deprived of the greater part of its authority[7] over them. China cowered in terror. Dbyar-mo-thang

Notes to Translation (continued)

6. Bell read *song*, which I followed; but re-examination of photographs—and the affix *de*—confirm *sod.* If this is from *gsod-pa* "to kill, the absence of a definite object is unusual and, although I have found no other example, I prefer to take is as a form of *bsod-pa* "to be fortunate, prosper".

7. *mnangs* here and in the inscription at the tomb of Khri Lde-srong-brtsan (p. 90) must be distinguished from *nam mnangs* (gnangs?) in the *Li-yul Chos-kyi lo-rgyus* 71 (Emmerick p. 86) and from the explanations in Dagyab's dictionary—*gtsigs che ba, rtsis che ba; brgyan pa, spras -pa* ("important, adorn"). Thomas TLTD III p. 150 has *mnangs= dmangs*, "people"; but gives no authority. Bacot in DTH p. 197 explains it as *nom-pa; srid,* probably on the basis of Sumatiratna's Tibetan-Mongolian Dictionary p. 1209. I have adopted *srid* which gives the best sense in the context of the elimination of Chinese authority over the 'A-zha. An apparent distortion of the phrase in the colophon of the *Mahavyutpatti* appears as *rgyal sa* (for *rgya las*) *gnang mang po bcad de* (Simonsson, *Indo-Tibetische Studien* p. 239.

South Inscription

46 :བཅོམ:སྟེ:བསྡུས:ནས། །རྒྱ:རྗེ:ཅེའུ:འོག:ཝང:

47 :དེ:རྗེ:བློན:སྐྱག:སྟེ། ལོ:གཅིག:ཅིང:རྟག:དུ:དཔྱ:

48 :དར:ཡུག:ལྔ:ཁྲི:ཕུལ:ཏེ། རྒྱ:དཔྱའ:འཇལ:དུ

49 :བཅུག:གོ། ། །དེའི:འོག:དུ། རྒྱ:རྗེ:ཡབ:ཅེའུ:འོག:

50 :ཝང:ཏེ:གྲོངས:སྟེ། རྒྱ:རྗེ:སྲས:ཝང:པེང:ཝང།

51 :རྒྱལ:པོར:ཞུགས:ནས། བོད:ལ:དཔྱའ:འཇལ:

52 :དུ:མ:རུང:སྟེ། །བཙན:པོ:ཐུགས:སྒྱུང:བའི:ཆེ:

53 :ངན:ལམ:ཀླུ:ཁོང:གིས། །རྒྱ:ཡུལ:གྱི:ཞིལད། རྒྱ:

54 :རྗེའི:ཕོ:བྲང:ཀེང:ཤིར། བོད:ཀྱིས:དམག:དྲང:

55 :བའི:བཀའ:གྲོས:ཀྱི:མགོ:ཆེན:པོ:གསོལད:ནུས།

56 :ཀེང:ཤིར:དྲང:བའི:དམག:དཔོན:ཆེན:པོར།།

57 :ཞང:མཆིམས:རྒྱལ:རྒྱལ:ཟིགས:ཤུ:ཐེང:དང།།

58 :བློན:སྟག:སྒྲ:ཀླུ:ཁོང:གཉིས། བཀའ:སྩལད:ཏེ།

59 :ཀེང:ཤིར:དྲངས:ནས། ཅིའུ:ཅིར:ཀྱི:རབ:ངོགས:

60 :སུ:རྒྱ:དང:ཐབ:མོ:ཆེན:པོ:བྱས:ཏེ། བོད:ཀྱིས:གཡུལ:

61 :བཟློག:ནས། །རྒྱ:མང:པོ:བཀུངས:པས། །རྒྱ:རྗེ:ཀྭང:

Translation

belonging to China . . . . and in the direction of Tsong-ka . . . . grain and barley etcetera . . . . many (taxes) were paid . . . . the enemies who had caused disorder . . . . great dominion . . . . gave great counsel . . . . . being loyal he took great trouble for the benefit of the kingdom. By the greatness of his counsel to the *btsan-po* Khri Srong-lde-brtsan who was of profound mind whatever was done in the administration of the kingdom turned out well. Many districts and fortresses belonging to China were brought into subjection. The king of China He'u-'ki 'wang-te[8] and his ministers were terrified. They offered regular tribute yearly of 50,000 pieces of silk. China was compelled to pay tribute. After that, the king He'u-'ki 'wang-te died and the Chinese king his son Wang-peng-wang[9] having succeeded to the throne did not deem it proper to pay tribute to Tibet. When the *btsan-po* was aggrieved at that, Klu-khong took the lead in advising that an army should be sent against the palace of the Chinese king at Keng-shi,[10] the very centre of China. Zhang Mchims-rgyal Rgyal-zigs shu-theng[11] and the minister Stag-sgra klu-khong were appointed chief generals for the campaign against Keng-shi. They attacked Keng-shi and a great battle was fought with the Chinese on the banks of the ford at Ci'u-cir.[12] The Tibetans put them to flight and many

Notes to Translation (continued)

8. He'u-'ki 'wang-te. Professor Hisahi Sato identifies him as Hsiao Kan Hwang-te, the title of the Emperor Su Tsung.
9. Wang-peng-wang (Kwang-peng wang in l. 61) : the Emperor Tai Tsung.
10. Keng-shi ; Kwang-hsi, capital city i.e. Ch'ang-an.
11. Rgyal-zigs shu-theng of the Mchims-rgyal clan later became Chief Minister (DTH 102/132).
12. Ci'u-cir : Chou-chih, about 32 miles south-west of Ch'ang-an on a tributary of the Wei river.

South Inscription

62 :ཡེང་ཐུང་ཡང་། ཀེང་ཤིའི་མཁར་ནས་བྱུང་སྟེའོ།

63 :སྙེམ་ཅི་ཙུར་བྲོས་ནས། ཀེང་ཤི་ཕབ་སྟེ་རྒྱ་རྗེའི་ནང་

64 :བློན་འབྲེའུ་×ིན་ཀེང་ལས་སྤོགས་ཏེ་དོང་ཀུན་དུ:

65 :ཐོ་ཀུན་ཡ ××× ××× ×××[1] ཙན་པོའི།

66 :འབ[2] ××××××××××× བོད་×ུ:[3] གང:

67 :དང་བྲ× ×××××× ×ཏེ། ཀེམ་ཤེང་ཀོ:

68 :ཅོའི་མིང:×ོ[4] ××××××× འབྲས་ཤུ:

69 ×××××××××××××× བློན་པོ:

70 ×××××××××× རྒྱལ་པོ་ཆེ་ཆུང:

71 ×××××××××× སྲིད་ཕྱུགས་སུ:

72 ×:བ:དང་གཏ[5] ×ུ ××× ×ུ སྐྱན་པར་བྱས་ཏེ། སྐྱུ་ཁེང་གློ:

73 :བ་ཅེ་ཞིང་ཆ××××××× ནད[6] པའི:×××[7] དཀའ:

74 :བ་བྱས་སོ།།

[1] བཙན: [2] འབངས: [3] རྒྱུ: [4] པོ: [5] Bell reads གཉ×

[6] ཆབ་སྲིད་ལ་དཔེ་ནད: [7] སེམས:

Translation

Chinese were killed. The Chinese king Kwang-peng-wang left Keng-shi and fled to Sshem-ci'u.[13] Keng-shi was taken and the Chinese king's inner minister 'Bye'u-tsin-keng[14] and others, Dong-kwan[15] and Bo-kwan . . . . subjects of the Btsan-po . . . . Tibet . . . . the brother of Kim-sheng Kong-co[16] . . . . being set up . . . . minister[17] . . . . kings great and small[18] . . . . the furthest part of the kingdom . . . . caused to be praised. Klu-khong being loyal took great trouble to benefit the kingdom.

Notes to Translation (continued)

13. Sshem-ci'u, Sato identifies this as Hsien-chou.
14. 'Bye'u, which Waddell read in 1904 is confirmed by Sato's identification of the minister as Miau Tsin Keng.
15. Dong-kwan is perhaps Tung Kuan, an eastern suburb of the capital.
16. Kim-sheng Kong-co; the Chinese princess married to Khri Lde-gtsug-brtsan. She died in 739 A.D. Her brother named in DTH 114/153 as Gwang-bu Hwang-te was set up briefly as emperor by the Tibetans in 763 A.D. He was Ch'eng Hung, prince of Kuang Wu, son of the prince of Pin.
17. "minister" may have been a reference to the appointment by the Tibetans of Yu K'o-feng as puppet minister.
18. "kings great and small" may have been a reference to the various princes who were compelled to welcome the Tibetans at the gate of the capital. (information from unpublished translation of T'ung Chien by Dr Chang Kun).

REIGN OF KHRI SRONG-LDE-BRTSAN 755–*c.* 794 A.D.

North Inscription

1 ༄།:།བློན་སྟག:སྒྲ:ཀླུ:ཁོང་།

2 :དགུ:རྒྱལ:གཙིགས:གནང་

3 :བའི:མདོ:རྡོ:རིངས:ལ:ཡིག:གྲུ:

4 :བྲིས:པའ།།

5 ༄།:།བཙན་པོ:ཁྲི:སྲོང་ལྡེ:བརྩན་

6 :གྱི:ཞ:སྔ:ནས:དབུ:སྙུང་གནང་

7 :སྟེ། །བློན་སྟག:སྒྲ:ཀླུ:ཁོང་གི་བུ:ཚ།

8 :རྒྱུད་འཕེལ་པད་ལ་ནམ:ནམ:ཞ:×× [1]

9 :དངུལ:གྱི:ཡི:གེ:ཆེན་པོ་གཅིག།།

10 ་ན་མྱི:དབབ:པར:གཡུང་དྲུང་།

11 ་དུ་སྩལ་པད་ཕར་གནང་ངོ་།།

12 ་བཙན་པོ:སྲས:དགོན་སྐུ:ཚེ:རབས:

13 ་རེ་ཞིང་ཡང་། ཀླུ:ཁོང་གི:བུ:ཚ་རྒྱུད་

14 ་འཕེལ་པད་ལས:གཙོག།ཞམ:འབྲི།

THE LHASA ZHOL *RDO-RINGS*

Translation

North Inscription

A summary of the edict for the ennoblement[1] of the minister Stag-sgra klu-khong is inscribed on this stone pillar in large letters.[2]

The *btsan-po* Khri Srong-lde-brtsan himself took an oath[3] and decreed that it should be granted forever to the descendants of the minister Stag-sgra klu-khong by a great silver letter[4] in perpetuity that they should never be degraded. And he decreed that in each generation of the *btsan-po* and his sons and grandsons one of the descendants of Zla-gong shall be appointed to be in personal attendance[5] ranking above the private retinue and be present always at the

Notes to Translation

1. *dku-rgyal.* Bell's equation *dku*= *sku*, which I adopted, is not tenable. A. Róna Tas in AOH 1955 p. 264 n. 39 interprets it as "the royal side, court". Without more evidence that inversion is not convincing and the sense of *rgyal* "to prevail" may be considered: cf. *dku-'phel* in TLTD II p. 53. However one arrives at it, the intention is that Klu-khong was honourably advanced to a position of privilege.
2. *yig-gru*, "square letters" presumably as distinct from cursive. I have seen no other instance of this word.
3. For comparable grants given on oath by a *btsan-po* see the Zhwa'i and Lcang-bu inscriptions (pp. 49, 51, 57, 59 and 97, 99) and DTH 106/138 and 110/146.
4. In such awards the order of precedence was turquoise, gold, *phra-men* (precious stone?), silver, brass, copper (Pell T. 1071). Klu-kong's senior colleague Rgyal-zigs shu-theng received a turquoise letter in 763 A.D. (DTH 60); the head of the Dba's clan held a gold letter (DTH 109); and it appears from DTH 60 that there was an even higher award than turquoise—viz *ke-ke-ru*, "a white precious stone" Das, Dictionary p. 30.)
5. *zham-'bring,* cf. *zha-'bring* in DTH 106/138; and *zham-ring* in TLTD II pp. 8 and 9.

North Inscription

15 :ན་ནང་གོར་ཡན་ཆད་དུ:གཞུག:

16 :རིང་ཚོལ:ཟར་ཏག:དུ་མཆིས་ལྔ:

17 :གནང་ངོ། །ཀླུ:ཁོང་གི:བུ:ཚ:རྒྱུད:

18 :འཕེལད་ལ་ཇེ:བླས:ཀྱི:རྗེ:ཐོག:པའི

19 :རྒྱམས:ཇེ:རྩིས:དུ་རྗེ:ཐོག:པར་བཀྱ།

20 :བཀུར་ཞིང་བསྟོད་པར་གནང་ངོ།

21 :ཀླུ:ཁོང་གི:བུ:ཚ:རྒྱུད་གྱིས། །བཙན་པོ།

22 :ཞ:སྔར། །སློ:བ:མ:རིངས:ན། །ཞོངས:

23 :སྡིག:གཞན་ཅི:བྱུང་ཡང་རུང་། སྲོག:

24 ·སྲིད་ལ:མྱི:དབབ:པར། །བཀའ་གྲོད་ཀྱི:

25 ·ཚིགས:ཅི:ལ:བབ:པ:ལས། །བཀའ་གྲོད:

26 ·ན་གཙིག:གིས:སྨད:ཅིང་བསྐྱུང་བར:

27 :གནང་ངོ། །ཀླུ:ཁོང་གི:བུ:ཚ:ཕེལད:ལྔ:

28 :ལ:ལ:ཞིག། །རབས:ཆད་ན་རབས:ཆད་

Translation

royal table.[6] And he decreed that those among the descendants of Zla-gong[7] who are suitable for the duty of *rje-blas* shall be honoured and exalted according to their ability. And he decreed that, provided the descendants of Zla-gong do not become disloyal to the *btsan-po*, whatever other offences they may commit they shall not forfeit their lives or position and whatever the terms of the charge against them they shall only be reprimanded and it shall be set aside. And he decreed that if in the case of some of the descendants of Zla-gong the

Notes to Translation (continued)

6. *tshal zar; stag-gi zar can pa* and *zar cung pa* in Pell T. 1089 1541 and 42 might be relevant. The term there seems to relate to a minor official or his insignia; and *zar* might be connected with *zar babs* "brocade" or *zar-bu* "tassel"; but further evidence is needed.
7. Although in this inscription he is not described as *blon*, Zla-gong might be the exterior minister of that name in the list of witnesses to the edict of Khri Srong-lde-brtsan in PT *ja* 109b; Klu-khong appears higher up in the list as an inner minister.

North Inscription

29 :ཀྱི་ཁོལ:ཡུལ:དང་། ནོར་ཕྱུགས། ཐར:སྨྱི།

30 :བཞེས:པར། ཕུ:ནུ:པོ:གང་ཉེ:བ:སྐལད་

31 :པར་གནངོ།། །བློན་སྟག:སྒྲ:ཀླུ:ཁོང་།

32 :གི་བུ:ཚ:རྒྱུད་ཕེལད་། དཀུ:རྒྱལ:གྱི:ཡི:གེའ:

33 :ལག:ན་འཆང་འཆང་བ:ཞིག:རབས:ཆད་

34 :དམ:བརྒྱུན་བབ་ན་ཡང་། དངུལ:གྱི:ཡི:གེ:

35 :ཐར:སྨྱི:བཞེས:པར་། བློན་སྟག:སྒྲ:ཀླུ:ཁོང་།

36 :དང་། ལྷ:གོང་གི:བུ:ཚ:རྒྱུད་གང་ཉེ:བ:གཅིག:

37 :དངུལ:གྱི:ཡི་གེ:ཆེན་པོ:གཡུང་དྲུང་དུ་སྐལད་

38 :པར་གནང་ངོ།། །བློན་སྟག:སྒྲ:ཀླུ:ཁོང་གི་

39 :ཕ་ལྷ:གོང་གི:བུ:ཚ:རྒྱུད་འཕེལད་ཀྱི:རྣམས།

40 :ཞང་ལོན་ཡོ:གེ:པའི:ཐང་དང། དམག:སུམ:རྒྱར།

41 :གནང་ངོ།། །སྐུ:སྲུངས:འཕན:ཡུལ:པའི།

42 :སྟོང་དཔོན་དུ་གཞན་སུ:ཡང་སྨེ:གཞུག:པར།

Translation

line should fail, the service-tenure[8] lands, the wealth and cattle[9] of the extinct line shall not be resumed but shall be granted to whichever of the kin[10] is the nearest. And he decreed that so long as one member of the descendants of the minister Stag-sgra klu-khong continues to hold the letter of ennoblement, even if the line be broken or he should incur a reprimand, the silver letter shall not be resumed but the great silver letter shall be given in perpetuity to whichever of the descendants of the minister Stag-sgra klu-khong and Zla-gong is the nearest. And he decreed to those[11] who are descendants of Zla-gong, the father of the minister Stag-sgra klu-khong, the rank of *zhang-lon yi-ge-pa*[12] and the command of three hundred soldiers. And he decreed that no one else should be appointed to the post of

Notes to Translation (continued)

8. *khol-yul*, DTH p. 110 supports the explanation in Bogoslovskij, *L'Histoire du Peuple Tibétain*, 1972, as "service tenure" rather than "servants and lands".

9. Bogoslovskij translates *nor-phyugs* as "bétail". Róna Tas (op. cit. p. 252 n. 9) infers that by this time it had become a permanent compound meaning "property" but the examples he cites from Tunhuang *mss* are not conclusive and there are others where each component has a separate meaning—e.g. TLTD II p. 162. The Lcang-bu inscription (p. 96) also shows a distinction between the two elements of property—*nor-rdzas* and *rkang-'gros.*

10. *pu-nu-po*, Róna Tas (op. cit) examines this relationship which covers essentially a wide group of blood relations.

11. *rnams* here is a substantive: see TLTD III p. 39.

12. Although there are instances where a *yi-ge-pa* is clearly a secretary (Pell T. 1089 and 1333) the *zhang-lon yi-ge-pa* here may be compared with the *zhang-lon yi-ge-can* in the Zhwa'i East inscription l. 27 where the probable meaning is someone holding a letter of entitlement to the rank of *zhang-lon*—the general body of ministerial officials, high and low (*che phra*). *Zhang* there is perhaps an equivalent of the Chinese *shang shu*, head of an office; and must be distinguished from *zhang*, maternal uncle, designating a marriage relationship between certain noble families and the Tibetan royal line. Ministers with that qualification are always known as *zhang blon*, not *lon*, see Richardson, *Names and Titles*, Sikkim Bulletin of Tibetology 1967.

North Inscription

43 ༔བློན་སྟག་སྒྲ་ཀླུ་ཁོང་གི་མྱེས་པོ་གསས་སླེབས་།

44 ༔ཁྲི་བུ་ཚེ་རྒྱུད་པེ་ལད་ལས་གང་ཇོ་ཚོག་པའ་།

45 ༔དམངས་འདྲང་བ་གཅིག །སྐུ་སྲུངས་འཕན་

46 ༔ཡུལ་པའི་སྟོང་དཔོན་གཡུང་དྲུང་དུ་སྐལད་

47 ·པར་གནང་ངོ། ། །ངན་ལམ་གསས་སླེབས་

48 ·ཁྲི་བུ་ཚེ་རྒྱུད་འཕེལད། ནམ་ཁར་གྲུང་སྟེ་སྐུ་།

49 ·སྲུངས་སུ་གནང་བ་ལས། སྟེ་ཆ་གྲུ་དུ་སྨྱི་སྤྱོའ་ཕྱི།

50 ·བསྒྱུར་བར་གནང་ངོ། ། །བློན་གོང་གི་བུ་ཚའ་

51 ·རྒྱུད་འཕེལད་ཀྱི་ལག་ན་བྲན་ཞིང་འབྲོག་སོག་

52 ༔ཚལ་ལས་སྟོགས་ཏེ་དབང་ངོ་ཚོག །བླར་ཕྱི་བཞེས

53 ༔ཕྱི་དགྲི་གཞན་གྱིས་ཕྱི་དཔྱོག་ཁོང་ཏ་བདག་སྤྱི་

54 ༔དགའ་ན་ཉེ་རིང་དང་བཟང་ངན་གྱི་བརྗེ་བར་

55 ༔གནང་ངོ། ། །བློན་གོང་གི་བུ་ཚ་རྒྱུད་འཕེལད་ལ་

56 ༔ལ་ལ་ཞིག་གིས་ཁ་ཁོན་གྱི་བག་དུ་སྨོག་སྤྱིད་ལ་།

Translation

Stong-dpon of the bodyguard from 'Phan-yul but that one of the descendants of Gsas-slebs, the grandfather of the minister Stag-sgra klu-khong, who is capable and a leader of the people shall be permanently appointed *Stong-dpon* of the bodyguard from 'Phan-yul. And he decreed that forever when the descendants of Ngan-lam[13] Gsas-slebs are appointed to the district bodyguard the district troops shall not be transferred elsewhere and shall not be changed. And he decreed that the bondsmen and fields, grazing ground, fallow land,[14] forest and so on, whatever is in the possession of the descendants of Zla-gong, shall not be resumed or diminished or taken by others; and if they themselves do not wish it, their nearness shall not be changed to distance nor good treatment for bad. And he decreed that if there should be any person who, harbouring a grudge, acts against the descendants of Zla-gong to cause detriment to their life and position,

Notes to Translation (continued)

13. Ngan-lam. Apart from Klu-khong, his father and grandfather, the only other member of the clan of whom I find mention in early *mss* is the monk Rgyal-mchog-dbyangs (TLTD II p. 86). The place Ngan-lam Tshal sar-pa appears in DTH 18. The family may have been of Sogdian origin. The name Ngan or An is Sogdian according to Pulleyblank (TP XLI) and there were Sogdian colonies in the Lop Nor region (Pelliot JA. 1916) and near the Kokonor (Stein, Epopée p. 306 n. 69).

14. *sog*. Uray in AOH 1960 p. 48 dismisses the meaning "grass, straw" and sees a connection with *sob* "empty". The best evidence for that is its equivalent in a Manchu dictionary which he cites.

North Inscription

57 :དམའ:བར:བྱེད་པ:ཞིག:ཡོད་ན། བཀའ:འོན་ལྷ:།

58 :ནས:མཇད་པར་གནང་ངོ།། །ལྷ:གོང་གི:བུ:ཚ:

59 :རྒྱུད་ཕེལད་ཀྱིས:གློ:བ:མ:རིངས:ན་ཕྲ:མ:སྨྲ:གསྡུ་ཐུ་

60 :ཀླན་ཀ:མྱི:བཙལ:སྨྲ:བརྒྱན་བར:གནང་ངོ།།།

61 :བུ:ཚ:འཕེལད་ཀྱི:ནང་ནས:ལ:ལ:ཞིག། །བཙན་པོ:

62 :ཞ:སྔར་གློ:བ:རིངས:ཡང་དག་པར་གྱུརད་ན་གང:

63 :ཉེས:པའི:སྐོར་། བཀའ:གྲོད་རྨ་འོ། །ཕུ་ནུ:པོ:གཞན:།

64 :ཁྲིན་ལ:སྨྲ:གདགས:སྒོག:སྲིད:ལ:སྨྲ:དབབ:པར་གནྡ་

65 :ངོ།།

66 ༄།:།མངོར་ནའ:བློན:སྟག:སྒྲ:ཀླུ:ཁོང་གི:ཕ:ལྷ:གོང་

67 :གི:བུ:ཚ:རྒྱུད་ཕེལད་སྒོག ×× དང་སྲིད[1]་དེ་པར་སྒྲུག:

68 :གོང་མཇད་དེ × × × × × × × × ×

[1] སྲིད་

Translation

an order to restrain him shall be given from above. And he decreed that if the descendants of Zla-gong do not become disloyal, slander against them shall not be listened to and they shall not be called to account or reprimanded. And he decreed that even if it be proved that one from among the descendants has become disloyal to the *btsan-po*, the charge shall be brought against only that one who is guilty; his other kinsmen shall not be brought to trial and their life and position shall not be adversely affected.

In short, having high regard for the life and position and the happiness[15] of the descendants of Stag-sgra klu-khong in this way . . . .

Notes to Translation (continued)

15. *skyid.* Following Bell, I originally read *srid.* Waddell in 1904 read *skyid* and photographs support this as the better reading: cf. *dbangs skyid par bya ba* in the inscription of Khri Lde-srong-brtsan at 'Phyong-rgyas (p. 88).

The Bsam-yas *rdo-rings*

[Plate 4]

The inscription is on a pillar of hard reddish stone standing on a worn lotus-shaped base of some softer light-coloured stone against the east wall of the great temple of Bsam-yas a little to the south of the main entrance. It is remarkably well preserved and the lettering, which is rather coarser than that of the Zhol *rdo-rings*, is undamaged. The text was copied for Sir Charles Bell in 1921 and was photographed for him on a later visit in 1935. I published it from his copy, as he had wished, in *JRASB* 1949. It was subsequently photographed and copied by me in 1949, and in the same year by Professor G. Tucci who published it in The Tombs of the Tibetan Kings (TTK) Rome, 1950.

Neither of those editions shows the original punctuation though it can be seen in that part of the inscription illustrated on plate 3 of TTK. Like that of the Zhol *rdo-rings* it uses a single and a double *tsheg* though not, as in Zhol, at the beginning of each line. A single *shad* is used to separate phrases and also in a rather random fashion in the middle of sentences. A double *shad* appears only in the *dang-kyog* at the beginning of the inscription.

Neither my edition nor Tucci's mentions that at the top of the pillar below a decorative scroll and not quite parallel with the main text is the mantra *OM A HUM* well carved in the Wartu character. The letters are smaller and more lightly incised than those of the main inscription and it appears to be a later addition.

The inscription, which is the earliest document relating to Buddhism in Tibet, records that the *btsan-po* made a vow to maintain the religion of the Buddha established in the temples of Ra-sa and Bsam-yas etcetera, and it states that a detailed text exists separately.

By great good fortune that detailed text has survived. In f. 111b of vol. *ja* of the Chos-byung of Dpa'-bo Gtsug-lag phreng-ba the inscription on the Bsam-yas *rdo-rings*, attributed to Khri Srong-lde-brtsan, is reproduced accurately apart from a few orthographical discrepancies. It is stated by PT to be a summary of two preceding documents which he describes as *bka' gtsigs.* Internal evidence, and a similar *bka' gtsigs* relating to a similar vow by Khri Lde-srong-brtsan (pp. 43, 72) confirm the authenticity of those documents. The first (PT *ja* ff. 108b–110a) is the detailed text of the edict, explaining why it was necessary and ending with the names of the ministers who witnessed it and were bound by it. There is also a list of the temples and religious communities to which sealed copies of the edict and of a secondary document, composed at the same time, were sent. In addition to the 'Phrul-snang of Ra-sa and Bsam-yas Lhun-gyis-grub, each of which received two copies, they are: Bkra-shis lha-yul of Khra-'brug, the religious community of the palace, the Rgya-btags Ra-mo-che of Ra-sa, Khams-sum mi-ldog sgrol in Brag-dmar, the religious communities of Bru-zha, Zhang-zhung and Mdo-smad, and those in the jurisdiction of the Sde-blon.

Khra-'brug, traditionally attributed to Srong-brtsan sgam-po, is in the Yar-lung valley. If "the palace" refers to a specific place it may be Pho-brang, also in the Yar-lung valley, associated with Khri Lde-gtsug-brtsan. The Ra-mo-che of Ra-sa can most probably be identified with the great *gtsug-lag-khang* founded, according to the *Li-yul chos-kyi lo-rgyus* (Emmerick, p. 85 (58) by the Chinese bride of Khri Lde-gtsug-brtsan some twelve years before her death in 739 A.D., that is to say about

727. Khams-sum Mi-ldog-sgrol is the three-storeyed temple, like a smaller version of the main temple, a little to the west outside the enclosing wall of the main temple complex at Bsam-yas. It is attributed in the *Rgyal-po bka'-thang* f. 34b and in the *Padma Bka'-thang* f. 182b under the name Khams-gsum Me-tog-sgrol, to Khri Srong-lde-brtsan's queen Tshe-spong-za Rma-rgyal ldong-skar, who is known in the *Bka-thang* and *Sba-bzhad* as Me-tog-sgron. Bru-zha, the Gilgit area, had been raided by the Tibetans as early as 719 A.D. and was dominated by them from 737 until the early part of the 9th century. Buddhism had been established there long before the Tibetan connection. Zhang-zhung was an imprecisely defined stretch of country to the north and west of Tibet inhabited by a complex of related tribes. The Tibetans conquered it between 634 and 660 A.D. Its capital seems to have been near Lake Manasarowar. Mdo-smad, mentioned as early as 653 A.D., was an eastern frontier province probably including what are now A-mdo and Sde-dge. The Bde-blon—for which "Sde-blon" in PT must be intended—headed the administration of five districts known as the *mthong-khyab khri-sde-lnga* which were set up at the time of the conquest of the Chinese borderlands between 758 and 763 A.D. In those regions many Buddhist temples had existed long before the arrival of the Tibetans who later founded their own temples and monasteries. Khri Srong-lde-brtsan is credited in the Skar-cung inscription (pp. 74, 75) and in DTH p. 114 with building temples "at the centre and on the borders, *dbung mthar*"; and some of those on the border, in the Tun-huang region, are named in TLTD II pp. 88–91.

The inscription and the detailed *bka'-gtsigs* together thus show the existence of a considerable number of Buddhist institutions of some sort throughout Tibet and its dependencies in the middle of the reign of Khri Srong-lde-brtsan. Further information about Buddhism at that time is added in the second document mentioned in the first edict as an account of the spreading of the doctrine in both early and recent times. Although in PT this is called the second *bka'-gtsigs*, the document identifies itself as a *bka'-mchid* i.e. not a sworn edict but a statement or exposition. Its purpose is to tell the history of the coming of religion—*chos 'byung-ba'i lo-drung*—and it can be seen as the first essay in that genre. The founding of the *pe-har*—vihara—of Ra-sa in the time of Srong-brtsan sgam-po is described as the beginning of the doctrine in Tibet; the building of a temple at Kwa-cu in Brag-mar is attributed to Khri Srong-lde-brtsan's father Khri Lde-gtsug-brtsan; there is confirmation of the tradition that there was a reaction against the practice of Buddhism on the death of Khri Lde-gtsug-brtsan; and there is a summary of what was seen as the essence of Buddhism at that time, inculcating the gradual acquisition of enlightenment through the active accumulation of merit.

It is largely due to the brief inscription at Bsam-yas that we can accept as authentic the valuable light thrown on the history of Buddhism in Tibet by these two documents in PT. The first of them, moreover, makes it possible to date the inscription to within a few years. The principal witness to the detailed edict was the Chief Minister Zhang Rgyal-zigs shu-theng who, according to the T'ang Annals, demitted office in 782 A.D. Accepting that the great temple at Bsam-yas was completed in the sheep year 779 A.D. the inscription and the other documents can be placed between those two years and therefore earlier than the culmination of rivalry between the Indian teaching of gradual and the Chinese of immediate enlightenment in a great debate, probably in 792 A.D. (Demiéville, *Le Concile de Lhasa*, and Tucci, Minor Buddhist Texts II).

REIGN OF KHRI SRONG-LDE-BRTSAN 755–*c.* 794 A.D.

Inscription

1 ༄།།ར་ས་དང་།བྲག་མར་གྱི་

2 གཙུག་ལག་ཁང་ལས་སྩོགས་

3 པར་།དཀོན་མཆོག་།གསུམ་

4 གྱི་རྟེན་བཙུགས་པ་དང་།སངས་

5 རྒྱས་གྱི་ཆོས་།མཛད་པ་འདི་།

6 ནམ་དུ་ཡང་མྱི་གཏང་མའ་ཞིག་

7 པར་བགྱི་འོ་།ཡོ་བྱད་སྦྱརད་།

8 པའ་ཡང་།དེ་ལས་མྱི་དགྲི་མྱི་

9 བསྐྱུང་བར་བགྱི་འོ་།དའ་ཕྱིན་

10 ཆད་།གདུང་རབས་རེ་རེ་ཞིང་ཡང་

11 བཙན་པོ་ཡབ་སྲས་ཀྱིས་འདི་།

12 བཞིན་ཡི་དམ་བཅའོ་།དེ་ལས་

13 མནའ་ཁ་དབུད་པ་དག་ཀྱང་།

14 མྱི་བགྱི་མྱི་བསྒྱུར་བར་།འཛིག་

THE BSAM-YAS *RDO-RINGS*

Translation

May the shrines[1] of the Three Jewels established in the temples of Ra-sa and Brag-mar and this practice of the religion of the Buddha never be abandoned or destroyed. The requisite properties that have been provided shall not be diminished or reduced. From now onwards each generation of the *btsan-po*, fathers and sons, shall make a vow in this way. And in order that there shall be no detraction from that oath and that it shall not be changed, the supra-

Notes to Translation

1. *rten* implying a support, container, image etc is difficult to translate satisfactorily.

Inscription

15 རྟེན་ལས:། འདའས:པའ:དང་།

16 འཇིག:རྟེན་གྱི:ལྷ་དང་། མི་མ:ཡིན:

17 པའ:། ཐམས:ཅད་ཀྱང:དཔང:དུ་།

18 གསོལ:ཏེ་། བཙན་པོ:ཡབ་སྲས:དང་

19 རྗེ་བློན་ཀུན་གྱིས་དབུ་སྙུང:དང་བྲོ:།

20 བོར་རོ:། གཙིགས:ཀྱི:ཡི:གེ:ཞིབ:

21 མོ:གཙིག:ཞི་གུད་ན་མཆིས་སོ།

Translation

mundane gods, the gods of the world, and the spirits[2] are all invoked as witnesses. The *btsan-po,* father and son, ruler and ministers[3] all have so sworn. A detailed account of the edict exists separately.

Notes to Translation (continued)

2. In the detailed edict in PT 109a the invocation has a more Buddhist appearance, beginning with the Buddhas of the ten directions, all the holy doctrine, the assembly of Bodhisattvas, the Pratyeka Buddhas and disciples; and ending with an array of autochthonous deities, gods of Tibet, Klu, Gnod-sbyin and Mi-ma-yin.

3. *rje-blon.* Thomas, TLTD II translates "eminent counsellor". Dagyab's dictionary gives "king and ministers" and see the Rkong-po inscription where the two words are separated by a *shad* (see p. 70).

REIGN OF KHRI SRONG-LDE-BRTSAN 755–*c.* 794 A.D.

The Bell at Bsam-yas

Hanging at the entrance to the *gtsug-lag-khang* of Bsam-yas is a fine bronze bell of Chinese design. An inscription in two lines runs round the upper part. It is divided into panels by vertical strapwork decoration. The text has been published by Tucci in TTK pp. 69 and 108 and by me in *JRAS* Oct. 1954 pp. 167, 168. There are photographs in TTK fig. 5 and in Tucci, *Transhimalaya* pl. 110.

The bell was the donation of Queen Rgyal-mo-brtsan and her son. I have not seen her name elsewhere in 8th/9th century sources and the fullest information about her is in PT which as has been seen (p. 26) makes use of early records, probably from Bsam-yas. In vol. *ja* f. 98b. he gives a list of the five queens of Khri Srong-lde-brtsan and names 'Bro-bza' Khri Rgyal-mo-brtsan as one of three who founded temples at Bsam-yas. Because she had no son and her homeland was far away there would be no one to maintain it so her temple was small in comparison with that of the Tshe-spong (properly Tshes-pong) queen who founded the Me-tog-sgron (Mi-ldog-sgrol, p. 26) and whose sons Mu-ne Btsan-po and Khri Lde-srong-brtsan succeeded their father. PT also states that because she had no son she became a nun with the name Byang-chub-rje (*ja* 104b) and in *ja* 116a Jo-mo Byang-chub is named as one of those present at the great religious debate between the Indian and Chinese doctrines. Demiéville in *Le Concile de Lhasa* proposes acceptably that the year of the debate was 792 A.D.; and in the dossier of the Chinese Master Mahayana, which he published, it is seen that "the Empress of the family of Mou-lou ('Bro") had been initiated by the Master into the Chinese doctrine and became a nun together with a maternal aunt of the king and thirty other noble ladies (Demiéville pp. 25–33). That apparently occurred some time before the debate. Jo-mo Byang-chub figures as the donor of another great bell, that at Khra-'brug, and its inscription shows that it was cast for her by a Chinese monk. The Khra-'brug bell is considerably later than that at Bsam-yas, having been set up in the reign of Khri Lde-srong-brtsan.

Although part of PT's account is substantiated by the early evidence, his statement that the 'Bro queen had no son is contradicted by the inscription on the Bsam-yas bell. In *JRAS* 1954 I drew attention to the record in DTH 58/65 of the birth of a son to Khri Srong-lde-brtsan in 760 A.D. and to the statement in PT *ja* 126 that the king had four sons, the first of whom died young. PT attributes them all to the Tshes-pong queen but that may be a mistake as by his account no more sons were born until Mu-ne Btsan-po in 774 A.D. It is probable that the child born in 760 was the son of the 'Bro queen and that he was alive when Bsam-yas was built, at which time his mother in dedicating the bell on their joint behalf used her lay name Rgyal-mo-brtsan. In the inscription on the Khra-'brug bell, in which no son is associated, the queen used her religious name, Byang-chub, which suggests that her son had died and she had taken orders as a nun before the accession of Khri Lde-srong-brtsan about 800–804 A.D.

In later histories there are a few references to a bell at Bsam-yas. The *Padma bka'-thang* f. 183 relates that when it was intended to hang a bell in the *lha-khang* the *mi-ma-yin* spirits prevented it until Padma Sambhava drove them out; whereupon it was possible to hang the bell. PT *ja* f. 76 tells of a *cong* that was taken from Mgrin-bzang of Brag-mar when it was destroyed in the anti-Buddhist reaction at the end of the reign of Khri Lde-gtsug-brtsan. It was first kept at Mchims-phu and then sent to Bsam-yas where it became the *dge-rgyas* bell. The Dge-rgyas *gtsug-lag-khang* is the name of the temple at Bsam-yas attributed to the 'Bro queen and among its furnishings PT *ja* f. 98b mentions a bell for making music, *rol mor cong*. It is impossible that the bell now at Bsam-yas could have been made thirty years or more before the foundation of the monastery for the inscription is part of the casting; but it might have been hung originally in the Dge-rgyas temple. There might, of course, have been other *cong* which have not survived. The *Padma bka'-thang* f. 183 mentions a *cong-khang*—bell house—in the temple of Me-tog-sgron attributed to the Tshes-pong queen; but it is likely that the various stories have developed around the bell now at the entrance to the main temple at Bsam-yas. The making of such large bells was a considerable undertaking and although the Tibetans had a reputation as metal workers there is no evidence that they had acquired by that time the art of metal casting. According to later tradition Chinese craftsmen were employed on the decoration of Bsam-yas. A Chinese monk supervised the casting of the Khra-'brug bell at the beginning of the 9th century. Chinese monks had been invited to Tibet in 781 A.D. according to the Tse Fu Yuan Kuei and it is possible that one of them, perhaps the same one who cast the Khra-'brug bell, was commissioned by the queen to make that at Bsam-yas with its unmistakably Chinese shape. As for its date, it may be placed in the decade between 780 and 790 A.D.

The two sections of the text below indicate the two lines of the inscription and the spaces show where it is divided by the panels on the bell. There are no punctuation signs between words. The last letter of *dbyal* in the second part of the second line is separated from the rest of the word by one of the bars dividing the panels but as it would be confusing to show it that way it has been joined up in my copy.

Inscription

ཇོ་མོ་རྒྱལ་མོ་བརྩན་ཁུམ། སྲས་ཀྱིས་ཚོགས་བཅུའི། དཀོན་མཆོག་གསུམ་ལ
མཆོད་པའི་སླད་དུ་ཅོང། འདི་བགྱིས་ཏེ་དེའི་བསོད། ནམས་ཀྱི་སྟོབས་ཀྱིས

ལྷ་བཙན་པོ་ཁྲི་སྲོང་ལྡེ། བརྩན་ཡབ་སྲས་སྟངས་དབྱལ། གསུང་དབྱངས་དྲུག་ཅུ
སྒྲ་དབྱངས་དང་ལྡན་ཏེ། བླ་ན་མེད་པའི་བྱང་ཆུབ། དུ་གྲུབ་པར་སྨོན་ཏོ།

THE BELL AT BSAM-YAS

Translation

"Queen Rgyal-mo-brtsan, the mother and her son, had this bell[1] made for the worship of the Three Jewels of the Ten Directions and pray that by the power of that merit the Divine King Khri Srong-lde-brtsan, father, son and consort,[2] may be endowed with the harmonious sound of the sixty attributes of the voice of the Buddha[3] and attain supreme enlightenment."

Notes to Translation

1. *cong* Chinese *c'ung*, Laufer 'Loan Words', see Tucci TTK p. 84 n. 125.

2. *Stangs dbyal.* Thomas (TLTD II p. 189), who mistakes this for a polite form of address, cites several variants: *stang dbyald; stangs byal; gtangs dbyal; stangs dgyal; stangs bsbyal.* DTH p. 20 has *btsan-po stangs dbyal.* The term also appears in later literature in the *rnam-thar* of the Fifth Dalai Lama and in a Sikkim *gnas-yig.* Professor D. L. Snellgrove informs me that it is found in early Bon-po works where according to Lopon Namdak it means "husband and wife" which is how it was explained in a verbal communication from the late Zurkhang Shappé who gave its modern form as *gtan zhal*—with the dubious etymology "constant companions". In early *mss* each component is found separately e.g. DTH p. 99 *btsan-po rje dbyal*; Pell T 1288 ed. M. Lalou *JA* 1958, l. 1 *dbyal mo gnyi*; l. 16 *ma dang yum gyi mtshan dbyal gun gun ma*; l. 59 *dmu'i pha yab gyi mtshan na'a gtangs brags cha dang ma yum gyi mtshan dbyal drum cha'i ngur ngur*; in AFL V l. 69 Thomas translates *gtan* in *gtan gyis rogs bza ni* as "husband"; in Pell T 1288 l. 119 *khab dang dbyal du bzhed* (took to wife) is echoed in Pell T. 1040 *khab dang dbyal du blangs ste* and AFL I B *khab dang dbyal du bgyis te*; cf. Lhasa Treaty inscription, E ls. 25 and 28 *khab du blangs.*

3. The sixty attributes of the Buddha are listed in the *Mahavyutpatti* XX (TTK p. 84 n. 126).

REIGN OF KHRI SRONG-LDE-BRTSAN 755–*c.* 794 A.D.

The *rdo-rings* near the bridge-head at 'Phyong-rgyas

[Plate 5]

This pillar stands in an exposed position to the south of a small bridge over the stream below the *rdzong* at 'Phyong-rgyas beside the track leading to the tombs of the kings (*bang-so*) about half a mile distant. The north face once bore an inscription; on the south face are carved the figures of a lion and a dragon now rather indistinct. When I visited the place in 1949 the north face had been so severely eroded by wind and sand that only a few letters could be read. I recorded them, so far as possible, line by line in their positions on the pillar. Some way down the pillar the name Khri Srong-lde could be made out; and local tradition attributed the inscription to Khri Srong-lde-brtsan but nothing was known of its contents. It seemed that a valuable historical record had been lost. But some time after I had left Tibet I received through the generosity of the distinguished Sikkimese scholar Rai Bahadur T. D. Densapa a copy of a manuscript collection of early inscriptions said to have belonged to the Ka-thog lama Rig-'dzin Tshe-dbang nor-bu (RT) a well-known man of learning in the 18th century (1698–1755)—see my *A Tibetan Antiquarian of the XVIIIth Century* in the Sikkim Bulletin of Tibetology IV 1967. In that collection is one headed *'Phyong-rgyas stag-rtse zam sna'i rdo-ring.* It proved possible to match the majority of the letters I had copied with RT's text in such a way as to restore, at least approximately, the original arrangement on the pillar, line by line, which is not shown in RT's copy. In a few cases I had been mistaken in copying damaged letters but enough survived to identify my fragments with RT's text.

The other inscriptions in the collection are those at Rkong-po De-mo-sa, Skar-cung, Khri Lde-srong-brtsan's tomb, and the Lhasa Treaty pillar. From a gloss on the last-named it appears that some of the copies date back at least to the 15th century.

From comparison of RT's copies with inscriptions of which photographs are available it is seen that his texts are generally reliable. In the copies, which were apparently made by different writers, archaic orthography has usually been modernised; the reversed *ki-gu, da-drag,* and *ya-btags* in such words as *myi* are for the most part, but not invariably, omitted; early forms have been changed to those with which the writer was familiar; sometimes words the copyist could not read were omitted without any indication; and the inevitable errors of copying by eye can be detected. But with those qualifications, the standard is good and it has been possible to restore several words where an inscription has been damaged since RT's copies were made.

I published RT's text of the 'Phyong-rgyas inscription in *JRAS* 1 and 2 1964 with a few modifications based on my own record of the remains and on comparison with contemporary inscriptions elsewhere. The reversed *ki-gu* has been shown where my record found it; *ya-btags* has been inserted, *la stsogs* corrected to *las stsogs* and *zhal snga* to *zha snga.* RT seems to have preserved the use of the *shad* in the original but there is no evidence for the *tsheg* so I have inserted this in single form. I may draw attention to an oversight in my article where on p. 4 I have said that the name Khri-lde-srong is visible; my notes show that this should be Khri srong-lde.

The inscription probably falls within the five years between 795 and 800. It might have been written after the king's death, the date of which is not certain but was perhaps 799 A.D.; but as it is stated in the 18th century account of Rang-byung rdo-rje that the tomb of Khri Srong-lde-brtsan was constructed while he was still alive, it is possible that the inscribed pillar was also set up in his lifetime. A photograph of the pillar may be seen on plate 5.

As I have commented in that article the inscription echoes strongly the account of Khri Srong-lde-brtsan's reign in DTH 114–15. There are also many similarities in the phraseology to that of the inscriptions at the tomb of Khri Lde-srong-brtsan and that at Rkong-po De-mo-sa (pp. 64–77). The burial rites at 'Phyong-rgyas were of pre-Buddhist character and I have drawn attention to the representation of the king as defending the faith and achieving the perfection of both the traditional religion and the new Buddhism. In this inscription the title *Chos-rgyal* is for the first recorded time applied to a Tibetan ruler.

Inscription

1 ༄། །ལྷ་བཙན་པོ་ཡབ་སྲས་ལྷ་དང་མྱིའི

2 རྗེར་གཤེགས་ཏེ། ཆོས་གཙུག་ལག་ཞི་

3 ལུགས་ཀྱིས་བཟང༌། །དབུ་རྨོག་བརྩན་པོ་ནི་

4 བྱིན་དུ་ཆེའོ། །

5 ༄། །ལྷ་བཙན་པོ་ཁྲི་སྲོང་ལྡེ་བརྩན་གྱི་ཞ་

6 སྔ་ནས་ཀྱང༌། ཡབ་མྱེས་ཀྱི་ལུགས་བཞིན།

7 ལྷའི་གཙུག་ལག་འོ་མ་ཉམས། གནམ་

8 པའི་ཆོས་དང་ནི་འཕྲུལ་པར་མཛད། སྐུ་

9 ཡོན་ཏན་ཡོངས་ཀྱིས་བརྗོད་པའི་ཡི་གེ།

10 ནམ་ཞིག་རྡོ་རིངས་ལ་བྲིས་སོ། །

11 ཆོས་རྒྱལ་ཆེན་པོས་ཕྲིན་ལས་སུ་ཅི་

12 མཛད་པ་དང༌། དབུ་རྨོག་བརྩན་པོའི་བྱིན་

13 ཀྱིས། ཆབ་སྲིད་སྐྱེས་པ་ལས་སྟོགས་པའི་

14 གཏམ་གྱི་ཡི་གེ། ཞིབ་མོ་གཅིག་ནི། གུད་

15 ན་ཡོད་དོ། །

16 ༄། །འཕྲུལ་གྱི་ལྷ་བཙན་པོ་ཁྲི་སྲོང་ལྡེ་

17 བརྩན་གྱི་ཞ་སྔ་ནས། མཐའ་བཞིའི་རྒྱལ་པོ་

THE *RDO-RINGS* NEAR THE BRIDGE-HEAD AT 'PHYONG-RGYAS

Translation

When the divine Btsan-po, the ancestors, came to rule over gods and men, religious learning and order were made excellent by their customs: their mighty helmet was great in glory[1].

The divine Btsan-po Khri Srong-lde-brtsan, too, in accordance with the custom of his ancestors did not impair the world order of the gods; he acted in agreement with the religion of heaven and earth. Of his meritorious achievement, praised by all, a record has been written on a stone pillar never to be destroyed. Of what deeds the great Religious King did, of the increase of his kingdom by the glory of his mighty helmet, and so on, an account recording them in detail exists elsewhere.

The supernaturally wise divinity[2], the Btsan-po Khri Srong-lde-brtsan, being beyond comparison with other kings of the four fron-

Notes to Translation

1. Madame A. Macdonald in *Une lecture des Pelliot tibétain 1286 etc.* (*Études Tibétaines, 1971*) has brilliantly analysed the cult words of the politico-religious system of the early Tibetan kings, especially *gtsug, lha, chos, 'phrul, byin* which are found in this inscription; *gtsug* and *gtsug lag*, in particular, defy exact translation.

2. *'phrul* in relation to the early, legendary kings, as Madame Macdonald argues (loc. cit.), describes magical powers but for the historical kings it implies, rather, intellectual qualities, though of a superhuman nature. That is confirmed for the expression *'phrul gyi lha* (which I formerly translated "divine manifestation") in *Un ensemble sémantique* by Professor R. A. Stein (*BSOAS* XXXVI, 1973) who shows that *'phrul* is there an analogue of Chinese *cheng* "sage" in the title of the Emperor, and in other instances also. The meaning of special wisdom is shared by the connected root *sprul*: e.g. *sprul-pa'i drang srong* (Pell. T. 992 l. 19) and *khye'u sprul-pas* (ibid. l. 75). But both *sprul* and *'phrul* also denote magical transformation. There are many examples of *sprul-pa* in that sense in Emmerick, *Tibetan Texts Concerning Khotan* (see his index); while in the *Mahavyutpatti* 3083, *'phrul* has the Sanskrit equivalent *nirmita.* Compliments in letters included in the Tun-huang *mss* include *lha dang 'dra* (TLTD II 382 (78) and *'phrul dang 'dra* (ibid. p. 185) which might suggest that *lha 'phrul* in the inscription at Khri Lde-srong-brtsan's tomb ll. 13 and 22 (pp. 86, 88 below) and in the Lhasa Treaty inscription East, l. 34 (p. 112 below) could mean "divine manifestation"; but as in the latter instance it occurs in the same inscription as *'phrul gyi lha*, it probably has the same meaning.

Inscription

18 གཞན་དང་མྱི་འདྲ་སྟེ། ཕྱིན་གྱི་སྐམ་དཀྱིལ་
19 ཆེན་པོ་དང༌། དབུ་རྨོག་བརྩན་པོས། ཡར་ནི་
20 ཏ་ཞིག་གྱི་མཚམས་མན་ཆད། མར་ནི་ལོང་
21 ཁན་གྱི་ལ་རྒྱུད་ཡན་ཆད། ཆབ་འོག་འདུ་
22 སྟེ། ཆབ་སྲིད་ནི་ལྷོ་བྱང་ཕར་ཟུབ།
23 མཐས་ཀླུས་པར་ཆེའོ། །དེ་ལྟར་ཆབ་སྲིད་
24 ཆེ་བའི་ཕྱིན་གྱིས། བོད་ཡོངས་ཡུལ་ཆེ། ཤིང
25 སྡུག་ཏུ་གྱུརད་པས། ནང་ནས་ཀྱང༌། ནམ་
26 ཞར་བདེ་ཞིང་སྐྱིད་པར་གནས་སོ། །
27 ཐུགས་ལ་བྱང་ཆུབ་སྤྱོད་པ་ལྷབས་པོ་
28 ཆེ་མངའ་བས། འཇིག་རྟེན་ལས་འདས་པའི་
29 ཆོས་བཟང་པོ་བརྙེས་ནས། ཀུན་ལ་བཀའ་
30 དྲིན་དུ་ཕྱིན་ནོ། །དེ་ལྟར་འགྲེང་དུད་
31 གཉིས་ལ། འཕྲུལ་ཡུན་གཉིས་ཀྱི་བཀའ་དྲིན་
32 ཆེན་པོས་མ་ཁྱབ་པ་མྱེད་དེ། །མྱི་ཡོངས་
33 ཀྱིས་མཚན་ཡང༌། འཕྲུལ་གྱི་ལྷ་བྱང་ཆུབ་
34 ཆེན་པོར་གསོལ་ཏོ། །

Translation

tiers, by his gloriously profound intellect and his mighty helmet from the borders of Ta-zhig[3] in the upper direction and from the line of passes of the Long Shan[4] in the lower direction all was drawn together beneath his sway and his dominion extended south, north, east and west beyond the furthest bounds. In this way, by the glory of the greatness of the dominion the whole of Tibet became great in territory and wealthy throughout. And within too, being always at peace it dwelt in happiness.

When through possessing in his mind the acts of enlightenment in great abundance he had found the excellent supramundane religion, he bestowed it as a favour on all. In this way, as to both men and beasts[5], there was none not covered by his great favour both for the present and the future. And all men gave him the name 'Phrul Gyi Lha Byang Chub Chen Po—the Great Enlightened Supernaturally Wise Divinity.

Notes to Translation (continued)

3. Ta-zhig. roughly the Khorasan and Transoxiana territories of the former Sassanian empire, dominated by the Arabs in the 8th century.
4. Long Shan: probably the mountains to the east of the Long-yu commandery on the present border between Shensi and Kansu.
5. *greng dud:* See my note in *JRAS* 1964 p. 9: the contrast between men and beasts is found in Pell T. 1038, *'greng 'go nag* and *dud rngog chag* (Macdonald ET p. 215).

REIGN OF KHRI LDE-SRONG-BRTSAN *c.* 800–815 A.D.

Inscriptions at Zhwa'i Lha-khang

[Plates 6–8]

Zhwa'i Lha-khang is a small temple about fifty miles north-east of Lhasa in a sheltered valley near the mouth of a stream which flows into the Skyid-chu from the direction of Nu-ma-ri in the east. On each side of the entrance is a tall stone pillar inscribed with a record of privileges granted at different times to Ban-de Myang Ting-nge-'dzin who founded the temple and who, as seen from the inscriptions, was the guardian of Khri Lde-srong-brtsan when young and later, as a minister of state, was instrumental in establishing him on the throne. When Khri Lde-srong-brtsan, following the example of his father, took an oath to maintain the Buddhist religion Ban-de Myang Ting-'dzin was one of the principal witnesses next to the great minister Ban-de Bran-ka Dpal-gyi yon-tan. A copy of his edict, like that of Khri Srong-lde-brtsan, is preserved in PT *ja* ff. 128b–130b.

Mention of Myang Ting-'dzin in later histories is not always reconcilable with the evidence of the Zhwa'i inscriptions. He was of special interest to 'Gos Lo-tsa-ba because of the tradition that he was the transmitter of the *snying-thig* which was taught to him by Vimalamitra. 'Gos was a later initiate of that doctrine. The account in *Deb-ther sngon-po Ga* f. 41a–41b, which does not appear to be in strict chronological order, is that Vimalamitra who came to Tibet in the reign of Khri Srong-lde-brtsan taught the *snying-thig* to the *btsan-po* and to Myang Ting-'dzin. He later went to China. When the *btsan-po* was young Myang Ting-'dzin acted as his guardian. After his ordination the king and ministers granted him an estate for monastic support (*rkyen-ris*).; 'Gos says he himself saw the charter, written on blue silk. At the age of 55 his mind having been purified, he died leaving no physical trace. 'Gos then relates, rather obscurely, that the guardian deity Rdo-rje legs-pa caused a hail storm in Khams and sent 500 camel loads as tax, which turned into grain. PT *ja* f. 108 has the version that the god turned a hail storm into grain which poured down a chimney through a hat placed there until it filled the lower rooms thus providing funds for the temple; and that a *bka'-gtsigs* giving Myang authority over the region was inscribed on a stone pillar. PT further records in *ja* f. 137b that Myang Ting-'dzin bzang-po was among those killed in the persecution of Buddhism by Glang Dar-ma; but that cannot be reconciled with the *Deb Sngon* and is perhaps due to the association of Myang Ting-'dzin with Bran-ka Dpal-yon who was the principal victim at that time. 'Gos would surely have reported the martyrdom of the transmitter of the *snying-thig* if that had been the authentic tradition.

There may be confusion between the names of Khri Srong-lde-brtsan and Khri Lde-srong-brtsan for it is certain that Myang Ting-nge-'dzin was guardian to Khri Lde-srong-brtsan and that he was alive as late as 812 A.D. and so, on 'Gos's statement that he died at the age of 55, he could not have been the guardian also of Khri Srong-lde-brtsan (b 742) although that is implied by PT in *tha* f. 21 as well as by 'Gos. On the other hand, although PT mistakes the reign in which the pillars were erected, it is not impossible that a *rkyen-ris* was granted by Khri Srong-lde-brtsan for the Zhwa'i inscriptions appear to confer privileges over an estate of which the Ban-de was already in possession.

REIGN OF KHRI LDE-SRONG-BRTSAN *c.* 800–815 A.D.

A possible sequence of events, putting together evidence from various sources, is: Myang Ting-nge-'dzin, born *c.* 760; ordained after the building of Bsam-yas *c.* 780; meditated for seven years (PT *tha* 21b); became guardian to Khri Lde-srong-brtsan (b 776) *c.* 788; granted a *rkyen-ris:* opposed Ye-shes dbang-po before the debate of 792 (*Sba-bzhad* p. 54); arranged for Vimalamitra to be invited to Tibet 794–6; helped Khri Lde-srong-brtsan in the troubles *c.* 800 and eventually established him on the throne *c.* 804; died *c.* 815.

The Myang clan whose origin may have been in the upper valley of the Myang-chu around Rgya-mda', was one of those that joined in the making of the Tibetan kingdom in the 6th century. As a reward its leader received estates including the castle of Sngur-ba (Pell T 1287 p. 191). It is likely that Zhwa'i Lha-khang was built on land belonging to the Myang clan; and near the temple are the ruins of a large building like an early fort, which may have been a palace of the Myang, perhaps even Mkhar Sngur-ba.

The *lha-khang* was the residence of another Myang Lama—Shes-rab 'byung-gnas (*Deb Sngon* 173–174) early in the 11th century; but by the 14th century it had fallen into neglect and the *dkar-chag* of the lha-khang records that the great Rnying-ma-pa Lama, Klong-chen-pa, also an exponent of *snying-thig*, repaired it and by his magical powers caused the *rdo-rings*, which had fallen to the ground, to rise upright. At a later date Sde-srid Sangs-rgyas rgya-mtsho, perhaps speculatively, connects Nyang (sic.) Ting-'dzin bzang-po with the Nyang valley near Se-ra and so with the 12th century teacher Mnga'-bdag Nyang Nyi-ma 'od-zer (VSP p. 415).

The inscriptions have a bearing on the obscure history of the period. Uncertainty surrounds the dates of the death of Khri Srong-lde-brtsan, the reign of his eldest surviving son Mu-ne btsan-po, the fate of the next son Mu-rug-brtsan, and the accession of the youngest, Khri Lde-srong-brtsan. Contemporary Tibetan sources provide no precise information and statements in the T'ang Annals are difficult to interpret in the light of later Tibetan histories. Without going into detailed discussion, I take the view that Khri Srong-lde-brtsan abdicated in 797 in favour of Mu-ne btsan-po and died perhaps *c.* 799 A.D. Mu-ne had a short and troubled reign until 799/800 when Khri Lde-srong-brtsan was chosen in preference to his elder brother Mu-rug-brtsan which led to disturbances before his rule could be consolidated. Dr Erik Haarh, in Acta Orientalia 1961, has ingeniously argued that Mu-rug was recognized as *btsan-po* by the Chinese, under the name Tsu-chih-chien, until his death in 804. The theory depends on the T'ang Annals and finds no support in early Tibetan records which know only Mu-ne and Khri Lde-srong-brtsan as successors to the throne of Khri Srong-lde-brtsan. The earlier of the Zhwa'i inscriptions—that on the west pillar (W) shows that Khri Lde-srong-brtsan felt himself able, as *btsan-po*, to bind his elder brother Mu-rug-brtsan by his oath to obey the edict. There is no indication that, as Haarh suggests, Mu-rug-brtsan was the king's guardian; that position is seen to have been held by Myang Ting-nge-'dzin. The date of the first inscription is not certain. The later inscription states that the second edict was made in "the later dragon year" *'brug-lo phyi-ma*, implying that it was the second such year in the reign, which can only be 812 A.D. That would show that Khri Lde-srong-brtsan claimed to have ruled since 800 A.D.; but it is also clear from the first inscription that there was much disturbance in the country before he could ascend the throne. It is probable that a considerable time elapsed between the two inscriptions and I suggest that the first may have been written *c.* 804/805 A.D.

The edicts are perhaps the earliest contemporary evidence of a monk acting as minister of state for the first date that can be assigned to the tenure of office by Bran-ka Dpal-yon is a letter to him from Po Chu-i in 808 A.D. (J. Kolmaś, Archív Orientální 1966); and although he figures as the principal witness to Khri Lde-srong-brtsan's edict to maintain Buddhism that seems to be later than the first Zhwa'i edict for there is no mention there of Mu-rug brtsan.

There is a uniquely personal character in the Zhwa'i inscriptions. The words "I". "me", "by me" etc. are used throughout and the expressions of gratitude have the ring of genuine warmth and affection. In the other inscriptions of the period *nged*(I) appears once only, in the Skar-cung edict.

The terms of the grants to Myang Ting-nge-'dzin may be compared with those of the grants to Stag-sgra klu-khong in the Zhol inscription and to Tshes-pong Stag-bzang nya-sto in that at Lcang-bu (pp. 93, 101). Since Ting-nge-'dzin was a monk and celibate the advantages of the edict were to be continued to his kinsmen who were descendants of his grandfather Myang Snang-bzang 'dus-kong. At the end of the edict there is a short addition extending the privileges previously granted to the family of Tin-nge-'dzin's grand-uncle Dbyi-gong. That branch of the clan appears to have benefited from the favoured position of Ting-nge-'dzin and the grant is explained as giving to the Myang clan similar privileges to those granted to the Dba's. The latter had been associates of the Myang in the establishment of the kingdom in the 6th century but, whereas Myang suffered eclipse with the fall of the great Myang Mang-po-rje Zhang-snang early in the reign of Srong-brtsan sgam-po, the Dba's continued to be leading figures in the state and frequently provided a Chief Minister. Prominent monks from the clan were Ye-shes dbang-po, who is said to have been opposed by Myang Ting-nge-'dzin (p. 44), and Dpal-dbyangs who, according to tradition succeeded Shantarakshita as head of religion. Both are named in a document from Tun-huang (TLTD II p. 85).

The texts, which were first published in *JRAS* 1952 and 1954, are based on copies and photographs made by me in 1948 and checked on a second visit in the following year. The inscriptions are finely carved and almost undamaged. There is slight flaking at the beginning of the last line of W; and in E the first letter of seven lines is effaced and two short passages are illegible but there is no difficulty in restoring the readings. Punctuation is not entirely consistent. A single *tsheg* is usual but a double *tsheg* is found at the end of some lines. A *tsheg* is sometimes used before a *shad* with letters other than *nga.* On both pillars the carving is similar but the texts may have been composed by different hands. In W there are six examples of the *da-drag* but none in E. Also the writing of *bka'* in W is unusual; it appears six times as *bk* (*b* on top of *k*) and only once correctly as *bka'.* In E its orthography is orthodox with one exception where the final letter is omitted. The differences may represent a conscious standardization during the reign of Khri Lde-srong-brtsan.

At the end of each inscription is a coffered recess which once held the king's seal; one of these can be seen in pl. 6.

REIGN OF KHRI LDE-SRONG-BRTSAN *c.* 800–815 A.D.

West Inscription

1 ༄། །གནམ་ལྷབ་ཀྱི་རྒྱལ་པོ། འཕྲུལ་གྱི་ལྷ་བཙན་པོ་ཁྲི་

2 ལྡེ་སྲོང་བརྩན་གྱི་།བཀས། བན་དེ་མྱང་

3 ཏིང་ངེ་འཛིན་། དབུ་སྨྱུང་གཙོགས་གཡུང་དྲུང་དུ་གནང་བ།

4 བན་དེ་ཏིང་ངེ་འཛིན་ལྷ་ཞིག། གདོད་ནས་མཐར་སྐྱིང་ཉེ་སྟེ།།ང་

5 སྐུ་ཆུང་ངུ་ནུས་ཆབ་སྲིད་མ་བཞེས་པའི་བར་དུ་ཡབ་ཡུཾ་ཀྱི་གོ་བྲ་སྟེ་

6 ལེགས་པ་ལ་ཞེན་པར་བྱས། ཞུ་དྲུང་པོའི་གོ་བྱས་ཏེ་སྐྱུ་བཙས།

7 ཡབ་སྲས་གཅེན་གཅུང་ཡུཾ་སྲས། བླ་འོག་དགྱེས་ཤི་འཐུན་བྱཿ

8 སྒྲུརད། ཕྱིར་ལེགས་པའི་བླ་གྲོས་གསོལ་ཅིང་། ལས་སུ་བྱས་པ

9 ལས་སྐོགས་ཏེ་། དཔེན་པ་བྱེད་བྱེད། སྐྱིང་ཉེ་ཉེའོ། །ཕྱིས་ཡབ་དང་

10 གཅེན་ཐུགས་ཞོངས་བརྟུད་པར་བྱུང་བའི་རྗེས། །ང་ཆབ་སྲིདཿ

11 མ་བཞེས་པའི་སྐབས་སུ་ཁ་ཅིག་ཕན་ཕུན་དུ། གདོན་སྐོན་པ་དག་

12 ཡོད་པ་ཡང། བན་དེ་ཏིང་ངེ་འཛིན་གྱིས་ཉི་དོད་བྱེན་ནས། དཔེན་ངཿ

13 པའི་བླ་གྲོས་གསོལ་ད་། ཁྲག་ཁྲུག་མྱེད་པར་བྱས། ལེགས་པ་བྱུའོ་ཆོག

14 གེ་གཞི་བཟུང་ནས། ངའི་ཆབ་སྲིད་ལས་སྐོགས་སྟེ། ཕྱིར་ལེགས་པའི་

15 ལས་ཆེན་པོ་བྱས་ཏེ། ངའི་ཞ་སྔར་། ཆབ་སྲིད་འདོན་འདོནད་། སྐྱིང་

16 ཉེ་ཉེ། བླ་འོག་ཀུན་གྱི་གཟུངས་བྱས་ཏེ། ཕྱོགས་སུ་འཁྲུག་པ་མྱེད་ཏུ་

INSCRIPTIONS AT ZHWA'I LHA-KHANG

Translation

West Inscription

By order of the king of mid-heaven,[1] the supernaturally wise divinity the *btsan-po* Khri Lde-srong-brtsan. For Ban-de Myang Ting-nge-'dzin a sworn edict granted immutably.

As regards Ban-de Ting-nge-'dzin: from first to last he has been loyal[2] and from my childhood until I obtained the kingdom he took the place of father and mother and acted with devotion to what is good. Taking the place of a wise uncle[3] he cared for me. He united happily in agreement, high and low, father and son, elder brother and younger brother, mother and child. Giving advice for the general good and in the performance of his duties and so on he continually rendered valuable service and was very loyal. Later, after my father and elder brother had fallen into repeated disagreement, before I obtained the kingdom there was some confusion and a contention of evil spirits; but Ban-de Ting-nge-'dzin, taking consideration about the matter, gave beneficial advice. He put an end to the disturbances. Making it his principle to do whatever is good, and doing many things for the general good and for my kingdom he continued to raise up the kingdom for my sake. He was very loyal; and acting in the interests of all, high and low, as there was no disturbance in any

Notes to Translation

1. *lhab*, which may mean "wide", is probably here for *lhabs*, "middle" cf. DTH p. 81 and note 7, p. 85.
2. *snying-nye*, the equivalent of *glo-ba-nye* in the Zhol inscriptions etc.
3. *zhang drung-po.* Although the Myang clan had no claim to the formal description of *zhang*, maternal uncle, in view of Ban-de Ting-nge-'dzin's activity as a family reconciler, and of the form *drung-po*, I take it to mean that he was assuming the responsibilities customarily falling upon true maternal uncles of a young *btsan-po.* But another interpretation might be possible for in Pell T. 1071 and TLTD II 353, there is mention of a high official, the *btsan-po'i zhang-drung* (= *zhang-lon drung-pa*?) which suggests one in constant attendance on the *btsan-po*—a minister-in-waiting or lord chamberlain.

West Inscription

17 བདེ་བར་བྱེད་བྱེད་དོ། །ཆབ་སྲིད་ཀྱི་བློན་པོ་ཆེན་པོ[1]་ལས་བྱས་ཀྱིས་

18 ཀྱང་། འཕྲུལ་ཡུན་གཉིས་སུ་སྨྲིར་ལེགས་ཤིང་དཔེན་པ་འབའ་ཞིག་

19 བྱེད་བྱེད་དོ། །འདི་ལྟར་སྔ་ཕྱི་གཉིས་སུ་གང་བས་ཀྱང་ལྷག་པར་སྙིང་

20 ཉེ་ཞིང་། ཆོ་ཕ་ཆེན་པོ་འབྱུང་འབྱུང་བ། སྔོན་གྱི་ལྷ་དཔེ་དྲུ་སྤྲུར་ཞིང་། བཀྲ་

21 དྲིན་འོས་པྲ་སྦྱིན་བྲ་དགོངས་པ་ལས། བན་དེ་ཉིད་རྗེས་འབངས་ཀྱི་

22 ལུགས་དུ། དགེ་སློང་གི་ཚུལ་འཛིན་ཅིང་། སྐ་དྲིན་གྱི་བོད་ཕྲ་གསོལ་གྱིས

23 ཀྱང། ཆོ་ཕའི་ལས། སྐ་དྲིན་སྦྱིན་པའི་ཆོས་ཡིན་བས། །ངའི།བཀས།

24 བན་དེ་ཏིང་ངེ་འཛིན། གཙིགས་བརྟན་བ་བྱིན་ཏེ། །སྲིད་གཡུང་དྲུང

25 དུ་གནང་བ། ཡུན་དུ་བརྟན་ཞི་བདེ་བར་བྱ་བ་དུ། ཀུན་ཀྱིས་ཤེས་པར་བྱ་

26 བའི་ཕྱིར། །དཀོན་མཆོག་གི་རྟེན། གཙུག་ལག་ཁང་འདིར། གཙིགས

27 ཀྱི་མཁར་བུ་བརྩིགས། རྡོ་རིངས་བཙུགས་ནས། །གཙིགས་ཀྱི་མདོ།

28 རྡོ་ལ་མངོན་བར་བྲིས་ཏེ་མཐུ་ཕྱག་རྒྱས་བཏབ་ནས་བཞག་པ་ཡི་གྲིས་

29 སྲུས་དགོན་ཕྱི་མ་མདྷ་མཛད་པ་རྫིས་དུ། ཆབ་སྲིད་ཀྱི་བློན་པོ་ཕྱི་མ་དབུ་

30 བྱེད་ལས་སྐོགས་པས་ཀྱང་། ཞིཾ་ཞིཾ་ཁ་ཁར་གཙིགས་ཀྱི་ཡི་གེ་ལས་འབྱུང་

31 བ་དུ། རྡོ་རིངས་ལ་བྲིས་པ་ལས་མྱི་དབྲི་མྱི་བཙོས་མྱི་བསྒྱུར་བར་གྱིས་སྒོ། །

32 ཞིཾ་ཞིཾ་ཁ་ཁར། །བཙན་པོ་གདུང་རབས་རྒྱུད་ཀྱིས། །བན་དེ་ཏིང་ངེ་འཛིན་དད་ཀྱི་

[1] པོ Cf. DTH pp. 17, 20, 21, etc.

Translation

quarter, he continually created peacefulness. In performance of his duties as great minister of the kingdom he continued to do only beneficial acts for the general good. In this way, both early and late, he was exceedingly loyal in everything and he frequently offered large gifts.[4] Although, in accordance with former precedents, I intended to bestow a suitable favour upon him, the Ban-de himself, adhering to the manners of a subject and the customs of a monk, requested that he should not receive any favour. Nevertheless, since it is a duty to bestow a suitable favour in return for gifts, by my order a firm edict has been given for Ban-de Ting-nge-'dzin granting him a privileged position for ever.

In order to ensure its long-lasting happiness and to make it known to all, in this temple the shrine of the Three Jewels, a small house[5] for the edict has been built and a stone pillar set up; and a summary of the edict, inscribed clearly on the stone and sealed at the end, has been placed here so that my sons and grandsons, who may rule hereafter, and the ministers of the kingdom who may later hold power, and all such persons, shall act for ever in accordance with the words of the edict and the inscription on the stone pillar, not diminishing, or modifying or altering them. And for ever and ever the

Notes to Translation (continued)

4. *zho sha* ''milk and meat'': probably regular offerings of produce —useful to feed the king's many retainers—rather than a money tax as I earlier suggested. Customary presents in Tibet up to recent times were sheep's carcases, butter, and grain.

5. *mkhar-bu*, a small stone shrine to hold the document: cf. *rten-mkhar* (Dagyab, p. 273.)

West Inscription

33 སློས་པོ་བློན་སྣང་བཟླ་འདུས་ཀོ་གི་བུ་ཆ་འཕེལ་རྒྱུད། །སྤྱན་རས་གྱིས:

34 བཙའ་ཕྱི་ཏོས་པ་ཞམ་འཁྲིང་དུ་གཞག་པ་དྲ། ཇི་ཙམ་དུ་ནུས་པར་བཀུར་

35 བསྟོད་པ་དྲ། གཞན་གྱིས་མནྲ་ཏོ། སྟོས་ལས་ཆད་ན། ལྷ་ཞོན་བླ་ནས་མཛད་

36 པ་དྲ། ཉེས་པྱ་དག་པ་མ་ཡིན་ན། འཕྲམ་མི་གསྟན། སྟོས་ལས་མྱི་གཅད་

37 པ་དྲ། སྣང་བཟླ་འདུས་ཀོ་གི་བུ་ཆ་འཕེལ་རྒྱུད། ལ་ལ་ཞིག་གིས་སྐྱ་དང་ཆབ:

38 སྲིད་ལ་སྙིང་རིངས་སོ། ཉེས་པ་གཞན་ཞིག་བྱས་ན་པྱ། གང་གིས་ཉེས་པ་ལ་མ།

39 ཕུ་ནུ་བུ་ཚ་མ་ཉེས་གཞུ་ལ་ཁྲིན་མྱི་མ། གྱོད་ལ་མྱི་གདགས། ལྷ་ནར་ད་མྱི་

40 མཛད། ཅི་ཉེས་ཀྱང་གྱོད་ན་གཅིག་གིས། བསྐྱང་བ་དྲ། ཡི་གེ་གཡུང་དྲུང་

41 མྱིང་མྱི་ནྒ་པར་བྱིན་པ་དྲ། ལས་སྣ་ཆེན་པོ་བདེ་བ་ཕུན་དུ་ཆང་ཀྱུར་བྱིན་བ

42 དྲ། སྟེའི་དཔོན་པོ་རྒྱུད་དུ་གནང་བ་དྲ། སྣང་བཟང་འདུས་ཀོ་གི་བུ་ཚ་འཕེལ

43 རྒྱུད་ཀྱི་བྲན་ཕྱི། འཁྲོག་སོག་ཆལ་ལས་སྩོགས་པ། ཞི་ཞར་རབས་ཆད་དེ། ལྷ:

44 གྱོད་ལ་ཐོགས་ན་ཡང། ཕྱག་དུ་མྱི་བཞེས། གཞན་གྱི་སྡེ་ན། མས་མ་ཕུལ་ཕན་

45 ཅད། ཅིའི་ཐབས་ཀྱིས་ཀྱང་མྱི་དགོག་མྱི་བཞེས་པར་གནང་བ་ལས་སྩོགས་སྟེ་

46 ཞི་ཞི་ཞེ་ཞར། བློན་སྣང་བཟང་འདུས་ཀོ་གི་བུ་ཚ་འཕེལ་རྒྱུད། སྲིད་བདེ་ཕྱི་བརྟན་

47 བའི་གཙོགས་གནང་བ་འདྲ། ཞི་ཞི་ཞ་ཞར་གནང་ཕྱི་མྱི་བསྒྱུར་གྱི་བཅོས་སྨྲ།

48 ངའི་ཞ་སྔ་ནས་ཀྱང་དབུ་སྙུང་གནང་། །གཅེན་སུ་རུག་བཙན་དྲ། ཇོ་མོ་མཆེད་དུ

Translation

royal line shall watch over the descendants of the minister Snang-bzang 'dus-kong,[6] the grandfather of Ban-de Ting-nge-'dzin, giving them suitable service near their person and honouring them according to their ability. And if others should harm or oppress them, a restraining order shall be given from above. And if no offence is proved against them, heed shall not be paid to slander, and they shall not be oppressed. If any of the descendants of Snang-bzang 'dus-kong is disloyal to our person and kingdom or commits any other offence, investigation[7] shall be made of the one who is guilty; there shall be no judicial investigation of relations and others who are not guilty; they shall not be brought to trial and no harsh order shall be passed against them. And whatever the offence, in the case of one charge,[8] it shall be set aside; and it is permitted that the title to the letter in perpetuity shall not be lost; and it is permitted that they shall hold various important posts in lasting peacefulness. And they are granted the succession to the governorship of a district. And the bondsmen, fields, grazing grounds, fallow lands, woodlands, and so on, belonging to the descendants of the minister Snang-bzang 'dus-kong shall never be resumed or given to another even if the line of descent be broken or they become involved in a criminal charge. Until the very last, by no means whatsoever shall they be forcibly taken away or resumed.

All this is granted. And I myself have sworn that for ever and ever this edict given for the peaceful maintenance of the position of the descendants of the minister Snang-bzang 'dus-kong, which has been granted for ever and ever, shall not be altered or modified. And binding by my oath my elder brother Mu-rug-brtsan, the sister queens,[9] the feudatory princes,[10] and all ministers great and small

Notes to Translation (continued)

6. Myang 'Dus-kong is named in DTH p. 26 in the year 745 A.D.
7. *rma*, "investigate, put to the question" rather than "punish".
8. *gcig-gis*, cf. Zhol N 26. "for one occasion only," or "merely".
9. Sister queens. According to DTH p. 32 Khri Lde-srong-brtsan's principal queen was 'Bro-za Lha-rgyal mang-mo-rje; but in the king's edict (PT *ja* f. 130a) the name is 'Bro-bza' Khri-mo-legs and the other queens are Mchims-rgyal-bza' Legs-mo-brtsan and Cog-ro-bza' Brtsan-rgyal.
10. The *rgyal-phran* are specified in PT ja f. 130a, as the 'A-zha-rje, Rkong-kar-po Mang-po-rje, and Myang-btsun Khri-bo.

West Inscription

49 རྒྱལ་ཕྲན་རྣམས་དང་། ཆབ་སྲིད་ཀྱི་བློན་པོ་མན་ཆད་། ཞང་ལོན་ཆེ་ཕྲ་ཀུན་ཀྱང་

50 མནས་བསྙག་སྟེ། གཙིགས་གཡུང་དྲུང་དུ་གནང་ངོ་། བན་དེ་ཏིང་ངེ་འཛིན

51 སྙིང་ཉེ་ཞུ་ཨོ་ཁ་ཇེ་ལྷར་ཕུལ་བ་དུ། དཔེན་པ་ཆེ་བགྱིས་པ་དུ། གཙིགས་ཅི་གནང་བ།

52 ཞིབ་མོ་ནི། གཙིགས་ཀྱི་ཡི་གེ་ལ་བྲིས་ཏེ། ཕྱག་སྦལ་དུ་བཞག། དཔེ་གཙིགཿ

53 ཕྱག་རྒྱས་བཏབ་སྟེ། གཙིགས་ཀྱི་མཁར་བུ་འདིར་བཞག་། དཔེ་གཅིག་ནི་།

54 ཕྱག་རྒྱས་བཏབ་སྟེ། ཏོག་དཔེར་འཆང་དུ་བརྒྱུག་གོ། །༄། །བན་དེ་ཏིང་ངེ་

55 འཛིན་ཀྱི་སྨྲས་ཕུ་པོ། དབྱི་གོང་གི་རྒྱུད་ཀྱང་། དབུ་སྙུང་གཙིགས་གནང་ངོ།།

56 སྔོན་སྲུང་དགུས་སྙིང་ཉེ་ཞུ་ཨོ་ཁ་ཕུལ་བར་འདྲ་བ་ལས། །དགུས་ཀྱི་ཟླ་དུ་སྩྲུར་ན།

57 སྲུང་བཀྲུ་དྲོན་ཆུངས་བ་འདྲ་ནས། ངའི། བཀས། །སྲུང་གི་གཙིགས་ཀྱང་ཟུར་

58 ཕྲུང་བརྟན་བསྐྱིད་དེ་གནང་ངོ་། ། ༄། །གཙིགས་ཀྱི་མཁར་བུ་འདི། ནམ་ཞིག

59 དབྱེ་དགོས་ན་ཡང་། །སྲས་དབོན་ཆབ་སྲིད་ཀྱི་མདྲ་གང་མཛད་པས་ངོང་ལྒུ

60 སྦུགས་ཆེས་པ་གཙིགས་བདག་འདྲུང་བ་གསུ་ཡན་ཆདཿ

61 བསྒོ་སྟེ། ལག་སྤྲུལ་ལ་དབྱུང་ཞིག། ཕྱིར་ཡུ་འདི་བཞིན་ཕྱག་རྒྱ

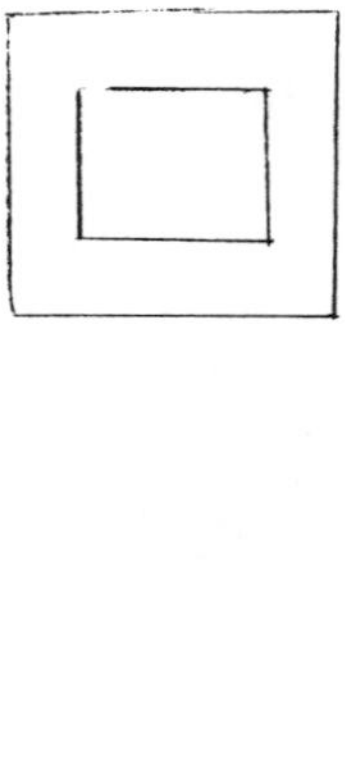

62 དུ། རིང་ལུགས་ཀྱི་རྒྱས་བཏབ་སྟེ། གཞག་པར་གནང་ངོ་།།

Translation

from the ministers of the kingdom downwards, this edict is granted immutably. And the text of the edict has been written in detail, describing how Ban-de Ting-nge-'dzin has been loyal and has offered gifts and the beneficial deeds he has done, and what edict has been granted; and it has been placed in the archives. One copy, duly sealed, has been placed in the edict-house here; and one copy[11], duly sealed, is allowed to be held as the secondary copy.

A sworn edict was granted also to the family of Dbyi-gong, the paternal grand-uncle of Ban-de Ting-nge-'dzin. Formerly Myang and Dba's, being loyal, were alike in the gifts they offered but compared with the example of Dba's it seems that Myang fell short in the matter of favour. Therefore, by my order, there has been granted a firm addition to the edict for Myang also.

If it is ever necessary to open this edict-house, whichever of my sons or grandsons may hold power shall appoint upwards of three trustworthy abbots[12] as custodians of the edict. They shall take it out jointly into their hands and afterwards shall seal it in the present manner and, adding the seal of the abbots, shall deposit it again.

Notes to Translation (continued)

11. *'og-dpe*, the copy to be held by the beneficiary.

12. *ring-lugs* is found in some Tun-huang *mss* apparently meaning a code of the rules and practice of justice (TLTD II pp. 59, 66; DTH pp. 23, 27) and in others as the title of a civil official administering that code and attesting decisions in judicial cases and business contracts (TLTD II pp. 56, 81, 139, 149, 162; and Pell. T. 1084, 1297). Such an official might be described as a registrar or commissioner. The term is also found in a religious context, e.g. *ring-lugs ban-de* (Pell T. 1002); and, as I understand it, in the present text and certainly in the Skar-cung and Lcang-bu inscriptions (pp. 78, 101) where it has the analogous implication of one who maintains or transmits the "law"—the doctrine—of the Buddha. "Abbot" may sometimes be a convenient rendering though it is not exact, for there might be more than one *ring-lugs* in a community.

East Inscription

1 ༄།། ཕྱིའི་རྒྱལ་པོ་ལྷས་མཛད་པ། །འཕྲུལ་གྱི་ལྷ་

2 བཙན་པོ་ཁྲི། ལྡེ་སྲོང་བརྩན་གྱི། བཀས། ། །

3 བན་དེ་སྨྱང་ཏིང་ངེ་འཛིན། ངེད་སྐུང་གཙོགས་སྐྱད་ཀྱིས་

4 གནང་བ། བན་དེ་ཏིང་ངེ་འཛིན། ངའི་ཆབ་སྲིད་འདོན་

5 ཅིང། ལོ་ཕྲ་ཆེན་པོ་འབུལ་འབུལ་བ། གཙོགས་སྤྲ་མ་

6 གནང་བའི་ཚེའང་བླ་དཔེ་དང་། ལོ་ཕྲའི་རྒྱུན་བཞིནཿ

7 བཀཱ་དྲིན་ངོས་པ་ཚམ་དུ་གནང་བ་ལས། བན་དེ་ཉིད་

8 ཀྱིས། བཀཱ་དྲིན་སྐྱུ་ཡོད་པར་གསོལ་ནས། །གཙོགསཿ

9 རན་པར་དཔགས་པ་ལསཿ ཁྲུང་ཕྲི་ཞིང་སྨད་པ་ལོ་

10 ཀའི་རྒྱུན་དུ་མ་བབ་སྟེ། བཀ་དྲིན་རྒྱུངས་ཤིང་ཡབ་མ་བར་

11 རྒྱུར་ད།། བན་དེ་ཏིང་ངེ་འཛིན་གྱིས། ངའི་ཁ་སྤར་ཆབ་སྲིད་

12 གསོལ་ནས། ངའི་སྐུ་རིང་ལ། སྐུ་དང་ཆབ་སྲིད་ལ་འཕྲུལཿ

13 ཕྱུན་གཉིས་སུ་ལེགས་པའི་བཀའ་གྲོས་གསོལ་ཡང་ཚང་

14 སྤྱིར་དཔེན་པའི་ལས་ཆེན་པོ་བྲུས་པ་དུ། བླ་འོག་ཛོ་གས་

15 སུ་བདེ་ལ་དང་། ཕན་བའི་ཡོད་ཆེན་པོ་བྱུང་བྱེད། །སྐྱིང་

INSCRIPTIONS AT ZHWA'I LHA-KHANG

Translation

East Inscription

By order of the supernaturally wise divinity, the *btsan-po* Khri Lde-srong-brtsan, a god acting as king of men.[1]

A further sworn edict granted for Ban-de Ting-nge-'dzin. Ban-de Ting-nge-'dzin raised up my kingdom and continually made great offerings. At the time of granting the former edict although I intended to bestow a suitable favour in accordance with precedent and as provision for his gifts, the *ban-de* himself requested that he should not receive any favour; so the favour was decreased and fell short of the measure of what was appropriate, and as it did not even amount to provision for his gifts, it was too small and inadequate. Ban-de Ting-nge-'dzin offered[2] me the kingdom and, in my reign, has given excellent advice for myself and my kingdom both for the present and the future and has performed great works for the general good. He has continuously brought about happiness and a great accumulation of benefits for high and low alike. He has been very

Notes to Translation

1. cf. Inscription at Khri Lde-srong-brtsan's tomb l. 2 *Lha las myi'i rjer gshegs pa:* Treaty Inscription E l. 8: and TLTD II p. 93 B 2.
2. *gsol* must mean "offered" rather than "served" the kingdom as I first took it (see p. 44).

East Inscription

16 ཉི་ཉི་སྟེ། ཆོས་ཁ་ཆེར་ཕུལ་བ། བཀའ་དྲིན་གཙིགས་

17 བསྐྱེད་པར། ངའི་ཐུགས་ལ་དགོངས་ན། བན་དེ་ནི་གཙིགས་

18 སྤར་གནང་བས་འཚལ་ཏེ་སྤྱི་བསྐྱེད་པར་གསོལ་གྱིས་

19 ཀྱུང་ཆོས་ཁ་ཆེན་པོའི་ལན། །བཀཱ་དྲིན་གྱི་འཕམ་པར་སྨིན་བའི་

20 རིགས་པར། རྗེ་བློན་མོལ་ནས། གཙིགས་སྤར་གནང་བ་

21 ཡཱ་དེ་བཞིན་གནང་བའི་སྙེང་དུ། བན་དེ་ཏིང་ངེ་འཛིན་སྙིང་

22 ཉེ་ཞིང་ཆོས་ཁ་ཆེན་པོ་ཕུལ་བའི་ཕྱིར། བཀཱ་དྲིན་འབྲུག་གི་ལོ་

23 ཕྱི་མ་ལ། ཕོ་བྲང་འོན་ཅང་དོ་ན་བཞུགས་པའི་ཚེ། གཙིགས

24 གསར་དུ་བསྐྱེད་དེ། ངའི་བཀས་གནང་བ།།ཡི་གེ་གཡུང་དྲུང་

25 སྤར་གནང་བ་བས་བསྟོད་དེ་ཆེར་གནཱ། བློན་སྤུང་བཟང་

26 འདུས་ཀཱོ་གི་བུ་ཚ་འཕེལ་རྒྱུད་དམངས་ཀྱི་རྣམས་ཀྱང་གཙཱ

27 [1]x་སྟོང་ལས་སྟོགས་པ་སྟོར་བདེ་བའི་ཉམས། ཞང་ལོན་ཡི་གེ་

28 རྩན་ཀྱི་ཐང་དུ་གནང་བ་དཱ། མ་ཉེས་པར་སྒྲོག་སྒྲིད་ལ་དཀུ་

29 དཱ། གནོད་པ་བྱེད་པ་ཞིག་ཡོད་ན། སུ་ལ་བབ་x x x[2]ུང། དཀུའ་

30 བ་དཱ། ཞེའུ་པའི་ཚོ་ཁར་ཀྱི་དོར་བར། དཀུ་བ་དུ་གཏོགས་པ།།

1 དཱ

2 ཀྱང་རུང་

Translation

loyal and has offered still greater gifts. When I considered that I should increase the favour granted by my edict the *ban-de* requested that I should not increase what had been granted by the former edict. Nevertheless, since it is right to bestow a favour that does not fall short, king and ministers consulted together and because Ban-de Ting-nge-'dzin has offered great gifts over and above what had been given when the former edict was granted, in the later dragon year while residing at the palace of 'On-cang-do I have by my order granted an increased favour by a new edict. I have granted even greater honour than that in the letter in perpetuity given earlier; and I have granted that those descendants also of the minister Snang-bzang 'dus-kong, who are of the ordinary folk and who personally enjoy the position of Gtsang and Stong officials,[3] shall be ranked as holders of a *zhang-lon* letter. And if anyone should intrigue[4] against them or harm them without offence on their part, to whomsoever it may happen, if the intriguer does not give up his intrigue in the

Notes to Translation (continued)

3. I formerly understood *sgor bde-ba* as equivalent to *mgo-bde-ba* "well qualified" (Das Dictionary p. 669) but the meaning "personal, private" is clear from Pell T. 16 26b l. 1 . . . . . *so so'i sgo sgor bde skyid pa'i drin*, the happiness of each in his own place"; see also Zhol inscription N. l. 63 and Vocabulary. The posts of *gtsang chen* and *stong dpon* are mentioned in Pell T. 1089; *stong dpon* and *stong chung* frequently in TLTD II; and *stong dpon* in Zhol inscription N ll. 42, 46.

East Inscription

31 བཀ་གྲོད་ལ་གདགས་པར་གནང་བ་དཱུ། ལྷ་xོ x xུ xོ[3] སྔོས་པ

32 xས་ཆེར་གྱུར་ཀྱང་། བླ་འོག་གཞན་གྱིས་དབྱེ་མྱི་བྱ་བར་གནཱ:

33 [4]x་ལས་སྐྱོགས་ཏེ། གཙིགས་སུ་མའི་སྟེང་དུ། གཙིགས་ཞྭི་མ

34 [5]x སྡུན་བསྐྱེད་དེ་གནང་བ་རྣམས་ཀྱང་། དེ་བཞིན་དུ། ནམ་ཞར་

35 [6]x རྒྱན་བར་གནང་སྟེ། འདི་ཞ་ལྷ་ནས་ཀྱང་དབུ་སྐྱུང་གནཱ་།།རྗེ་མོ་

36 [7]x ཆེད་དུ། རྒྱལ་ཕྲན་དང་། ཆབ་སྲིད་ཀྱི་བློན་པོ་རྣམས་དཱུ། ཞང་

37 ལོན་ཕྲ་མོ་ཐམས་ཅད་ཀྱང་བརྟན་ཏེ། མནས་བསྐགས་ནས།

38 གཙིགས་བསྟན་བསྐྱེད་དེ་གནང་བ་ཡཱ་ ཡུན་ཏུ་བརྟན་ཞཱི་མཆོན་

39 བར་བྱ་བའི་ཕྱིར། མདོའ་རྡོ་རིངས་ལ་བྲིས་ཏེ་མཐའ་ཕྱག་རྒྱས་

40 བཏབ་ནས། གཙུག་ལག་ཁང་དཱུ། གཙིགས་ཀྱི་མཁར་བུའི:

41 སྣང་དུ་བཞག་པ་ཡིན་ཀྱིས། །རྗེ་བློན་ཕྱི་རབས་མདཱ་མཛད་པ་

42 རྣམས་ཀྱིས་ཀྱང་། ནི་ནི་ཞ་ཞར་གཙིགས་ནི་གཉིས་ཀྱི་ཡི་གེ་ལས་

43 འབྱུང་བ་དང་། རྡོ་རིངས་ནི་གཉིས་ལ་བྲིས་པ་ལས་གྱི་དབྱེ་མྱི:

44 བཅོས་མྱི་བསྒྱུར་བར་གྱིས་ཤིག། །གཙིགས་སུ་མའི་སྟེང

45 དུ་ཞྭིས་གཙིགས་བསྟན་བསྐྱེད་དེ། །གནང་བ་ཡང་། ཞིབ་ཏུ་ནི་

[3] རོས་སུ་བསྔོས་
[4] བ
[5] བསྡུན་
[6] བརྒྱན་
[7] མཆེད་

Translation

presence of a mediator[4] he shall be brought to trial. And what has been dedicated as monastic property, whatever may happen, shall not be subjected to anyone else, high or low. Giving order thus, I swore solemnly that the terms of this edict should be firm for ever. And binding strictly by my oath the sister queens, the feudatory princes, the ministers of the kingdom, and all lesser ministers, in order that the edict granted in augmentation also may be known and maintained forever, a summary inscribed on a stone pillar and sealed at the end has been set up near this temple and the edict-house. Therefore, later generations of rulers and ministers, also, who may hold authority shall so act as never to decrease or modify or alter the purport of the words of the two edicts and the inscription on the two stone pillars.

The order granting the later edict in addition to the former edict

Notes to Translation (continued)

4. In ll. 28–30 *dku, dku' ba* and *dku ba* present problems. Róna Tas loc. cit. (see p. 17) suggests that the homophones *dku* "ruse, trap" and *dku* "side" are both represented here, the former presumably in *dku ba la gtogs pa.* But *dku ba*, as distinct from *dku*, does not seem to be found with the meaning "side" and I regard all three instances as the same word and translate "intrigue". *Phe'u pa'i ngo khar myi dor ba* is obscure. Mr Ngawang Thondup Narkyid suggests a parallel with *dngos skyes kyi ngo la mi dor ba* referring to the refusal of a bribe and meaning "in the face of a present do not give up (your honour)". *'Phe-u* in Sumatiratna's dictionary is explained as *gsol ba;* and Dagyab has *'phe'u debs pa = skad chen pos 'debs pa.* In Pell T. 1132 l. 11 the meaning seems to be "recommend, intercede"; and pending further elucidation, I have translated it as "mediate".

East Inscription

46 གཙིགས་ཀྱི་ཡི་གེ་ལ་བྲིས་ཏེ། ཕྱག་སྦལ་དུ

47 བཞག། དཔེ་གཅིག་གཙིགས་སྐུ་མ་དུ་སྦྱོག་ཀུ་

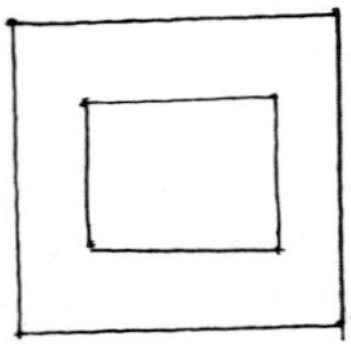

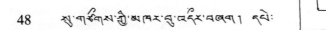

48 སྐུ་གཙིགས་ཀྱི་མཁར་བུ་འདིར་བཞག། དཔེ་

49 གཅིག་ཏོག་དཔེར་འཆང་དུ་བཅུག་གོ། །

Translation

has been written in detail in the words of the edict and has been deposited in the archives. One copy has been deposited beside the former edict in the edict-house here; and one copy has been allowed to be held as the secondary copy.

Inscription

1 x x x x x x ཡང་ནས་ x x x x x x x

2 པད་ x x x སྤྱིའི་མགོན་དུས་ལ་གཤེགས་ན x

3 གཙོཾ་དུ་བཞུད་པ་ནོ། །ཁ་ཐབས་བརྗོད་དུ་སྨྲི

4 x ང་ཡུ[1]བས་ཐྲིཾ་དུ་སྨྲི་བརད་དེ། ཁྡེར་མ་སློས

5 ༄།།ལྷ་ཇེ་ཆེན་པོ་གཙིཾ་ལྷའི་སྲས་ལས། ཚོ་ལྡེ་ཚེ་གསུཾ་དང་།

6 མདའ་སྨྲི་ཚེ་གསུཾ་དུ། ཚེ[2]ཚེ་གསུཾ་དང་། ལྷུག་པོ་ཚེ་གསུཾ་དང་།

7 ཁྲིམ་པོ་ཚེ་གསུཾ་ལས་སྐོགས་པ་སྤྱན་སྨྲ་འཕ x x x

8 x x སུ་གྲིས་སོ།

9 x x x ང་གི་སྤྱུས་པོ་སྔེ། པོ་ལྡོང་ཚེ་སྤྱག། རྗོར་ཁྲིང་ x x x

10 x x x x པོ་སྔེ་ཆ་གར་གྱི་ཞལ་བུ་འདིའི་བར་དུ་སྨྲི x x x

11 x x x x བར་ཚེའི་ནི་བདག་པོ། སྤྲེ་ཨཾ་པའི་ནི་རྒྱུ་ x x x

x x x x x[3]

1 not quite clear ? སྨྲ

2 ? ཚེ་

3 ? གཉིས་དེ་ ལ x

Fragmentary Inscription near Zhwa'i Lha-khang

This cannot be clearly dated to the reign of Khri Lde-srong-brtsan but it is included here because it comes from within half a mile of the *lha-khang* where there are remains of a large stone building, perhaps a former palace of the Myang family. Lying there was what appears to be the top part of an inscribed pillar (photograph in *JRAS* 1953, where the text is published). The rest of the pillar could not be found. The stone is roughly dressed but the lettering is well carved and rather similar to that of the inscriptions at the *lha-khang* and, like them, makes much use of the *anusvāra*.

What remains of the text contains the genealogy of some family tracing its origin to a god. It does not echo the legendary genealogy of the Tibetan kings and, in view of its proximity to Myang Ting-nge-'dzin's foundation, it may be that of the Myang clan. It mentions some tribal names known in later histories and also some seen in documents from Tun-huang: *mda'* (Stein, Tribus Anciennes, pp. 5, 17); *phyug* (Stein, p. 16); *tse* (*tshe-mi*? Stein p. 16); *gyim-po* (Thomas, AFL, pp. 16, 17, 19, 41); *cho-phyi* (*cho-pyi*, AFL p. 18); *po-ldong* (*po-chu-ldong*, Stein p. 15). Though most of the first part can be translated, the last three lines are too obscure to attempt.

Translation

. . . . how (some divine personage) came to earth to rule over men and then returned to heaven cannot be told in words . . . . it is not spoken here.

From the sons of the great Lha-ji, a god of heaven, were descended the . . . . brothers: three generations[1] of Cho-phyi and three generations of Mda'-myi and three generations of Tse and three generations of Phyug-po and three generations of Gyim-po, and so on.

The ancestor of (Myang),[2] Po-ldong-tse myag . . . ."

Notes to Translation

1. *Tshe,* (*tse*), "lifetime" perhaps meaning "generation".
2. It is tempting to read *Myang* but only the final letter is legible.

REIGN OF KHRI LDE-SRONG-BRTSAN *c.* 800–815 A.D.

The Rkong-po Inscription

I have not seen this inscription which is said to be carved on a rock face by the side of the Gtsang-po in a part of Rkong-po known as De-mo-sa, about fifteen miles downstream from Rtse-lha-sgang (see map at p. 152 in *No Passport to Tibet* by F. M. Bailey, 1957). I was able to get a copy through the kindness of the learned Rnying-ma-pa Lama, Bdud-'joms Rin-po-che to whom I explained that I wanted an accurate copy showing the length of any words or passages that might be illegible. It was found that the greater part of the inscription had been engulfed in sand and the Rin-po-che arranged to have it cleared. His copyist certainly took great trouble and the result is reproduced in my article in *JRAS* 1954 nos. 3 and 4. Later when RT's collection came into my possession, his copy of the inscription not only supplied a number of missing words but gave a standard for comparison with Bdud-'joms's text. RT's copy must have been made some time before the 18th century for various glosses and notes imply that he had acquired a complete text and that when someone (probably himself) went to check it on the spot the last six lines were buried in sand so that only the first fifteen lines bear his corrections.

In light of the new evidence I published a revised text in *JRAS* 1972 no. 1, based on comparison of the work of three hands—that of the maker of the first copy (O); the corrections by RT; and that of Bdud-'joms' copyist (D). The variants are listed in that article. In chosing between them I tried to establish to what type of mistake each person was prone, accepting readings where RT and D agreed as against O; but having a more open choice where O and D conflicted and there was no correction by RT. In some instances I may have chosen wrongly but that is nowhere likely to have affected the meaning. In the text below I have changed my mind on one reading and have noted two others where there may be some doubt.

The inscription records an edict given to a feudatory prince, the ruler of Rkong-po by Khri Lde-srong-brtsan confirming one by his father Khri Srong-lde-brtsan. The former edict appears to have been a brief instruction to the *btsan-po's* officers not to cause trouble to the prince of Rkong-po following a petition in which the prince and his ministers cited the legendary origin of the divine ancestors from whom the rulers of Rkong-po and the royal line shared a common descent. The confirmatory edict by Khri Lde-srong-brtsan is of special interest in throwing light on the relationship between a *rgyal-phran*—feudatory prince—and the *btsan-po.*

I have discussed the legendary figures of Ya-bla (Yab-bla) bdag-drug, Nya Khri (Nyag Khri) btsan-po, Dri-gum btsan-po, Sha-khyi and Nya-khyi in AHE pp. 47–9 and in *JRAS* 1954 and 1972. They have been exhaustively studied by Dr Haarh in *The Yarlung Dynasty* and most recently by Madame A. Macdonald in a remarkable essay in *Études Tibétaines* where she has brought new insights into the mystique of the ancient Tibetan kingship and its cult figures such as the *sku-bla* which figure in the Rkong-po inscription. Her translation of some passages there differs from mine and although it provides new ideas, I have not been able to accept it completely as it seems to postulate an unusually involved and allusive grammatical structure. At all events, whatever one may make of the details, the purport of the edict is that the prince of Rkong-po had invoked his common descent and ancestral cult in an appeal to the *btsan-po* to maintain his established rights.

One point I noticed formerly is that whereas Khri Srong-lde-brtsan is given the title Khri, that is not applied to his son Lde-srong. It is possible that this might imply that the latter was not fully established on the throne when the inscription was written; but too much need not be made of that. Feudatory princes may not have been so meticulous in matters of protocol as were the kings and their ministers. Lde-srong is described as *rje* and is in a position to be asked for and to grant a valid edict.

A few changes in the translation from that in *JRAS* 1972 are mentioned in the notes. Other points in the notes in *JRAS* 1972 are not repeated here.

Inscriptions

1 ༄། །ལྷ་བཙན་པོ་ཁྲི་སྲོང་ལྡེ་བརྩན་དང་། ལྡེ་སྲོང་ཡབ་སྲས་ཀྱི་རིང་ལའ།

2 ། །ཀོང་དཀར་པོ་ལེ་གཙོགས་གནང་བའ། །

3 ༄། །ཀར་པོ་མང་པོ་རྗེ་དང་། །བློན་པོ་ལྷའི་ཟུང་གིས་གསོལད་བའ། །ཐོག་མ་ཕྱྭ་

ཡ་བླ་བདག་དྲུག་གི་སྲས་ལས།

4 ཉ་ཁྲི་བཙན་པོ་མྱི་ཡུལ་གྱི་རྗེར། །ལྷ་རི་གྱང་ཏོར་གཤེགས་པ་རྒྱན་ཆད། དྲི་གུམ་

བཙན་པོ་ཡན་ཆད་། གདུང་རབས་བདུན་གྱི་བར་དུ། །ཕྱིང་བ་སྟག

5 རྩེ་ན་བཞུགས་བཞུགས། །དྲི་གུམ་བཙན་པོའི་སྲས་གཅེན་ཉ་ཁྲི་དང་། །གཅུང་ཤ་ཁྲི་

གཉིས་ལས། གཅུང་ཤ་ཁྲི་ནི། ལྷ་བཙན་པོ། གཅེན་ཉ་ཁྲི་

6 ནི་ཀོང་ཡུལ་དུ་བཞུགས་སྟེ། གཅེན་ཀར་པོ་ནི། ཐོག་མ་ཡས་གཤེགས་པའི་ཆེ། །

མཆེད་གཉིས་ཀྱི། སྐུ་བླ་གཉན་པོ་གསོལ་བ་དང་། སྐུ་བླ་དེ་མོ་དང་བཤོས་པའི་

7 ལྷ་བདག་བསྐྱོད་ཀྱིས་ཀྱང་། ལྷ་སྲས་ཀྱི་སྐུའི་རིམ་གྲོ་ལ། བདགི་སྲོག་ལའ་བབ་པ་མན་

ཆད་ཀྱི་ཆོ་གར་མཛད་པ། སྲོག་ཡོངས་མ་བསྒྱིས་ཏེ། །ལྷ་སྲས་ཀྱི་ཆབ་

8 སྲིད་འདི་ལྟར་མགོ། དབུ་རྨོག་བརྩན་།[1] ཡོང་ལྷ་སྲས་གནམ་དང་འདྲ་བའི་ཆགས་

འོག་ན། གནམ་ཀོལ་དུ་གནང་བའང་ཙོབས་ཞིག་མཆིས་ན། བདག་

Notes to Text
1. *brtsan* of RT's text seems better here than *brtsan pa* which I formerly preferred.

THE RKONG-PO INSCRIPTION

Translation

In the time of the divine *btsan-po* Khri Srong-lde-brtsan and Lde-srong father and son. An edict given to Rkong dkar-po.

Kar-po Mang-po-rje and the minister Lha'i-zung made this petition: "At first from the time when Nya-khri btsan-po, who was of the lineage of the Auspicious Ya-bla bdag-drug, came to Lha-ri Gyang-do to rule over the land of men for seven generations the kings continued to dwell at Phying-ba stag-rtse[1]. Of the two sons of Dri-gum btsan-po the younger brother Sha-khyi became the divine *btsan-po* and the elder brother Nya-khyi dwelt in Rkong-yul. As for that elder brother Kar-po, at the time when he first came from above he worshipped the Gnyan-po the patron spirit[2] of the two brothers and acting as divine master[3], as consort to the patron spirit De-mo, in allegiance to the divine prince[4] he performed due service even to the risk of his life. He was not even sparing of his life. In this way the dominion of the divine prince was exalted and his helmet was firm. Further, being beneath the sway of the divine prince who was like to

Notes to Translation

1. Phying-ba Stag-rtse, the old castle at 'Phyong-rgyas overlooking the royal burial ground.
2. In a damaged Tun-huang *ms*, Pell T. I line 3 there is the phrase *sku-bla gnyen zhing* which may mean "the *sku-bla* being his helper"; but in the inscription both readings agree on *gnyan-po*.
3. My translation here, differing from *JRAS* 1972, regards Kar-po himself as the divine master (*lha-bdag*).
4. The *btsan-po*.

Inscriptions

9 ཅག་ལྷ་ཞིག །ཐོག་མ་མཆེད་གྲོས་ནས། །ཕ་མྱེས་དང་པོ་ལྷ་མྱི་མ་ལྡེ་བ་རྒྱུན་ཆད།

བདེ་སྐྱིད་ཚོང་། ཆུ་སྲིད་གཡུང་དྲུང་དང་འདྲ་བར་གནང་གིས་ཀྱང་། །དེང་སང་

10 དུ། །ཁབ་སོ་དཔོན་སྣ་དགོས། །ཁྲལ་གྱི་སྣ་འཚལ་ཏེ། །གཏོས་ཤིང་མཆིས་ན་། ནམ་དུའང་

བདེ་བར་ཐུགས་བག་མཛོད་པའི། །གཙོགས་ཚོ་ ཞིག་ཚོ་གནང་ཞེས་

11 གསོལད་ནས། དེ་བཞིན་དུ་གནང་སྟེ། གཙོགས་འཕྲུ་མེན་སྒྲོམ་བུ[2]་སྣ་ལད་བའི་དཔེར་

བྲིས་པའ།

12 ༄། །བཙན་པོ་ལྷ་སྲས་ཁྲི་སྲོང་ལྡེ་བརྩན་གྱི་རིང་ལ།[3] །ཀར་པོའི་གཙོགས་གནང་བ་ལས་

13 ལྷ་སྲས་ལྡེ་སྲོང་གི་སྐུ་རིང་ལ། གཙིགས་སྟ་མ་བས་བསྐྱེད་པར། བཀའས། གནང་བའ།

14 ༄། །ནམ་ཞར་ཀྱང་། ཀོང་ཀར་པོའི་རྒྱལ་པོར་གཞན་མྱི་གཞུག་པར། ཀར་པོ

མང་པོ་རྗེའི་བུ་ཚ་འཕེལ་རྒྱུད་ལས་སྣ་ལད་བར་གནང་ངོ་།

15 ཀར་པོ་མང་པོ་རྗེའི་རྒྱུད་རབས་ཆད་ན། གཅེན་རྒྱལ་པོ། ཀར་པོའི་མྱིང་མྱི་ཉག་པར།

རྒྱལ་པོར་ཡང་། །ཀར་པོ་རྒྱལ་བརྩན་གྱི་རྒྱུད་ལས།

16 བསྐོའོ། །རྒྱལ་བརྩན་གྱི་རྒྱུད་ཀྱང་རབས་ཆད་ན། །ཉེ་འཚམས་ལས། །ཁ་ཆེམས་

ཀྱིས་གང་། གསོལད་བའི་ནང་ནས། སྣུས་དང་

Notes to Text (continued)

2. *bur* as in O is more attractive but RT and D are both against it; and cf. Lcang-bu inscription 2, line 12.

3. O's copy shows the whole sentence in large letters.

Translation

heaven, in whatever he did he acted as a subject of heaven. So, as regards ourselves, from the first when the brothers had their origin[5] and from the time when among our ancestors there was no separation between gods and men we have lived in happiness and have maintained our status, unchangeable as the swastika. But nowadays because the chief officers of the royal government are putting us to trouble by demanding different kinds of taxes, an edict may please be granted to ensure our perpetual contentment." A petition having been made in those words, it was granted and this has been written as a copy of the edict which is kept in a box of *phra-men.*

Arising out of the edict for Kar-po which was granted in the time of the *btsan-po* the divine prince Khri Srong-lde-brtsan, an edict has been given in the time of the divine prince Lde-srong, by order, in addition to the former edict.

It is ordered that never shall any other be appointed as king of Rkong kar-po except for the descendants of Kar-po Mang-po-rje. If the line of Kar-po Mang-po-rje should be broken, in order that the name of Kar-po the king, the elder brother, should not fail there shall be appointed as king one from the line of Kar-po Rgyal-brtsan. If the line of Rgyal-brtsan be broken, whichever one of those from among the near relations, who are mentioned in the will, is recommended for his qualities[6] and is suitable, he shall be appointed.

Notes to Translation (continued)

5. In 1972 I translated *gyes* as "parted" but in a similar context in the Zhwa'i fragment (p. 63) it appears to mean "originated"; cf. Das' Dictionary p. 294 '*gye-ba* (2).
6. *spus*, cf. TLTD II pp. 23, 24, etc.

Inscriptions

17 སྒྲུརད་ཏེ།།གང་འོས་པ་གཙིག་སྤྱལད་བར་གནང་ངོ་།།

18 ༄།།ཀོང་ཀར་པོའི་བྲན་དང་།།ཞིང་འབྲོག་།སྨན་ཆད་མྱི་དགྱི་ཞིང་།།རྗེ་བླས་

དང་།།དཔྱལ་ཁྲལ་བླ་སྐྱེས་ཀྱི་དབབ་པ་དང་།

19 སྣང་ར་སྤྲུ་ནས་དང་།།འབྲས་གང་འབུལ་ཡང་རུང་།།འབུལ་བའི་ས་ཚིགས།།

ད་ལྟར་ཀྱི་ལས་མི་བསྒྱིད་བར།། ལྷ་སྲས་[4]

20 ཡབ་ཀྱི་བཀའ་ལས[5]།།གནང་བ་བཞིན་དུ།། ལྷ་སྲས་ལྡེ་སྲོང་གི་སྐུ་རིང་ལ། །

རྗེ[6]། །བློན་མོལ་ཏེ།

21 བཀའས[7] ། །གནང་ངོ་། །

Notes to Text (continued)

4. and 5. are also shown in large letters.
6. from *Lha sras* to *Rje* also in large letters.
7. *bka's* in large letters.

THE RKONG-PO INSCRIPTION

Translation

The bondsmen of Rkong Kar-po, his fields and grazing grounds, shall not in future be diminished. The duty of *rje-blas*[7], tribute, taxation and the offering of presents shall not be imposed; and the granary where the fine barley, rice and whatever is paid shall not be placed at a greater distance than it is now[8]. In accordance with the order to that effect by the divine prince the father, so it was decreed by order in the time of the divine prince Lde-srong, the son, after consultation between ruler and ministers.

Notes to Translation (continued)

7. *rje-blas*, see note p. 5. This function seems to imply a greater degree of subordination to the *btsan-po* than a feudatory prince was willing to admit.

8. In this difficult passage I think *stsang-ra* must mean ''granary'' rather than ''grain'' as I previously took it. *Phywa nas* was explained by Bstan-'dzin rnam-dag as ''fine barley''; but perhaps *dpya' nas* ''tax barley'' was intended. *Da ltar gyi las* also presents a question: perhaps *las* here means ''work, duty''.

REIGN OF KHRI LDE-SRONG-BRTSAN *c.* 800–815 A.D.

The Skar-cung *rdo-rings*

[Plates 9–10]

This pillar stands outside a small temple near the village of Ra-ma-sgang on the south bank of the Skyid-chu about two miles south-west of Lhasa. It records the renewal by Khri Lde-srong-brtsan of his father's vow to maintain the Buddhist faith; and it names the *gtsug-lag-khang* of Skar-cung as his own foundation. The text was copied and checked by me and by Tibetan helpers on several occasions and I also have photographs of it. I published it first in *JRASB* 1959. In 1960 Professor Tucci published it again in TTK where he raised a tentative question about the age and authenticity of the inscription. In *JRAS* 1973, 1. I slightly revised the text and upheld the attribution to the 9th century which, I think, is now generally accepted.

There are, as mentioned in my previous articles, various statements in later histories about the site of Khri Lde-srong-brtsan's *gtsug-lag-khang* but there is no good reason to doubt that the *rdo-rings* in which the foundation of Skar-cung is mentioned was set up at the temple of that name. Rig-'dzin Tshe-dbang nor-bu was clearly of that opinion for in his collection of inscriptions the text is headed *skar-cung rdo-rings kyi yi-ge;* and ends with the note *ces-pa 'di skar-cung rgyal sde'i rdo-rings kyi yi-ge.*

The present-day temple is very small and neglected but it stands inside an extensive area bounded by four large ancient *mchod-rten* which show traces of having been covered by tiles of the colour appropriate to their position as are those at Bsam-yas. A great accumulation of sand, which made it impossible to see whether there were the remains of other buildings, had covered the stone pillar. It had apparently been forgotten by the people of Lhasa and was rediscovered by the 'Brug-pa Bka'-rgyud-pa Yongs-'dzin Bde-chen Chos-'khor Rin-po-che who very kindly shared with me his interest in early history, rare among modern Tibetans. With his help I had enough of the sand cleared away to be able to copy the whole text; and some time later I was able also to clear the base on which the pillar stands and which was seen to be a massive block of stone carved with a pattern of mountains in the Chinese style. Photographs of the pillar can be seen in my article *Early Burial Grounds in Tibet* (*CAJ* VIII (2) 1963). Inside the courtyard of the little temple were a stone capital, similar to that on the pillar, and the remains of what appeared to be the base of another pillar which may be buried somewhere in the sand.

The inscription is in good condition and slight damage in a few places hardly affects the readings. Punctuation is similar to that of the Zhwa'i inscriptions except that the *anusvāra* is not used and no letters are written below the line.

In this edict renewing the vow to maintain Buddhism, Khri Lde-srong-brtsan repeats the exact words of Khri Srong-lde-brtsan in his inscription at Bsam-yas and ends with the statement that a detailed copy has been deposited alongside the edict written in the time of his father. Like Khri Srong-lde-brtsan's edict that of Khri Lde-srong-brtsan, also, has been preserved by PT (*ja* pp. 128b–130b.). It shows many close parallels with the Skar-cung inscription and can confidently be accepted as authentic. That reinforces the authority of PT's copy of the detailed edict attributed to Khri Srong-lde-brtsan. This body of interrelated evidence in the inscriptions at Bsam-yas and Skar-cung and the three *bka'-gtsigs* as recorded in PT is of primary importance for the early history of Buddhism in Tibet. For this, Tibetologists are greatly indebted to Bde-chen Chos-'khor Rin-po-che. His determined effort to find for me a complete copy of the *Chos-'byung mkhas-pa'i dga'ston* of Dpa'-bo Gtsug-lag 'phreng-ba led to the discovery of the wood-blocks in Lho-brag Lha-lung monastery; and the Tibetan Government agreed to have a number of copies printed and distributed to interested persons. Before that, all that was available of the work in Lhasa was a manuscript copy of vols *ka* to *ja* in the possession of the Bshad-sgra household which was seen by Sir Charles Bell in 1920 and later lent to me and to Professor Tucci. It was generously given to me in 1950 by the grandson of Blon-chen Bshad-sgra as a parting present.

One new item of information in the inscription which is not found in the detailed edict is that a temple was founded at Gling Khri-rtse by 'Dus-srong who is not generally regarded as a patron of Buddhism. The detailed *bka'-gtsigs* throws further light on the hostility towards Buddhism, mentioned in l. 31 of the inscription, by showing that there was a strong reaction against the faith after the death of Khri Srong-lde-brtsan just as there had been after the death of his father Khri Lde-gtsug-brtsan. That was presumably among the troubles mentioned in the first Zhwa'i Lha-khang inscription as having to be overcome before the succession of Khri Lde-srong-brtsan could be assured.

Inscription

1 ༄།།འཕྲུལ་གྱི་ལྷ་བཙན་པོ་ཁྲི་ལྡེ་སྲོང་བརྩན་གྱི་རིང་

2 ལ། །དམ་པའི་ཆོས་ཡུན་དུ་བརྟན་པར་གཙིགས་

3 བརྣན་པ།།

4 ༄། །འཕྲུལ་གྱི་ལྷ་བཙན་པོ། མྱེས། ཁྲི་སྲོང་བརྩན་གྱི་

5 རིང་ལ། །སངས་རྒྱས་ཀྱི་ཆོས་མཛད་དེ། །ར་སའི་གཙུག་

6 ལག་ཁང་ལས་སྩོགས་པ་བརྩིགས་ཤིང་། །དཀོན་མཆོགཿ

7 གསུམ་གྱི་རྟེན་བཙུགས་པ་དང་། །མྱེས། ཁྲི་འདུས་སྲོང་གི་

8 རིང་ལ། །ཁྲིང་གི་ཁྲི་རྩེ་ལས་སྩོགས་པར། གཙུག་ལག་

9 ཁང་བརྩིགས་སྟེ། །དཀོན་མཆོག་གསུམ་གྱི་རྟེན་བཙུགས་

10 པ་དང། །མྱེས། ཁྲི་ལྡེ་གཙུག་བརྩན་གྱི་རིང་ལ། །བྲག་མར་གྱི་

11 ཀ་ཆུ་དང་མཆིང་ཕུར་གཙུག་ལག་ཁང་བརྩིགས་སྟེ།།དཀོན་

12 མཆོག་གསུམ་གྱི་རྟེན་བཙུགས་པ་དང་། །ཡབ། ཁྲི་སྲོང་ལྡེ་

13 བརྩན་གྱི་རིང་ལ། །བྲག་མར་གྱི་བསམ་ཡས་ལས་སྩོགས་

14 པ། །དབུང་མཐར་གཙུག་ལག་ཁང་བརྩིགས་སྟེ། །དཀོན་

15 མཆོག་གསུམ་གྱི་རྟེན་བཙུགས་པ་དང། །ལྷ་བཙན་པོ་ཁྲི།

THE SKAR-CUNG *RDO-RINGS*

Translation

In the time of the supernaturally wise divinity, the *btsan-po* Khri Lde-srong-brtsan: an edict confirming that the holy religion shall be maintained for ever.

In the time of the supernaturally wise divinity, the ancestor Khri Srong-brtsan, in practising the religion of the Buddha, shrines of the Three Jewels were established by building the temple of Ra-sa and so on; and in the time of an ancestor Khri 'Dus-srong shrines of the Three Jewels were established by building the temple of Khri-rtse in Gling and so on; and in the time of the ancestor Khri Lde-gtsug-brtsan shrines of the Three Jewels were established by building the temples at Kwa-cu and Mching-phu in Brag-mar and so on; and in the time of the father Khri Srong-lde-brtsan shrines of the Three Jewels were established by building temples at the centre and on the borders, Bsam-yas in Brag-mar and so on; and in the time of the

Inscription

16 ལྡེ་སྲོང་བརྩན་གྱི་རིང་ལ་ཡང་། །སྐར་ཅུང་གཙུག་ལག་ཁང་

17 ལས་སྩོགས་པ་བརྩིགས་སྟེ། །དཀོན་མཆོག་གསུམ་གྱི་རྟེན་

18 བརྩུགས་པ་ལས་སྩོགས་པ། །གདུང་རབས་རྒྱུད་ཀྱིས་།

19 འདི་ལྟར་སངས་རྒྱས་ཀྱི་ཆོས་མཛད་པ་འདི། །ནམ་དུ་ཡང་མ

20 ཞིག་། མ་བཏང་ན། །ལེགས་པ་དཔག་དུ་མྱེད་པར་འགྱུར་།།

21 བཏང་སྟེ། ཞིག་གམ། མྱེད་པར་གྱུར་ན། །སྡིག་པ་གྲངས་མྱེད

22 པར་འོང་བས། །ད་ཕྱིན་ཆད་ནམ་ནམ་ཞ་ཞར། །འཕྲུལ་གྱི་ལྷ

23 བཙན་པོ། ཡབ། ཁྲི་སྲོང་ལྡེ་བརྩན་གྱི་རིང་ལ། །དཀོན་མཆོག

24 གསུམ་གྱི་རྟེན་བརྩུགས་པ་དང་། །སངས་རྒྱས་ཀྱི་ཆོས་མཛད་པ

25 མྱི་གཏང་མ་ཞིག་པར། །གདུང་རབས་རྒྱུད་ཀྱིས་ཡི་དམ་བཅའོ

26 ཞེས་འབྱུང་བ་ལས་སྩོགས་པ། །བཙན་པོ་ཡབ་སྲས། །རྗེ

27 བློན། ཀུན་གྱིས་དབུ་སྙུང་དང་བྲོ་བོར་ཏེ། །གཙིགས་ཀྱི་ཡི་གེ་དང་།

28 རྡོ་རིངས་ལ་བྲིས་པ་བཞིན་དུ་ཡང་མཛད་དོ། །འདི་ལྟར། །ཡབ

29 མྱེས། གདུང་རབས་རྒྱུད་ཀྱིས། །དཀོན་མཆོག་གསུམ་གྱི་རྟེན

30 བརྩུགས་ཤིང་། སངས་རྒྱས་ཀྱི་ཆོས་མཛད་པ་འདི་། །གཉིས་སྲས་ཅི

Translation

divine *btsan-po* Khri Lde-srong-brtsan also, shrines of the Three Jewels were established by such acts as building the temple of Skar-cung and so on. As for the practice of the religion of the Buddha in this way by successive generations, if it is never destroyed or abandoned, good beyond measure results; but if it is abandoned or destroyed and done away with, there come sins beyond number.

Therefore, from now onwards, for ever and ever, following the pronouncement in the time of the supernaturally wise divinity, the *btsan-po* the father, Khri Srong-lde-brtsan that each generation should take a vow not to abandon and not to destroy the shrines of the Three Jewels and the practice of the religion of the Buddha, the *btsan-po,* father and sons, ruler and ministers, all together have sworn an oath that they shall act in accordance with the words of the edict and the inscription on the stone pillar. And so, if someone should say "This practice of the religion of the Buddha by establishing shrines of the Three Jewels by the father and ancestors in successive generations, to hold it in esteem for whatever purpose is a

Inscription

31 ལ་ཡང། སྡིག་པོ་ཞེའམ་། མ་ལེགས་སོ་ཞེས། །མི་དང་ཕྱི་ལྟུས་ལས་

32 སྐོགས་སྟེ། ཚེའི་ཕྱིར་ཡང་རུང་སྟེ། མུ་གཞིག་གོ། མུ་སྟང་ངོ་། །དེ་སྐད་

33 ཅེས། ཆེ་ཆུང་ཞུས་གསོལད་ཀྱིས་ཀྱང་། དེ་ལྟར་མི་མཛད་དོ། །བཙན་

34 པོ་དབོན་སྲས། །སྐུ་ཆུ་ངུར་བཞུགས་པ་ཡན་ཆད། །ཆབ་སྲིད་ཀྱི་

35 མངའ་བདག་མཛད་པ་མན་ཆད་ཀྱང། །དགེ་སློང་ལས། དགེ་བའི་

36 བཤེས་ཉེན་བསྒོས་སྟེ། ཆོས་ཐུགས་སུ་ཅི་ཆུད་ཆུད་དུ་བསླབ་ཅིང། །བོད་

37 ཡོངས་ཀྱིས་ཀྱང་ཆོས་སློབ་ཅིང་སྤྱད་པའི་སྒོ་སྒྲིག་གཅད། ནམ་དུ་ཡང་བོད་ལ་

38 རབས་མན་ཆད། བོད་འབངས་ལས་ཐར་པར་གཟུད་པའི་སྒོ་སྒྲུ་བགགཿ

39 པར་། དད་པའི་རྣམས་ལས་ཐར་པར་བརྩོད་དེ། །དེའི་ནང་ནས་

40 ཞུས་པ་ལས། །བཅོམ་ལྡན་འདས་ཀྱི་རིང་ལུགས་རྟག་དུ་བསྒོ་

41 ཞིང། །བཅོམ་ལྡན་འདས་ཀྱི་རིང་ལུགས་བྱེད་པའི་རྣམས་ཆོས་འཁོར་

42 ནས་བྱུའོ་རྟོག་གི་བཀའ་ལེ་ཡང་བཏགས་སྟེ། །ཆོས་འཁོར་ཀྱི་ལས་དང་

43 དབང་བྱེད་ཅིང་། དགེ་བའི་བཤེས་ཉེན་བྱེད་པར་བསྒོའོ། །རབ་དུ་བྱུང་བའི་

44 རྣམས། །ངེད་ཡབ་སྲས་ཀྱིས། མཆོད་གནས་སུ་གནང་བ་བཞིན་དུ་བྱས་

45 སྟེ། །བཙན་པོའི། ཞོ་ཤང་ན་དཀོན་མཆོག་གསུམ་ཀྱི་རྟེན་བརྩུགས་ཤིང་།

Translation

sin'' or ''it is not good'', whether that be said because of divination or omens in dreams or for any reason whatsoever, it shall not be destroyed, it shall not be abandoned. And whoever utters such words, be he great or small, let nothing of that sort be done. But from the time when the *btsan-po*, sons and grandsons[1] are young until the time they become rulers of the kingdom and thereafter, too, teachers of virtue shall be appointed from among the monks and by teaching religion as much as can be absorbed into the mind, the gate of liberation for all Tibet, through the learning and practice of religion, shall not be closed. And when for all Tibetan subjects, from the nobles downwards, the gate leading to liberation is never obstructed and the believers have been led towards liberation, from those among them who are capable there shall always be appointed abbots to carry on the doctrine of the Buddha; and the abbots who carry on the doctrine of the Buddha, adhering to all such conduct as is commanded in the Wheel of the Law, shall be appointed to act as teachers of virtue. As for those who enter the priesthood, in accordance with their appointment by us, father and sons, as chaplains, they shall perform their duty as chaplains by establishing shrines of the Three Jewels in the

Note

1. *dbon sras* In a paper read at Oxford in July 1979 Dr Helga Uebach examined this phrase, which appears again in l. 48 and also in DTH 110 and in the inscription at the tomb of Khri Lde-srong-brtsan l. 18 (p. 88), and distinguishes it from *sras-dbon* in- e.g. the Zhwa'i inscription W ll. 29 and 59 (pp. 29, 52). In both uses the intention is to bind the king's descendants by his oath.

Inscription

46 མཆོད་པ་ཡང། །ཀུ་དུ་སྒྲོ་སྟང་གྱི་བསྐར་ཞིང་། མཆོད་གནས་སུ་བསྒྱུར་རོ།།

47 མདོར་ན། །བཙན་པོའི། ཡོ་བྱད་དང་། བོད་ཁམས་ན་། དཀོན་མཆོག་གསུམ་སྤྱོད་

48 པ་དང། སྟང་བའི་ཐབས་ཆོ་ཡང་སྒྲོ་མཛད་དོ། །ཡབ་སྲས་དབོན་སྲས་

49 གང་གི་རིང་ལ་ཡང་རུང་སྟེ། དཀོན་མཆོག་གསུམ་གྱི་རྐྱེན་བཙད་པའི་རྣམས་

50 ཀྱང་མ་དམའས་མ་ཞིག་པའི་ཆོས་སུ། །ལྷ་རིས་ཀྱི་ཁྲིམ་ཡིག་གི་མགོ་ནན་ལས

51 འབྱུང་བ་བཞིན་དུ་ཆེས་མཛད་དོ། །ད་ཕྱིན་ཆད་གདུང་རབས་རེ་རེ་ཞིང་ཡང་།

52 བཙན་པོ་ཡབ་སྲས་ཀྱིས། འདི་བཞིན་དུ་ཡི་དམ་བཅའོ། །དེ་ལས་མནའ་ཁ་

53 དབུད་པ་དག་སྒྲོ་བསྒྱུ་སྤྱི་བསྒྱུར་བར། །འཇིག་རྟེན་ལས་འདས་པ་དང་། འཇིག་

54 རྟེན་གྱི་ལྷ་དང་ཀླུ་མ་ཡིན་པ་ཐམས་ཅད་ཀྱང་། དཔང་དུ་གསོལ་ཏེ། །བཙན་པོ།

55 རྗེ་བློན་ཀུན་གྱིས་ཀྱང། དབུ་སྙུང་དང་། །བྲོ་བོར་རོ། །གཙིགས་བརྡུབ་པའི་

56 ཡི་གེ་ཞིབ་མོ་ནི། ཡབ་ཀྱི་རིང་ལ་གཙིགས་ཀྱི་ཡི་གེ་བྲིས་པའི་ཟླ་ལ་

57 བཞག་གོ། །

Translation

palace of the *btsan-po* and by not neglecting or restricting the offerings of worship.

In short, in the palace of the *btsan-po* and in the land of Tibet no means whatsoever shall be employed to destroy or abandon the Three Jewels. And in the time of father, grandfather, grandsons and sons[1], whoever it may be, in their religious duty not to reduce or destroy property assigned to the support of the Three Jewels they shall administer it in accordance with the principal instructions in the register of households in the monastic estates. And from now onwards, also, in each generation the *btsan-po,* father and son, shall take an oath accordingly. And so that there shall be no falling off from that sworn pledge and no change to it, the *btsan-po,* the ruler and his ministers, all together invoking as witnesses the saints, the supramundane gods, the gods of this world, and all spirits, have sworn a solemn oath. As for the detailed text of the confirmatory edict, it has been deposited alongside the text of the edict written in the time of the father.

1. See p. 79, note 1.

The Bell at Khra-'brug

The temple of Khra-'brug lies about seven miles up the valley of the Yar-lung river which runs from the south into the Gtsang-po near Rtse-thang. From the roof of the outer gateway opening on to a courtyard in front of the main temple hangs a bronze bell. It is larger than that at Bsam-yas but less graceful and part of it has been broken off as can be seen in the photograph opposite p. 174 of Tucci's *Lhasa and Beyond.* An inscription in two lines runs round the upper part but the top of the bell is close under the roof of the portico so copying had to be done by eye, from a ladder. Both my Sikkimese assistant and I made copies and I returned to Khra-'brug the following day to check doubtful readings.

Tucci, who was unable to secure a copy, has described the contents of the inscription in TTK p. 70; and I published the text in *JRAS* 1954. Khra-'brug, which is attributed to Srong-brtsan sgam-po, enjoyed prestige almost equal to the Jo-khang of Lhasa, the Ra-mo-che, and Bsam-yas; and special offerings made there are regularly mentioned in the *rnam-thar* of the Fifth Dalai Lama. Tucci (TTK p. 71) questions the attribution to Srong-brtsan sgam-po because the inscription on the bell suggests to him that Khri Lde-srong-brtsan was the founder. But Khra-'brug was already in existence and regarded as important at the time of Khri Srong-lde-brtsan's edict of *c.* 782 A.D. (p. 26). Although it is said to have been damaged by the Dzungars in the 18th century and repaired by the late Dalai Lama, there is no reason to suppose that the original structure has been basically altered.

The inscription shows that the bell which, unlike that as Bsam-yas is described as a *dril* not a *cong,* was dedicated by Queen Byang-chub for Khri Lde-srong-brtsan who was her step-son. One passage is slightly damaged and there is uncertainty about the meaning of Tshal in the last line which perhaps refers to Tshal-ka in Brag-mar where there was a royal palace (DTH 18/38). The name of the abbot Rin-cen who cast the bell, is presumably translated from the Chinese. Demiéville op. cit. p. 33 refers to a distinguished monk of the same persuasion as the Master Mahayana, who was active at the time of the religious debate and whose name Pao-chen is a fair approximation; but his family name, Yi (Rngegs?) is said to be not Chinese. A Dge-slong Rin-cen Bla-ma is named in Pell T. 103 and a Ban-de Rin-cen in Pell T. 2125 but there is nothing to identify either with Khra-'brug.

Presumably the bell was dedicated by Queen Byang-chub after Khri Lde-srong-brtsan had overcome the opposition to Buddhism mentioned in his edict in PT (p. 73). Khra-'brug may have been near the queen's place of residence. Her former association with Chinese doctrines and the presence of a Chinese abbot suggest the continuance in Tibet of the school of teaching which later histories would have us believe was banished as a result of the great religious debate of *c.* 792 (p. 27).

Like that at Bsam-yas the inscription is divided into panels by ornamentation on the bell. There is one correction in the text below from that in *JRAS* 1954—*rnga* for *rda;* and the translation has been slightly revised. Some orthographical irregularities are mentioned in notes.

THE BELL AT KHRA-'BRUG

Inscription

དྲིལ ཆེན པོ འདི ཡང ལྷ   བཙན པོ ཁྲི ལྡེ སྲོང བརྩན

གྱི དུ × × [1] སྣན འགྲངས   པ བཞུགས སོ སོལ [2] ལྷའི རྔ སྒྲ བར

སྣང ལ   གྲག པ དང འདྲ བར

ཡོན བདག ཇོ མོ བྱང ཆུབ གྱིས   བགྱིས ནས མཁེན [3] ཕོ རྒྱའི

དགེ སློང རིན ཅེན གྱིས བླུགས སོ   ཚལ གྱི སྐུ ཡོན དང   སེམས ཅན

ཐམས ཆད   དགེ བ ལ བསྐུལ བའི ཕྱིར །

Notes to Text
1. *dus la*?
2. for *gsol.*
3. for *mkhan.*
4. Although there is no indication on the bell, an alternative and possibly preferable arrangement of the lines, without altering the meaning, would be:
(i) Lha'i rnga sgra bar snang la grag pa dang 'dra bar dril chen po 'di yang lha btsan po khri lde srong brtsan gyi du . . snan 'grangs pa bzhugs so sol
(ii) Tshal gyi sku yon dang sems can thams chad dge ba la bskul ba'i phyir yon bdag jo mo byang chub gyis bgyis nas mkhen pho rgya'i dge slong rin cen gyis blugs so

Translation

This great bell was installed[1] here to tell the increase of the life-time[2] of the divine btsan-po Khri Lde-srong-brtsan. The donor Queen Byang-chub had it made to be like the sound of the drum roll of the gods in the heavens and it was cast by the abbot, the Chinese monk Rin-cen as a religious offering from Tshal and to call all creatures to virtue.

Notes to Translation
1. literally ''invited''.
2. *dus* meaning ''life'' is found in *dus las 'das so* Pell T. 996.

REIGN OF KHRI LDE-SRONG-BRTSAN *c.* 800–815 A.D.

Rdo-rings at the tomb of Khri Lde-srong-brtsan

[Plate 11]

An impressive stone pillar bearing on its south face an inscription in commemoration of Khri Lde-srong-brtsan stands a little way from one of the great tumuli (*bang-so*) at the burial ground of the Tibetan kings near 'Phyong-rgyas. The mound was identified by a local monk who accompanied me as that of "Sad na legs". The inscription was first published in TTK by Professor Tucci who had visited the site, not long before me, in 1949. The lower part of the pillar was buried in the ground and only twenty-one, rather damaged, lines were to be seen. After copying and photographing them I was able to have a narrow, sloping trench dug down to what appeared to be the end of the inscription; and in dark cramped conditions a companion and I copied separately, with difficulty, what could be made out of a further twenty-five lines. The reward was tantalizingly small. Only a complete clearance, which was not possible at that time in so hallowed a place, could have secured a better result. Even that might have been disappointing for RT's copy, which I acquired later, shows that when someone—probably himself—visited the place he noted at the twenty-ninth line "above this are 29 lines of writing; below are 14 which are not clear; after that, how much goes down into the ground has not been written." From my notes it seems that only three more lines were buried at the time of RT's visit. This shows that not later than the middle of the XVIIIth century, although the greater part of the pillar was visible, the inscription on the lower part was already largely illegible. Nevertheless from what my companion and I were able to recover some two hundred years later it seems that even if much of the text was effaced RT could have recorded many useful words and passages.

In *JRAS* 1969 (1) I published an edition of the text on the basis of RT's copy and my notes and photographs. That gave an acceptable reading for the twenty-nine lines covered by RT. For the rest I had given Tucci provisional readings which he published in TTK. I hesitated to reproduce that patchwork in my article in *JRAS* but I have examined again my notes and photographs. Unfortunately the negatives of the lower part were destroyed in an attempt to have them intensified; but I think it worth publishing a revision of those fragments provided it is understood that although some words and letters are certain, the degree of reliability is less than that of the first twenty-nine lines.

Another source for comparison—and one that inspires a good deal of speculation—is the *Rgyal-po bka'thang* (GK) ff. 21–2 where in an account of the reign of Khri Lde-srong-brtsan there are many close parallels showing that the author must have been acquainted with the inscription or with connected documents. In *JRAS* 1969 I quoted a long extract from GK and in the notes on the text of the inscription below I have compared relevant passages. It may be seen that the passages are not in the same order as their parallels in the inscription; but the similarities illustrate the value of GK as a historical source though with the caution that while early material has clearly been used, it has been adapted to the needs of a verse form and appears to have been re-arranged, enlarged on probably with later material, and perhaps sometimes misunderstood. So, although it is possible that names such as those of the Ta-zhig kings, La Mer Mu and Hab Gdal, and the Dru-gu place name Ong-ngu-man-chod may have been drawn from lost parts of this inscription, it cannot be asserted with confidence.

The stately mystic language of the qualities of kingship and the divine origin of the kings is like that of Khri Srong-lde-brtsan's memorial inscription (pp. 38–41) and the Lhasa Treaty inscription E. (pp. 108–111); also of DTH pp. 112–15 and 118.

Rang-byung rdo-rje in his description of the *bang so* refers to this pillar as recording the establishment of peace in the kingdom, *rgyal khams la bde khod pa'i dkar chag*. His eye was probably caught by the phrases *'bangs skyid do* and *'bangs skyid par bya ba* in the 18th and 19th lines; but the expression is not unique to Khri Lde-srong-brtsan for it is found also in the inscription of Khri Srong-lde-brtsan (p. 40) and in DTH pp. 113 and 118 referring respectively to the reigns of Khri Lde-gtsug-brtsan and Srong-brtsan sgam-po.

The importance of this inscription has been discussed by Tucci in TTK and in my article in *JRAS* 1969 but I may observe further that the statement in lines 25 and 26 implying that warfare against China began as soon as Khri Lde-srong-brtsan had assumed power, throws some light on the date of his accession. From the T'ang Annals it appears that Tibetan forces were fighting the Chinese continuously between 799 and 803 A.D. so that agrees with the view that Khri Lde-srong-brtsan was on the throne *c.* 800 A.D. The inscription goes on to state that, later, a lasting peace was made. Although the T'ang Annals record an exchange of envoys and a series of negotiations, in which the Chinese took the first step, from 803 onwards, and although hostilities appear to have ceased, there is no mention of a formal treaty having been achieved. That agrees with the Lhasa Treaty Inscription (E. lines 40–46 where it is said that Khri Lde-srong brtsan discussed a treaty, *mjal dum mol*, and that good relations were restored but it was not possible to proceed to a full treaty.

REIGN OF KHRI LDE-SRONG-BRTSAN *c.* 800–815 A.D.

Inscription

1 ༄།།བཙན་པོ་ལྷ་སྲས། །འོ་ལྡེ་སྤུ་རྒྱལ། །གནམ་གྱི་

2 ལྷ་ལས། མིའི་རྗེར་གཤེགས་པ། །ཆོས་ལུགས་བཟང

3 པོ་ནི་གཞན་གཙུག་གྱི་འགྱུར། །མངའ་ཐང་ཆེན་པོ་ནི་ནམ་

4 ཀུང་ཁྲིན་མི་ཉམས་སྟེ། །ཆབ་སྲིད་ནི་ཁྱེར་ཞིང་ཆེ། །དབུ་རྨོག་

5 ནི་ཡུན་དུ་བརྟན་པའི། །གཡུང་དྲུང་གི་གཙུག་ལག་ཆེན་པོ་

6 བཞིན་དུ[1] །བཙན་པོ་ལྷ་སྲས། ཁྲི། ལྡེ་སྲོང་བརྩན། མིའི་རྗེ་

7 མཛད་པ། །ལྷའི་ལུགས་དང་མཐུན་པར་ནི་མངའ་ཐང་ཆེ།

8 གནམ་གྱི་ཆོས་དང་མཚུངས་པར་ནི། བཀའ་བརྟན་ཏེ།

9 ཐུགས་རྣམ་པོའི་ལྡབས་དང་། བཀའ་ལུང་བཟང་པོའི་

10 ལུགས་ཀྱིས། །ཕྱི་ནང་གཉིས་སུ་ལེགས་ཤིང་། །ཆབ་སྲིད་ཆེ་

11 བའི་རྒྱལ། །ནམ་དུ་ཡང་། མི་འོངས་ཀྱིས་ཤེས་པར། །མདོ་

12 རྩམ་ཞིག་རྡོ་རིངས་ལ་བྲིས་པའོ།།

13 ༄། །བཙན་པོ་ལྷ་སྲས། ཁྲི་ལྡེ་སྲོང་བརྩན། ལྷ་འཕྲུལ་གྱི་

14 ཞལ་སྔ་ནས། །ཐུགས་རྣམ། ཕོང་ཡངས།[2] བཀའ་བརྟན། ཐུང་ཐུབ།

15 ཐུགས་སྟོབས་ཆེའོ། །རང་ཉིད་དེ་ལྟ་བས་ན། །འགྲིང་[3]གི་

16 རྗེ་མཛད་ན་ཡང་། །མི་ཆོས་པའི་ལས་ཀྱི་ལྷ་བསྐྱངས་པས་

Translation

The following translation covers only the first 29 lines: the fragments of the remainder have not been attempted.

The *btsan-po,* the divine prince, 'O-lde spu-rgyal came from among the gods of heaven to be ruler of men[1]. His religious customs were good: the order of the world was unchangeable. His power was great: its splendour was never impaired. And so the kingdom increased in extent and his helmet was firm. Even so, in accordance with that everlasting great order of the world[2], the *btsan-po,* the divine prince Khri Lde-srong-brtsan became ruler of men. His power, being in agreement with the way of the gods, was great: his orders, being in accordance with the religion of heaven, were firm. Through the outflowing of his profound spirit and the manner of his excellent commandments there was well-being both within and without; and his dominion was great. In order that this may be known for ever to all men a short account has been written on a stone pillar.

The *btsan-po,* the divine prince Khri Lde-srong-brtsan, the divinely wise himself, was great in his profound spirit, magnanimous heart, firm command, strength of body, and force of mind. His nature being thus, in his governance of men, by reducing the limits of

Notes to Translation

1. cf. TLTD II p. 93; Lhasa Treaty Inscription E ls. 5–8; and DTH p. 81.
2. Macdonald ET p. 353, see note 1 p. 39.

Notes to Text

1. cf. Lhasa Treaty Inscription E. lines 5–8; TLTD II p. 93.
2. cf. GK 19b (3) *thugs sgam bka' btsan khong pa yangs pa dang . .* also ff. 42a; 60b; 69a; and 85a.
3. '*greng*, cf. Khri Srong-lde-brtsan pillar, l. 30 (p. 40).

Inscription

17 ནང་དུ་འཁྲུག་པ་དང་། །སྨི་བདེ་བ་སྐྱིད་ཚོང་། །བོད་ཡོངས་ཀྱིས་

18 ཁོངས་ལ་ཡུལ་ཕྱུག་སྟེ། །འབངས་སྐྱིད་དོ། །ཞམ་ཞར། དབོན་

19 སྲས་རྒྱུད་ཀྱི་ཆབ་སྲིད་བརྟན་ཞིང་། །འབངས་སྐྱིད་པར་བྱ་བའི་

20 གདམས་ངག་དང་། །ཕྱིའི་དགྲ་འདུལ་བའི་ཕྱིན་གྱི་དཀྲའ་ཐབས་

21 སྟོན་སྨྱིད་པའི་བཟང་པོ་བཀའ་ལུང་དུ་བཞག་སྟེ། །ཡུན་ཀྱི་ལེགས་

22 པ་ཡང་རྒྱ་ཆེར་དགོངས་སོ། །ལྷ་འཕྲུལ་གྱི་ཞལ་སྔ་ནས་མཐའ་

23 བཞི་ཕྱོགས་བརྒྱད་དུ། །བཀའ་བརྩན། །ཆབ་སྲིད[4]ཆེ་སྟེ། །ཤར་ཕྱོགས་

24 ༄།།རྒྱལ་པོ་ཆེན་པོར་རྒྱ་འདུག་པ་དང་། །བར་དུ་བཀའ་ལོན་བྲུང་ནས་

25 དགྲར་བསྡོ་བ་ལས[5]། །དང་པོ་ཆབ་སྲིད་ཕྲུག་དུ་བཞེས་མ་ཐག་དུ[6]། །བོད་

26 ཀྱི་དམག་གིས། །རྒྱའི་ཡུལ་ཐོག་ཕྱོགས་སུ་དྲངས་པས་སྤྱ་བཏོ[7]། །

27 དེ་ཚུན་ཆད་ཀྱིས་ཆབ་སྲིད་ཀྱི་མངའ་བདག་མཛད་མ་ཐོག་ལ་

28 ནར་དུ་ལན་འགའ་རྒྱས་ཆབ་སྲིད་ལ་མ་བསྡོ་སྟེ། །རྟག་ཏུ་མཐལ་

29 དུམ་གསོལ་ལོ། །ལྷོ་ཕྱོགས་ཀྱི་རྒྱལ་པོར་རྒྱ་གར་འདུག་

30 པ་ཡང་།། [8] ཀྱིས་ མཛད་

31 ཆབ་སྲིད

32 ཕྱུང

Translation

harmful actions, he did away with internal dissension and unease. All Tibet being wealthy within the land, the people were happy[3]. Making the dominion firm for ever for the succession of his sons and grandsons, he established by his command, more excellently then before, the precepts of conferring happiness upon his subjects and the glorious strategy for subduing outer enemies; and he took ever-increasing thought for enduring welfare. The divinely wise himself extended his powerful commands and his dominion to the four quarters and the eight directions. In the east with China, which is the great king there, disagreements arose and they contended with him as enemies. And so, at first, just when he obtained the kingdom the armies of Tibet, thrusting into the upper part of China, caused terror. But after that, as soon as he himself was exercising authority over the kingdom, having come of age, when on some occasions China did not contend with his dominion, a lasting treaty was made. India being the great king of the southern direction . . . .

Notes to Translation (continued)

3. *skyid* happiness'' is the outcome of divine kingship and world order; cf. Khri Srong-lde-brtsan's inscription l. 26 (p. 40); I.O. 735 (Macdonald ET p. 360); and Treaty Inscription W ls. 55, 58, 59 where *skyid-rtag* is the name of a regnal era.

Notes to Text (continued)

4. cf. GK 21b (3) *mtha' bzhi phyogs brgyas bka' btsan chab srid la.*
5. cf. GK 21b (3) *phyogs bzhir rgyal po sde bzhi gnas pa yang bar du bka' khon byung na dgra ru bsdo.*
6. cf. GK 21b (2) *dang po chab srid ma khad du ni.*
7. cf. GK 21b (5) *rgya yul gshog pa'i phyogs su dmag gis phul* and 22a (5) *bod dmag shar phyogs rgya nag yul du phab.*
8. cf. GK 21b (6) *lho phyogs rgya gar rgyal po bzhugs pa yang.*

Inscription

33 བོད་གཉིས་

34 ཧྲེ   དང   ཞིན   དུ

35 ཡང་   སྨི   ད་

36 ×ོང་སྒྱ×× ཉི་འོག་ཏུ་ཆབ་

37 ཙ   མན་ཅད་×ཞི×[9]སྦྱོར་ཞིང

38 ཕྱོགས་×དྲུ་གུ་འདུག་[10]

39 བར་དུ་བཀའ་ལོན་བླུང་ནས་ཆབ་སྲིད་

40 བསྐོ་བ་ལས་ ༧༧༧ རྒྱ×འི་   དང་པོ་མན་ཚུན་ཅད་དུ།།བོད་[10]

41 དམ   པོ་ཆེ   །།མནངས་བཅད་[11] རྒྱ

42 དང། ཡུལ་གྱི་སྐུ་ཆེ   ×དོང   ཚུན་ཅད་སྟོད་ཕྱོར་ཁ་ག[12]

43 གྱིས་བྲུང་ཆབ་སྲིད་ལ་   བསྐོ་སྟེ།།མཇལ་དུམ་དུ་གསོལ་ལོ།།འདི་དག་

44 ལས་སྟོགས་པ་རྒྱལ་པོ།   འོག་ཏུ

45 ཆབ་སྲིད   ད ་པའི་ཆོས་[13]

46 ×གྱིད་རབ་ཏུ རྒྱལ ×ུ ×ུ   ང

RDO-RINGS AT THE TOMB OF KHRI LDE-SRONG-BRTSAN

(*not translated*)

Notes to Text (continued)

9. My notes suggest *ta-zhig* but it is not clear.
10. cf. GK 22a (3) *byang phyogs ge sar gru gu bzhugs pa yang bar du bka' khon byung nas bsdo ba la . . . . . . gru gu yul gyi ong ngu man chod du.*
11. *mnangs bcad* cf. Zhol S. l. 31.
12. *Hor kha*(*gan*)? cf. Pell T 1188.
13. *dam pa'i chos* is possible but not quite clear enough in my notes.

REIGN OF KHRI GTSUG-LDE-BRTSAN 815–836 A.D.

The Lcang-bu Inscriptions

[Plate 12]

In the courtyard of the great Karma-pa monastery of Stod-lung Mtshur-phu there is a stone pillar of which a photograph may be seen among the illustrations to my *Tibetan Burial Grounds, CAJ* 1963. It bears two inscriptions relating to the building of a *gtsug-lag-khang* (temple) at Stod (Stod-lungs) Lcang-bu by Zhang Tshes-pong Stag-bzang nya-sto. The name Lcang-bu was not traceable in the neighbourhood of the monastery and the monks had no reliable information about the origin of the pillar or the contents of the inscription in which they showed little interest; but there can be no doubt that Mtshur-phu was built on or near the site of the earlier Lcang-bu *gtsug-lag-khang.*

It is recorded in the Tibetan Annals that in 757 A.D. Khri Srong-lde-brtsan stayed in the palace of Lcang-bu of Stod (DTH p. 57). The founder of the Lcang-bu *gtsug-lag-khang* was a noble of the Tshes-pong clan from which Khri Srong-lde-brtsan took his principal wife, the mother of Mu-ne, Mu-rug, and Khri Lde-srong-brtsan. It is probable that the temple would be built on the founder's own estates, so perhaps in 757 the king, recently enthroned and then fifteen years old, was visiting the palace of the family from which he had taken or was about to take a wife; alternatively, a royal palace could have been bestowed on his wife's family.

The title "Zhang", maternal uncle, by which Tshes-pong Stag-bzang nya-sto was known, was accorded to leading members of a clan from which a Tibetan king had chosen a queen who then bore him an heir. Tshes-pong was one of the clans which had helped the Myang and Dba's in establishing the Tibetan kingdom at the end of the 6th century (DTH p. 104). A lady of that clan was the mother of Srong-brtsan sgam-po and a member was among his leading councillors (DTH 82 and 110). Thereafter, the clan does not figure prominently in the Tibetan Annals, only one member being mentioned as holding the office of *brung-pa* in 714 A.D. (DTH p. 21). Neither he nor the earlier councillor of Srong-brtsan sgam-po is distinguished by the title *zhang* which does not appear in the Tibetan Annals until 710 A.D. and perhaps did not come into use until the ascendancy of the 'Bro clan with the marriage to Mang-srong mang-rtsan of the lady 'Bro Khri-ma-lod whose influence lasted long after the death of her husband in 676 A.D. until her own death in 712 A.D. as can be seen from frequent mention of her in the Tibetan Annals for those years. In Chinese eyes, too, she was of such importance that the Emperor sent a special representative to her funeral (Ts'e-fu yuan kuei 979 4a: information from Dr Chang Kun). Not surprisingly several members of the Tshes-pong clan are named among the leading officials in the religious edict of Khri Lde-srong-brtsan (PT *ja* f. 130a and b); and one of them Zhang Lha-bzang klu-dpal, won a great military reputation in association with Zhang Khri-sum-rje of 'Bro (TLTD II pp. 94, 96 etc.). It may be remarked that in the personal names (*ming*) of members of the clan the final syllable *sto* appears frequently and is perhaps exclusive to them.

The principal inscription records the foundation of the *gtsug-lag-khang* of Lcang-bu as a religious donation for the benefit of the king in return for favours granted by him; and to link it more closely with the king, it was dedicated as a dependency of his great temple of 'On-cang-do in the Skyid-chu valley not far from Lhasa. This inscription was written at the order of the king and the principal copy of the list of property assigned to the *gtsug-lag-khang* and of the document of dedication were deposited with the *Bcom-ldan 'da's ring lugs kyi 'dun sa* which was perhaps the assembly hall of a governing council for Buddhism, either at Lhasa or Bsam-yas; other copies were given to the Gnas-brtan—the Elder, or Abbot, of 'On-cang-do and the Mngan, who seems to have been a civil district administrator; and one copy was to be kept at the *gtsug-lag-khang* itself.

The second, short, inscription on a narrow side of the pillar records the disposal of copies of the *gtsigs,* that is the royal decree directing the writing of the first inscription, and its terms. The word *gtsigs* used in all inscriptions directly attributed to a king, does not appear in the main inscription. In the second inscription there is no mention of Zhang Nya-sto by name but only of the descendants of Zhang Tshes-pong Gsas-sto who was probably his father. The practice of mentioning the forebears of a person for whom a decree was granted is seen in the Zhol inscription (N) where both the father and grandfather of Ngan-lam Stag-sgra klu-khong are named and in the Zhwa'i Lha-khang inscriptions which mention the grandfather of Ban-de Myang Ting-nge-'dzin and also his paternal grand-uncle. The principal copy of the decree (*gtsigs*) was deposited (*bzhag*) at Phying-ba'i kun-mkar, a royal palace near the burial ground at 'Phyong-rgyas and another at the *Bka'i-sa,* perhaps the office of the councillors of state, who are described as *bka' la gtogs-pa* (p. 9). The secondary copy was to be deposited (*gzhag*) at the *gtsug-lag-khang* where it was to be treated with greater respect than the other documents for its resting place was to be the *mdzod,* the treasury.

I first saw the pillar on a visit to Mtshur-phu in 1946 but my photographs were not successful and it was not until 1948, when I was sent a fine rubbing by the kindness of the Rgyal-dbang Karma-pa Rin-po-che, that I was able to complete an edition of the inscription which was published in *JRASB* XV. 1, 1949, that being my first, inexpert, essay in Tibetan epigraphy. Professor Tucci, who also acquired a copy in 1948, published it in TTK with a much improved translation. The original inscription is almost undamaged and the text below differs from the former versions only in a few small instances of punctuation.

There is no indication of the date of the inscription but if, as seems likely, Khri Gtsug-lde-brtsan came to the throne in 815 A.D. at the age of nine, it may be supposed that some years elapsed before the foundation of the temple of 'On-cang-do with which Lcang-bu was connected.

The only passage I have seen in later literature that appears to refer to this temple is in f. 27b of the *Sngon gyi gtam me tog phreng ba* by Ne'u Pandita published at New Delhi in 1974 from the collection of rare texts in the library of Tsepon W. D. Shakabpa. It attributes to Zhang Tshe-spong rtag-bzang nya-lto (*sic*) the foundation of a temple in Stod-lungs as a sort of annex to that of 'On-cang-rdo: *'on cang rdo tshar ba'i lhag mas stod lungs lhag ma'i lha khang bzhengs;* "from what was left over when the *lha-khang* of 'On-cang-rdo was completed, he built the Stod-lungs Lhag-ma'i *lha-khang.*"

REIGN OF KHRI GTSUG-LDE-BRTSAN 815–836 A.D.

Inscription

1 ༄།།ཞང་ཆེས་པོང་སྟག་བཟང་ཉ་སྟོས།

2 སྟོད་ཀྱི་ལྕང་བུར། གཙུག་ལག་ཁང་བརྩིགས་

3 པའི་ལོ་རྒྱུས། །རྡོ་རིངས་ལ་བྲི་བར།:།བཙན:

4 པོའི་བཀའས་གནང་སྟེ་བྲིས་པའོ།:།

5 ༄།།བཙན་པོ་ལྷ་སྲས་ཡབ་མྱེས་ཀྱི་སྐུ་རིང་ལ།

6 དམ་པའི་ཆོས་བརྩེས་ནས། །གདུང་རབས:

7 སུ་དམ་པའི་ཆོས་ཀྱི་གཏང་ཞིང་མཛད་པར:

8 ཆོས་གཙིགས་དང་། བཀའི་ལུང་སྩལད་པ

9 ལས་འབྱུང་བ་བཞིན། །ཞང་ཆེས་པོང་ཉ་སྟོས།

10 དམ་པའི་ཆོས་ཉམས་སུ་བླངས། །བཙན:

11 པོ་ལྷ་སྲས། ཁྲི་གཙུག་ལྡེ་བརྩན་འཕྲུལ་གྱི:

12 བཀའ་དྲིན། །ཞང་ཉ་སྟོ་ལ་ཆེར་སྩལད་པས

13 །བཀའ་དྲིན་ཆེན་པོ་བསབ་པའི་ཕྱིར།།

THE LCANG-BU INSCRIPTIONS

(1)

Translation

The *btsan-po* having ordered that it should be inscribed on a stone pillar, a record of the founding of the temple at Lcang-bu of Stod by Zhang Tshes-pong Nya-sto has therefore been inscribed.

In accordance with the edicts concerning religion[1] that since the holy religion was received in the time of the *btsan-po,* the sons of god, father and grandfather, in succeeding generations the holy religion should be practised and not abandoned, and with the commandment in consequence thereof, Zhang Nya-sto accepted the holy religion in his heart. The favour of the *btsan-po,* the son of god, Khri Gtsug-lde-brtsan having been greatly bestowed on Zhang Nya-sto, in

Notes to Translation

1. *Chos-gtsigs,* the edicts of Khri Srong-lde-brtsan and Khri Lde-srong-brtsan cited in the inscriptions at Bsam-yas and Skar-cung (pp. 38, 76).

Inscription

14 བཙན་པོ་སྐུ་ཡོན་དུ་བསྔོས་ཏེ། །སྨོན་ལམ་

15 རྒྱ་ཆེར་བཏབ་ནས། །སྟོད་ལྗོངས་ཀྱི་ལྷུང་བུར་

16 །གཙུག་ལག་ཁང་བརྩིགས་སྟེ། །དཀོན་

17 མཆོག་གསུམ་གྱི་རྟེན་བཙུགས། །དགེ་

18 སློང་བཞི་གནས་པར་སྦྱར་ནས། །རྐྱེན་གྱི་

19 ཟས་དང་། །ཞིང་འབྲོག་དང་། ལྷ་ཆ་དང་། །ནོར་རྫས་

20 དང་། །རྐང་འགྲོས་ལས་སྩོགས་པ། ཚང་བར་

21 བཙད་དེ། །བཙན་པོ་ཁྲི་གཙུག་ལྡེ་བརྩན་

22 གྱི་སྐུ་ཡོན་རྒྱུན་མྱི་འཆད་པར་བྱེད་དོ།།

23 གཙུག་ལག་ཁང་འདིའི་མཚན་ཡང་།།

24 བཙན་པོའི་བཀའ་ཞལ་ཕྱིས་བཏགས་སྟེ།

25 ཀོན་ཙང་དོའི་ཐུགས་དམ་གྱི་གཙུག་ལག་

26 ཁང་ཆེན་པོའི་མདུག་ལ་གདགས་སོང་།

Translation

order to repay that great favour, having offered great prayers he founded the temple at Lcang-bu and set up shrines of the Three Jewels, dedicating it as a benefaction on behalf of the *btsan-po*[2]. And he arranged for four *dge-slong* to live there; and assigning for its support in full measure, bondsmen, fields and grazing grounds, sacred vessels and treasure, cattle and so on, he acted so that the benefaction of the *btsan-po* Khri Gtsug-lde-brtsan should never be discontinued. The name of this temple was given by the personal command of the *btsan-po* and it was ordered that it should be attached as a dependency of the temple of the (king's own) vow at

Notes to Translation (continued)

2. The spiritual merit of the pious act is conferred on the *btsan-po*.

Inscription

27 ཆེས་གྱུང་། །ལྷ་ནས་མཛད་པར། །བཀའ་ཙས་

28 གནང་། །ལྷ་རིས་ཀྱི་འབངས་དང་། དཀོར་

29 ལ། །ཁྲལ་སྤྱི་དཔབ་པ་དང་། ཁྲ་དང་། ཆད་ཀ:

30 སྤྱི་བཞེས་པ་ལས་སྩོགས་པ་ཡང་། །ལྷ་རིས:

31 ཆེན་པོའི་ཐང་དུ། །བཀའ་ཙས་གནང་ངོ། །

32 གཙུག་ལག་ཁང་འདིའི་རྐྱེན་རིས་བསྡོ་ཞིང་

33 སྲིད་པ་ཡང་། །ཐང་ཉ་སྟོས། ཇོ་ལྷར་གྲུས་ཤིང་།

34 བསྟོས་པ་བཞིན་བརྩན་པར། །བཀའ་ཙས་གནངོ།

35 །ནམ་ཞིག་ན། །ཐང་ཉ་སྟོ་ལ། བུ་ཚ་རྒྱུད་ཡོང:

36 སྐྱིད་པ་ཞིག་དུ་གྱུར་ན། །ཁོལ་ཡུལ་ལས་སྩོགས

37 པ་དབང་ངོ་ཚོག། །ལྷར་ཡང་སྤྱི་བཞེས།

38 [1]གྱུང་སྤྱི་སྦྱིན་པར། །གཙུག་ལག་ཁང་འདི་རྐྱེན།

39 དུ་བསྔན་པར། །བཀའ་ཙས་གནང་ངོ།

[1] གྱུང་ for རྒྱུང་

Translation

'On-cang-do and that its administration[3] should be directed by the superior authority. It was ordered that by reason of its rank as a great religious estate, taxation should not be imposed on the subjects of the property of the religious estate and that they should not be liable to duties or fines. It was ordered that with regard to what has been done in dedicating property for the support of this temple, that dedication should be confirmed just as Zhang Nya-sto has made it. It was ordered that if the future descendants of Zhang Nya-sto should ever happen to die out, the service-tenure land and so on, whatever they may hold, shall not be resumed nor shall it be given away but it shall

Notes to Translation (continued)

3. *chis,* see my *Tibetan chis and tshis* in Asia Major XIV 2, 1969 pp. 254–6.

REIGN OF KHRI GTSUG-LDE-BRTSAN 815–836 A.D.

Inscription

40 གཙུག་ལག་ཁང་གི་རྐྱེན་བཅད་པའི་དཀར:

41 ཆག་དང་། བསྒྲིམས་ཡིག་བླ་དཔེ་ནི། །བཅོམ་ལྡན་

42 འདའས་རོང་ལུགས་ཀྱི་འདུན་སར་བཞག། །

43 ཚོག་དཔེ་ནི། །ཚོན་ཅང་དེ་གཙུག་ལག་ཁང་གི:

44 གནས་བརྟན་དང་། མངན་ལ་སྐྱལད། །དཔེ:

45 དེ་དང་འདྲ་བ་གཙོག་ནི། །གཙུག་ལག་ཁང:

46 འདིར་གཞག་པར། །བཀའ་གཙིགས་གནང་ངོ། །

Translation

be added to the property of this temple. And by order, a list of the property assigned to this temple, and the principal copy of the deed of dedication have been deposited in the assembly hall of the abbots who maintain the tradition of the Buddha[4]; a secondary copy has been given to the Elder[5] of the temple of 'On-cang-do and also to the Mngan[6]; and a similar copy is kept in this temple.

Notes to Translation (continued)

4. *ring-lugs* see p. 53 note 12.
5. *gnas-brtan;* sthavira.
6. *mngan,* chief administrative officer of a district? see TLTD III, Vocabulary, p. 126.

Inscription

1 ༄། ཁང་ཆེས་པོང་

2 གསས་སྟོའི་བུ་

3 ཚེ་། །གཙོགས:

4 གནང་བའི། ལྷ་

5 དཔེ་ནི། །ཕྱིང་བ

6 འི་སྐུན་མཁར:

7 ན། །གཙོགས:

8 ཆེན་པོ་གཞན་གྱི་

9 ལྷ་ལ་བཞག། །དེ་

10 དང་འདྲ་བ་རྣམ:

11 གཙོག་ནི། གཙོགྶ:

12 གཞན་གྱི་ལྷ་ལ།

13 བཀའི་སར་བཞུྒ:

14 །གཙོགས་ཀྱི །

THE LCANG-BU INSCRIPTIONS

(2)

Translation

By order: the principal copy of the edict granted for the descendants of Zhang Tshes-pong Gsas-sto has been deposited at the castle of 'Phying-ba alongside the other great edicts; a copy, just like that one, has been deposited alongside the other edicts in the council

Inscription

15 རྫོག་དཔེ་འཕྲུ

16 མེན་གྱྀ་སྒྲོམ་བུཿ

17 ནྀ་། གཙུག་ལགཿ

18 ཁང་འདིའི་མཆོད་

19 དུ་བཞག་པར།

20 བཀའས་གནང་

21 ངོ།།

Translation

chamber; and a secondary copy of the edict in a box of *'phra-men*[1] is to be deposited in the treasury of this temple.

Note to Translation

1. *'phra-men* (also in the Rkong-po inscription l. 11.) appears as a precious substance used as one of the insignia of nobility ranking third after turquoise and gold and before silver (Pell. T. 1071). A list in the T'ang Annals places "silver-gilt" in that position; but another Chinese list (Demiéville, *Concile,* p. 285.) omits silver-gilt altogether. In current Tibetan *phra* means "jewel" or "bejewelled object"; but Dagyab's dictionary has *khra-men* as a blue stone like turquoise, and also *mu-men* as a precious blue stone. That suggests lapis lazuli which Schafer (*The Golden Peaches of Samarkand,* p. 333, n. 88) identifies with sê sê, highly valued in China and by the Tibetans. The 9th-century Japanese pilgrim Ennin found many reliquaries of lapis lazuli at Wu-tai Shan (E Reischauer, *Ennin's travels in T'ang China).* Sê sê comes first in the T'ang Annals, the place given to turquoise in Pell T. 1071; but DTH p. 60 shows that the Tibetans had an even higher ornament than turquoise, *viz ke-ke-ru;* that, however, is identified by Das as a precious white stone. In so much uncertainty it seems best to leave *'phra-men* untranslated.

REIGN OF KHRI GTSUG-LDE-BRTSAN 815–836 A.D.

The Treaty of 821/822 A.D.

[Plates 13–14]

The bilingual inscription on a stone pillar outside the Jo-khang at Lhasa recording a treaty between Tibet and China is probably the most widely known and in many ways the most important of the early inscriptions from Tibet. In *JRAS* 1978 I published in transcription what I hope may be a generally acceptable text. There are several earlier editions the best being that of Li Fang-kuei (T'oung Pao 1956) which includes both the Tibetan and Chinese texts. The reason for yet another edition was that in RT's collection there is a copy of much earlier origin than the 19th and 20th century estampages on which Li's and other editions are mainly based and which contains passages that are effaced or illegible in those estampages.

The text below is, in Tibetan letters, that of my article in *JRAS* with a few corrections where there were lapses in proof reading. I have here omitted details of the critical comparison between RT's and other texts and also most of my notes on the translation; but I add a few further comments on the historical setting to those in earlier editions.

During the two hundred years or so of relations between the kings of Tibet and the T'ang dynasty of China almost continuous hostilities were interspersed with diplomatic negotiations leading now and then to the conclusion of a short-lived treaty of peace. The T'ang Annals mention many of these beginning with the matrimonial alliance in the time of Srong-brtsan sgam-po and including two, in 708/710 and 733 A.D., in the reign of Khri Lde-gtsug-brtsan and four during the particularly warlike reign of Khri Srong-lde-brtsan in the years 756, 762, 766 and 783. Those treaties seem to have been of more significance to the Chinese, who record in some detail the process of negotiating and concluding the agreements, than to the Tibetans who may have regarded them simply as breathing space. In the Tibetan Annals, which cover the years up to 756, there is no mention of any treaty; and in the East inscription below, where a rapid *coup d'oeil* is cast over past relations, apart from the matrimonial alliances of 640 and 710 only the infructuous negotiations between Khri Lde-srong-brtsan and the Emperor Tê-tsung are mentioned. That reference must be to the years 804/805 when Khri Lde-srong-brtsan, having established his succession, sent envoys to the Chinese court and it is presumably that occasion which is described in the inscription at his tomb (pp. 88, 89) where it is said that the Chinese sought a treaty.

The Emperor Tê-tsung died before an agreement could be concluded and for the next fifteen years, in spite of occasional overtures, hostilities went on sporadically with neither side gaining a lasting advantage. It was not until the accession of the emperor Mu-tsung in 820 that purposeful negotiations were resumed, leading to the treaty of 821/822.

There is no evidence that any of the earlier treaties was ratified at Lhasa itself. It may be chance that this is the only such document to survive in Central Tibet; but perhaps the growing political influence of Buddhism from the beginning of the 9th century had led to special regard being given to an agreement in which the principal Tibetan participant was a monk-minister. And from the same cause, a new spirit of peace-making may have inspired the complete silence in the east inscription on the reign of Khri Srong-lde-brtsan in which the Chinese emperor suffered the humiliation of having to flee from his capital and to see on his throne, albeit for only a few days, a puppet emperor appointed by the triumphant Tibetans.

The treaty was solemnized with both Buddhist and non-Buddhist rites. In the attestation not only the holy ones of Buddhism are invoked but also the sun, moon, planets and stars. The oath-taking was accompanied by the sacrifice of animals and, according to the T'ang Annals, all the participants except the Poch'ep'u smeared their lips with the blood. That was a regular part of Tibetan ceremonial on such occasions—e.g. at the annual oath of loyalty to the *btsan-po* (Demiéville p. 256) and had been practised at the conclusion of the treaty near Ch'ing-shui in 783. But the religious character of the ceremony then and at Lhasa was underlined by the taking of a separate oath in front of an image of the Buddha; and it is strongly stressed in prayers offered at the founding of a chapel on the border with China to commemorate the treaty (TLTD II pp. 92–104 and Pell T. 16). Mainly owing to increasing weakness on both sides the treaty held good until the collapse of the authority of the *btsan-po* in the civil strife that followed the death of Glang Darma *c.* 842 A.D.

The Chinese texts of the inscriptions on the west, south and north faces reproduced in Li Fang-kuei's edition throw valuable light on the interpretation of the Tibetan; and I have depended entirely on his translation and explanation of the proper form of the official titles, posts, and personal names of the Chinese ministers in the south inscription.

Of the several later histories which mention the pillar and the treaty, the *Rgyal-rabs gsal-ba'i me-long* f. 92a gives the longest account and quotes, not always accurately, several passages from the terms of the treaty on the west face. The *Deb-ther sngon-po* vol. *nya* f. 107b cites the opening passage of the east inscription.

East Inscription

1 ༄། །འཕྲུལ་གྱི་ལྷ་བཙན་པོ་ཁྲི་གཙུག་ལྡེ་བཙན་དང༌། །རྒྱ་རྗེ་བྷུན་བྷུ་ཧེའུ་

2 ཏིག་ཧྭང་ཏེ་གཉིས། །ཆབ་སྲིད་གཅིག་དུ་མོལ་ཏེ་མཇལ་དུམ་མཛད་པའི་

3 ཚེ། །བོད་རྒྱ་གཉིས་ཀྱི་རྩུལ་ཅི་འདྲ་བ་དང༌། །མཇལ་དུམ་མཛད་པའི་

4 གཏན་ཚིགས་རྡོ་རིངས་ལ་བྲིས་པའོ།།

5 ༄། །འཕྲུལ་གྱི་ལྷ་བཙན་པོ་འོ་ལྡེ་སྤུ་རྒྱལ། །ཡུལ་བྱུང་ས་དོད་ཚུན་ཆད

6 གདུང་མ་འགྱུར་བར། །བོད་ཀྱི་རྒྱལ་པོ་ཆེན་པོ་མཛད་པ་ཡང༌། །གངས་རི་

7 མཐོན་པོའི་ནི་དབུས། །ཆུ་བོ་ཆེན་པོའི་ནི་མགོ། །ཡུལ་མཐོ་ས་གཙང༌།།

8 ཞེས། །གནམ་གྱི་ལྷ་ལས། །མིའི་རྒྱལ་པོར་གཤེགས་ཏེ། །གཙུག་ལག་

9 ཆེན་པོས་ནི། །ཡུནད་ཀྱི་སྲིད་བཙུགས། །ཆོས་ཁྲིམས་བཟང་པོས་ནི། །མིའི་

10 ལུགས་བསྲང། །བྱམས་པའི་བཀའ་དྲིན་གྱིས་ནི་ནང་གི་ཆིས་སྐྱུརད།།

11 དགྲ་ཐབས་མཁས་པས་ནི་ཕྱིའི་དགྲ་བཏུལ་ཏེ། །ཆབ་སྲིད་ནི་ཕྱིར་ཞིང་ཆེ།།

12 དབུ་རྨོག་ནི་བརྟུར་ཞིང་བརྟན་པས། །ནམ་ཞར་གཙུག་མྱི་འགྱུར། །ཕྱོན་མྱི་

13 ཉམས་པའི་གཡུང་དྲུང་གི་རྒྱལ་པོ་ཆེན་པོ་ཡིན། །དེའི་ཕྱིར། །ལྷོ་ཕྱོགས་

THE TREATY OF 821/822 A.D.

Translation

East Inscription

At the time when the supernaturally wise divinity, the *btsan-po,* Khri Gtsug-lde-brtsan and the Chinese king B'un B'u He'u Tig Hwang Te conferred about the alliance of their dominions and made a treaty, the nature of the relations between Tibet and China and the purport of the treaty were inscribed on a stone pillar.

From the time when the supernaturally wise divinity, the *btsan-po.* 'O-lde spu-rgyal obtained the country and came to high estate his line, unchanging, has ruled as great kings of Tibet[1]. Saying "it is the centre of high snow mountains, the source of mighty rivers, a high country, a pure land" they came from being gods in heaven to be lords of men. By the great world order they established an enduring dominion. By excellent religious laws they set right the ways of men. By loving benevolence they brought harmony to the affairs of the interior. Subduing external enemies through knowledge of the arts of war they increased the extent of their dominion. Through the ever-increasing might of their helmet their wise order was immutable. They were great kings of the Eternal Swastika of unsullied glory.

Notes to Translation

1. *Deb-ther sngon-po* vol.*nya* f. 107b quotes this paragraph describing the achievements of the descendants of 'O-lde spu-rgyal. Unlike the inscriptions at the tombs of Khri Srong-lde-brtsan and Khri Lde-srong-brtsan, the *btsan-po* Khri Gtsug-lde-brtsan is not specifically named here as following the customs of the first ancestor.

East Inscription

14 གྱི་མོན་རྒྱ་གར་དང་། །ནུབ་ཕྱོགས་ཀྱི་ཏ་ཞིག་དང་། །བྱང་ཕྱོགས་ཀྱི་དྲུ་གུ་ནོ་

15 མྱིལ་ལ་སྩོགས་པ། །གཡལ་གཡོའི་རྒྱལ་པོ་སྡེ་ཆེན་པོར་བླ་བ་ཀུན་ཀྱང་། །

16 འཕྲུལ་གྱི་ལྷ་བཙན་པོའི་དབུ་རྨོག་བརྟན་པོ་དང་ལུགས་བཟང་པོ་ལ། །ཕྱི་

17 ཕྱོགས་ཀྱིས་གུས་ཤེད་དེ། །ཕན་ཚུན་དགྱེས་ཤིང་། །བཀའ་སྒྲལད་ཏོ་ཆོག་

18 ཉན་པ་ཡིན། །ཤར་ཕྱོགས་ན་རྒྱ་འདུག་པ། །མཚོ་ཆེན་པོའི་བར། །ཉི་མ་

19 ཤར་བ་ཡོགས་ཀྱི་རྒྱལ་པོ་སྟེ། །ལྷོ་བལ་གཞན་དང་མི་འདྲ་བར། །སྲིད་དང་

20 ཆོས་བཟང་། །གཙུག་ལག་ཆེ་བས། །བོད་དང་ཡང་། །འཐབ་ཀྱི་དགྲ། །གཉེན་

21 ཀྱི་དོ་སྟེ། །དང་པོ་རྒྱ་རྗེ་ཡི་རྒྱལ་སར་ཞུགས་ནས། །དེའེ་ཏང་གི་སྲིད་ལོ་ཉི་ཤུ་

22 རྩ་གསུམ་ལོན། །རྒྱལ་རབས་གཅིག་གི་འོག་ཏུ། །འཕྲུལ་གྱི་ལྷ་བཙན་པོ་

23 ཁྲི་སྲོང་བརྩན་དང་། །རྒྱ་རྗེ་ཐའེ་ཙོང་བུན་བུ་ཤེང་ཧྭང་ཏེ་གཉིས། །ཆབ་

24 སྲིད་གཅིག་ཏུ་མོལ་ནས། །ཅེང་ཀྭན་གྱི་ལོ་ལ། །ཀུན་ཤེང་ཀོང་ཅོ། །

25 བཙན་པོའི་ཁབ་ཏུ་བླངས། །ཕྱིས་འཕྲུལ་གྱི་ལྷ་བཙན་པོ་ཁྲི་ལྡེ་གཙུག་

26 བརྟན་དང་། །རྒྱ་རྗེ་སམ་ལང་ཁའེ་འགྭན་ཤེང་བུན་ཤིན་བུ་ཧྭང་ཏེ་དང་། །

27 ཆབ་སྲིད་གཅིག་ཏུ་མོལ་ཏེ། །གཉེན་བརྩེགས་ནས། །ཀེང་ལུང་གི་ལོ་ལ་

THE TREATY OF 821/822 A.D.

Translation

Thus[2], India of the borderland in the south, the Ta-zhig in the west, the Dru-gu No-smel and so on in the north, all those known as the great kingdoms of the right and left, and every inhabited region without exception did not fail to revere the mighty helmet and excellent customs of the supernaturally wise divinity, the *btsan-po;* and on all sides, with happiness, they hearkened to whatever commands he gave.

In the east is China, extending to the great ocean, the king of the region where the sun rises, unlike other barbarians[3], by the excellence of its dominion and religious customs and the greatness of its wisdom and method, a match even for Tibet in war and a partner in friendship. From the time when the first Chinese emperor Li ascended the throne twenty-three years of the De'e Tang dynasty having passed, after one royal generation, the supernaturally wise divinity Khri Srong-brtsan and the Chinese king The'u-tsong B'un Bu Sheng Hwang Te conferred about the alliance of their kingdoms and in the Ceng Kwan year Mun Sheng Kong Co was received as bride of the *btsan-po*. Later, the supernaturally wise divinity, the *btsan-po* Khri Lde-gtsug-brtsan and the Chinese king Sam Lang Kha'e B'un Shin B'u Hwang Te conferred about the alliance of their dominions and

Notes to Translation (continued)

2. Madame Macdonald in Études Tibétaines p. 340 shows convincingly that *de'i phyir* here means "because of" rather than "after that".

3. Together with Tucci and F-K Li I formerly understood *lho bal* to mean Nepal but in his impressive article *Saint et Divin* in *JA* 1981 R. A. Stein shows from comparison of Chinese and Tibetan texts that it translates the Chinese *jong-yi* "barbarians". So the Tibetans here are paying the Chinese in their own coin. "Barbarian" makes good sense also in the second edict of Khri Srong-lde-brtsan in PT *ja* f. 110 where opponents of Buddhism describe it as *lho bal gyi lha dang chos* "the gods and religion of the barbarians", and in Pell T. 1077 and 1085 where subjects of the Chinese at Sha cu (Tun-huang) call themselves "we humble *lho-bal*"; while in Pell T. 1089 which deals with administrative arrangements on Tibet's north-east frontier—far distant from Nepal—an official has the Turkic title of *to dog* of the *lho bal.* And in Pell T. 1071 and 1072 where penalties for offences are listed according to social status, *lho bal gyi btson* "captive barbarians" are classified last of all with the *g-yung,* the lowest order of Tibetan society.

East Inscription

28 ཀིམ་ཤང་ཀོང་ཅོ། །བཙན་པོའི་ཁབ་དུ་བླངས་ནས། །དབོན་ཞང་དུ་གྱུར

29 ཏེ་དགྱེས་པ་ལས། །བར་འགའ་ཕན་ཅུན་ཀྱི་སོའི་བློན་པོས་གནོད་པ

30 དག་ཧྲུལ་གྱིས་ཀྱང༌། །གཉེན་བའི་ཆབ་གང་དུ་བྱ་བ། །ཐུགས་ཕྲེ་ལ་ཆེ་ནས

31 དོའ་དག་གི་ཆེ། །དམག་སྟོངས་ཀྱིས་ཕན་ཐོགས་པར་བྱས་པ་དང༌། །ཕན་ཅུན

32 ཐུགས་ཞེངས་སྲུང་ངོ་ཚོག་ན། །དགྱེས་སྣང་དག་ཀྱང་མ་ཆད་པར་བསྲིས་ཏེ།།

33 འདི་ལྟར་ཉེ་ཞིང་གཉེན་པ་ཡིན་ན། །དབོན་ཞང་གི་ཚུལ་ལོ་ན་ལྟར། །ཐུགས

34 ཡི་དམ་ཞབས་པ་ལས། །བཙན་པོ་ཡབ་ལྷ་འཕྲུལ་ཁྲི་ལྡེ་སྲོང་བཙན་གྱི་ཞ

35 སྔ་ནས། །སྙམ་དཀྱིལ་ཆེན་པོས་ནི། །ཆོས་སྲིད་ཏེ་ལ་ཡང་མཁས་ཤིང་གསལ

36 བྱམས་པའི་བཀའ་དྲིན་གྱིས་ནི། །ཕྱི་ནང་མེད་པར། །ཕྱོགས་བརྒྱད་དུ་ཁྱབ་སྟེ།།

37 མཐའ་བཞི་རྒྱལ་པོ་ཀུན་དང་ཡང་མཛལད་ཅིང་འདུམ་པར་མཛད་ན། །རྒྱ་དང་ལྷ

38 ཞིག། །གཉེན་རྩེག་མ། །ཡུལ་ཁྲིམ་ཆེས་ཡིན་བས། །ལྷག་པར་ཆབ་སྲིད

39 གཙུག་དུ་དགྱེས་ཏེ། །ཕན་ཅུན་དབོན་ཞང་དགོངས་པ་མཐུན་ནས། །རྒྱ་རྗེ་ཞེང

40 ཤིན་བྱུན་བྱུ་ཧྭང་ཏེ་དང༌། །མཛལ་དུམ་མོལ་ཏེ། །བཀའ་ལོན་ཆེང་པ་ཉེ

41 སྤྱངས་ཤིང་བསལད། །དགྱེས་པ་གསར་ནི་བརླས་ཤིང་བསྡུད་ནས། །དེ་ཅུན

Translation

when they had increased their friendly connexion Kim Shang Kong Co was received in the Ken Lung year as the bride of the *btsan-po*. They rejoiced at becoming Nephew and Uncle[4] and, although now and then the frontier ministers on both sides caused[5] some mischief, at that time when with great unity of mind they vied in acting according to the spirit of their relationship beneficial measures were taken by sending military assistance; and whatever disagreement might arise on either side care was taken not to interrupt the display of cordiality. And since they were thus connected as kinsmen, the *btsan-po* my father, the supernaturally wise divinity Khri Srong-lde-brtsan himself, having taken a firm resolve in strict accordance with the relationship of Nephew and Uncle, knowing through the great profundity of his mind everything that pertained to religious law and government, and by the grace of his conspicuous loving-kindness embracing the eight directions without distinction of inner and outer, came to an agreement and made treaties with all the kings of the four frontiers. And as for China in particular, since there was one bond of kinship after another and since the countries were neighbours, he took pleasure that the dominions should be specially united and Nephew and Uncle being agreed in their thoughts one with the other, he conferred about a treaty with the Chinese king Zheng Shin B'un B'u Hwang Te. The old animosity was purged and cleared away. The new happiness was conjoined and increased. From then onwards

Notes to Translation (continued)

4. The princess was in fact a great niece of the Emperor. *Dbon-zhang* came to be used as a formal description of the relationship between successive Tibetan rulers and Chinese emperors.

East Inscription

42 ཅད། །བཙན་པོ་དབོན་ཤི་སྐྱ་ཆེ་གཙིག། །རྒྱ་རྗེ་ཞང་ཤི་གཏུང་རབས་གསུམ་གྱི་

43 བར་དུ། །བཀའ་ལོན་གྱི་གཙུགས་ཤི་མ་བྱུང། །དགྱེས་པའི་སྤྱི་ཞུ་ཤི་ཕན་ཚུན་

44 ཕྱད་དེ། །ཕོ་ཉ་གཅེས་པ་ལས། །བཀའ་ཕྲིན་སྙན་པ་དང་། །དཀོར་ནོར།།

45 བཟང་པོས་ནི། །རྒྱུན་དུ་འདྲུལ་ན། །མཇལ་དུམ་གྱི་མདོ་ཆེན་པོ་གཙིགས་

46 བཅ་བ་ལྟ་བུ་ཡང་མ་གྲུབ། །དབོན་ཞང་མི་ལེད་པའི་རྗེས་གྲུང་ཚོར་མ་ཕྱིན་པར།།

47 ཐུགས་ནོངས་ཀྱིས་བརྩལ་ཏེ། །བར་གྱི་གཙུགས་རྙིང་པ་ཕྲན་ཆེགས་ཀྱི།།

48 རྡོགས་ཕྲིག་གིས། །ཞིགས་པ་ཆེན་པོའི་སྐྱུ་དོན། །ཕྱི་ལྡིགས་པ་ཤེ་དག་དུ་གྱུར་

49 ནས། །དཔྲ་ཆོས་ཀྱི་ཐབས་དང། །དམག་བརྩན་པོ་དག་གྲང་སྐྱི་རྟུལ་དུ་མ་

50 རུང་སྟེ། །དཔྲ་ཟུན་གྱི་ཚུལ་དུ་གྲུར་ཏ་ཀྱིས་གྲང། །ཡོང་ཏེ་ཞིང་གཉེན་ལ།།

51 འཕྲུལ་གྱི་ལྷ་བཙན་པོ་ཁྲི་གཙུག་ལྡེ་བརྩན་གྱི་ཞ་སྔ་ནས། །མཁྱེན་པ་ནི།།

52 འཕྲུལ་གྱི་ཚུལ་ཆགས། །མཛོད་པ་ཤི་ལྷའི་ལུགས་དང་མཐུན་ཏེ། །བཀ་

53 དྲིན་ཆེན་པོས། །ཕྱི་ནང་གཉིས་སུ་སྙོམས་ཤིང་། །དབུ་རྨོག་བརྩན། །བཀའ་

54 ལུང་གཟན་ཏེ། །རྒྱ་རྗེ་བུན་བུ་ཧེ་ཧུ་ཏེག་ཧྭང་ཏེ་དང་དབོན་ཞང་གཉིས།།

55 འཕྲུལ་གྱི་དགོངས་པ་ཤི་མཐུན། །ཞིགས་པའི་ཆབ་སྲིད་ཤི་གཅིག་སྟེ།།

Translation

during the life of one *btsan-po*. the Nephew, and three generations of the king of China, The Uncle, there was no harbouring of resentment. Pleasant courtesies continued on either side and there were constant exchanges through respected envoys of friendly messages and splendid treasures. But the full terms of a treaty were never actually achieved as a ratified agreement. Even after consultation between Nephew and Uncle the matter did not proceed to completion; yet, although some troubles intervened and mutual suspicions arose out of trifling ancient resentments, the purpose of great good was merely postponed. Since it was not possible to keep powerful armies inactive[5] and as there had come about a state of neither war nor peace, on account of their truly close relationship, the supernaturally wise divinity, the *btsan-po* Khri Gtsug-lde-brtsan himself, whose knowledge springs from supernatural inspiration, whose acts are in conformity with the ways of the gods, who with great kindness treats outer and inner alike, whose helmet is mighty and whose commands are strict, he together with the Chinese king B'un B'u He'u Tig Hwang Te, Nephew and Uncle, agreed in the supernaturally wise thoughts; and the kingdoms being united in pros-

Notes to Translation (continued)

5. Ngawang Thondup Narkyid relates *rngul* to *sgul* "cause to move, agitate" which supports the interpretation that the frontier ministers caused trouble. *Rngul (drngul)* is found repeatedly in Pell T. 1071 in the phrase *mda'* (or *mda's*) *rngul* "to shoot an arrow".

East Inscription

56 བོད་རྒྱ་གཉིས།།རབས་ཁྲིར་བདེ་སྐྱིད་པའི་མཇལ་དུམ་ཆེན་པོ་མཛད་ནས།།

57 རྒྱ་ཡུལ་དུ་ནི།།ཀང་ཤིའི་ནུབ་ཕྱོགས་ཤེག་སང་སིའི་ཐུང་དུ།།བོད་ཆེན་

58 པོའི་ལོའི་མྱིང་ནི་སྐྱིད་རྟག་ལོ་བདུན།།རྒྱ་ཆེན་པོའི་ལོའི་མྱིང་ནི།།

59 ཅང་ཀང་ལོ་དང་པོ་ལྟགས་མོ་གླང་གི་ལོའི་དཔྱིད་ཟླ་ར་བ་ཚེས་བཅུ་ལ།།

60 དཀྱིལ་འཁོར་ལ་འཛེགས་ནས།།རྒྱས་གཙིགས་བཟུང་ངོ།།བོད་

61 ཡུལ་དུ་ནི།།ཡེ་བྲང་ལྷ་སའི་ཤར་ཕྱོགས་སྦྲ་སྟོད་ཚལ་དུ།།བོད་ཆེན་པོའི་

62 ལོའི་མྱིང་སྐྱིད་རྟག་ལོ་བརྒྱད།།རྒྱ་ཆེན་པོའི་ལོའི་མྱིང་ཅང་ཀང་ལོ་

63 གཉིས།།ཆུ་ཕོ་སྟག་གི་ལོའི་དབྱར་ཟླ་འབྲིང་པོ་ཚེས་དྲུག་ལ།།དཀྱིལ་

64 འཁོར་ལ་འཛེགས་ཏེ།།བོད་ཀྱིས་གཙིགས་བཟུང་ངོ།།གཙིགས་ཀྱི་

65 མདོ་རྡོ་རིངས་ལ་བྲིས་པ་འདི་ཡང་།།བོད་ཆེན་པོའི་ལོའི་མྱིང་སྐྱིད་རྟག་

66 ལོ་དགུ།།རྒྱ་ཆེན་པོའི་ལོའི་མྱིང་ཅང་ཀང་ལོ་གསུམ།།ཆུ་མོ་ཡོས་

67 བུ་ལོའི་དཔྱིད་ཟླ་འབྲིང་པོ་ཚེས་བཅུ་བཞི་ལ།།རྡོ་རིངས་ལ་ཡི་གེ་བྲིས་སོ།།

68 རྡོ་རིངས་ལ་འདྲི་བའི་སྤྱན་ཡང་།།རྒྱའི་ཕོ་ཉ་ཐབས།།འགུ་

69 ཤི་ཙུང་ཤིང་ཡོད་པ།།དོ་ཆེའི་དང་།།ཐབས་ཅན་ཤན་དེ་ཀླུ་ཡོད་པ།།

70 ལི་ཁྲི་ཀླུ་ལ་སྐོགས་པས་ཟུས་སོ།།གཙིགས་ཀྱི་མདོ་རྡོ་རིངས་ལ་བྲིས་པ་འདི་

71 དང་འདྲ་བ་གཅིག།།རྒྱའི་ཡུལ་ཀང་ཤིར་ཡང་བཙུགས་སོ།།

perity, a great treaty was made to bring happiness to both Tibet and China for ten thousand generations.

In China near Sheg Sang Si'i to the west of Keng Shi, on the 10th day of the first winter month of the female iron-ox year which is called the 7th year of Continuous Happiness in great Tibet and the first year of Cang Keng in great China, the Chinese ascended the altar and solemnized the agreement. In Tibet, in the Sbra-stod park to the east of the palace of Lhasa[6], on the 6th day of the middle summer month of the male water-tiger year which is called the 8th year of Continuous Happiness in great Tibet and the second year of Cang Keng in great China, the Tibetans ascended the altar and solemnized the agreement. And this account of the agreement which is inscribed on the stone pillar was inscribed on the stone pillar on the 14th day of the middle month of spring in the female water-hare year which is called the 9th year of Continuous Happiness in great Tibet and the third year of Cang Keng in great China. And an examination of this inscribed stone pillar was made by the Chinese envoys Do Tse'e, who has the rank of 'Gu Shi Cung Shing, and Li Kri B'u, who has the rank of Tsan Shan De B'u, and others. And a copy of the terms of the agreement inscribed on the stone pillar has been set up also at Keng Shi in China.

Notes to Translation (continued)

6. "Lha-sa" here, not "Ra-sa" as in the Bsam-yas and Skar-cung inscriptions. The passage in the New T'ang Annals (Bushell p. 521) which seems to imply that the treaty ceremony took place at the summer residence 100 *li* south of the Lo so valley (?Brag-mar) is probably a fusion of separate events.

REIGN OF KHRI GTSUG-LDE-BRTSAN 815–836 A.D.

West Inscription

༄།།བོད་ཀྱི་རྒྱལ་པོ་ཆེན་པོ་
འཕྲུལ་གྱི་ལྷ་བཙན་པོ་དང༌།།
རྒྱའི་རྒྱལ་པོ་ཆེན་པོ་རྒྱ་རྗེ་ཧྭང་ཏེ།
དབོན་ཞང་གཉིས།།ཆབ་སྲིད་
གཅིག་དུ་མོལ་ནས།།མཇལ་དུམ་
ཆེན་པོ་མཛད་དེ་གཙིགས་བཅས་
པ།།ནམ་ཞར་ཡང་མྱི་འགྱུར་བར།
ལྷ་མྱི་ཀུན་གྱིས་ཤེས་ཤིང་དཔང་བྱས
ཏེ།།ཚེ་ཚེ་རབས་རབས་སུ།།བརྗོད་
དུ་ཡོད་པའི་ཕྱིར།།གཙིགས་
ཀྱི་མདོ་རྡོ་རིངས་ལ་བྲིས་པའོ།།

༄།།འཕྲུལ་གྱི་ལྷ་བཙན་པོ་ཁྲི་གཙུག་
ལྡེ་བཙན་གྱི་ཞ་སྔ་ནས།།རྒྱ་རྗེ་
བུན་བུ་ཧེའུ་ཏིག་ཧྭང་ཏེ་དང༌།།འཕྲུལ་དབོན་
ཞང་གཉིས།།སྙམ་དཀྱིལ་ཆེན་པོས་

THE TREATY OF 821/822 A.D.

Translation

West Inscription

The great king of Tibet, the supernaturally wise divinity, the *btsan-po* and the great king of China, the Chinese ruler Hwang Te, Nephew and Uncle, having consulted about the alliance of their dominions have made a great treaty and ratified the agreement. In order that it may never be changed, all gods and men have been made aware of it and taken as witnesses; and so that it may be celebrated in every age and in every generation the terms of the agreement have been inscribed on a stone pillar.

The supernaturally wise divinity, the *btsan-po,* Khri Gtsug-lde-brtsan himself and the Chinese ruler, B'un B'u He'u Tig Hwang Te, their majesties the Nephew and Uncle, through the great profundity

West Inscription

16 ནི། །འཕྲུལ་ཡུན་གཉིས་ཀྱི་ལེགས་

17 ཉེས་རྟོ་ཡང་མཁྱེན། །ཐུགས་རྗེ་ཆེན་

18 པོས་ནི། །བཀའ་དྲིན་གྱིས་དགབ་པ་

19 ལ་ཕྱི་ནང་མྱེད་པས། །མང་པོ་ཀུན་བདེ་

20 སྐྱིད་པར་བྱ་བ་ལ་ནི་དགོངས་པ་གཅིག།

21 ཕྱུན་རིང་པོར་ལེགས་པའི་དོན་ཆེན་པོ་

22 ལ་ནི་བཀའ་གྲོས་མཐུན་ཏེ། །གཉེན་

23 ཞིང་པའི་སྲི་ཞུ་ནི་བསྟུད། །ཁྲིམ་ཆེས་

24 དགྱེས་པའི་ཚད་ཁ་ནི་བརྟེག་མར་

25 མོལ་ནས། །མཛལ་དུམ་ཆེན་པོའ་

26 མཛད་དེ། །བོད་རྒྱ་གཉིས། །ད་ལྟར་

27 སུ་མངའ་བའི་ཡུལ་དང་མཚམས་སྲུང་

28 ཞིང་། །དེའི་ཤར་ཕྱོགས་ཐམས་ཅད་ནི།

29 རྒྱ་ཆེན་པའི་ཡུལ། །ནུབ་ཕྱོགས་ཐམས་

30 ཅད་ནི་ཡང་ཐག་པར་བོད་ཆེན་པོའི་

Translation

of their minds know whatsoever is good and ill for present and future alike. With great compassion, making no distinction between outer and inner in sheltering all with kindness, they have agreed in their counsel on a great purpose of lasting good—the single thought of causing happiness for the whole population—and have renewed the respectful courtesies of their old friendship. Having consulted to consolidate still further the measure of neighbourly contentment they have made a great treaty. Both Tibet and China shall keep the country and frontiers of which they are now in possession. The whole region to the east of that being the country of Great China and the whole region to the west being assuredly the country of Great Tibet,

West Inscription

31 ཡུལ་ཏེ། །དེ་ལས་ཕན་ཆུན་དགྲ་ཟི་

32 འཐབ། །དམག་མྱི་དྲང་། །ཡུལ་མྱི་

33 མནམ། །ཡིད་མ་ཆེས་པ་ཞིག་ཡོད་

34 ན། །མྱི་བཟུང་ཞིང་གཏམ་དྲིས་ཏེ། །

35 བཟངས་ནས་ཕྱིར་གཏང་ངོ། །

36 ད་ཆབ་སྲིད་གཅིག་ཅིང་། །མཇལ་

37 དུམ་ཆེན་པོ་འདི་ལྟར་མཛད་པས། །

38 དབོན་ཞང་དགྱེས་པའི་བཀའ་ཕྲིནད

39 སྙན་པས་ཀྱང་འདྲུལ་དགོས་ཏེ། །

40 ཕན་ཆུན་གྱི་ཕོ་ཉ་འདོང་བ་ཡང་། །ལམ་

41 རྙིང་པར་བསྲུང་ནས། །སྔ་ལུགས་བཞིན་

42 །།བོད་རྒྱ་གཉིས་ཀྱི་བར། །ཙོང་ཀུན་

43 ཡོག་དུ་རྟ་བརྗེས་ལ། །སྩེ་ཞུང་ཆེག་དུ

44 རྒྱ་དང་ཕྲད་པ་མན་ཆད་ནི་རྒྱས་ཕྲུ་དྲུང་

45 བྱ། །ཙོང་ཀ་ཁྲུན་དུ་བོད་དང་ཕྲད་པ་

Translation

from either side of that frontier there shall be no warfare, no hostile invasions, and no seizure of territory. If there be any suspicious person, he shall be arrested and an investigation made and, having been suitably provided for, he shall be sent back.

Now that the dominions are allied and a great treaty of peace has been made in this way, since it is necessary also to continue the communication of pleasant messages between Nephew and Uncle, envoys setting out from either side shall follow the old established route. According to former custom their horses shall be changed at Tsang Kun Yog which is between Tibet and China. Beyond Stse Zhung Cheg, where Chinese territory is met, the Chinese shall provide all facilities; westwards, beyond Tseng Shu Hywan, where

West Inscription

46 ཡན་ཆད་ནི་བོད་ཀྱིས་ལྷ་དུད་བླ་སྟེ།།

47 དབོན་ཞང་ཆེ་ཞིང་གཉེན་བའྀ་ཚུལ་བཞིན་

48 དུ།།སྲི་ཞུ་དང་བཀུར་སྟིའི་ལུགས་

49 ཡོད་པར་སྣུར་ཏེ།།ཡུལ་གཉིས་ཀྱི་

50 བར་ན་དུད་རྟུལ་ནི་མྱི་སྣང་།།གློ་བུར་

51 དུ་སྣང་བ་དང་དགྲའི་སྡྱིང་ནི་མྱི་གྲག་སྟེ་

52 ས་མཚམས་སྲུང་བའྀ་མྱི་ཡན་ཆད

53 ཀྱང་དོགས་ཤིང་འཇིགས་པ་མེད་པར་

54 ས་ས་མལ་མལ་ན་བག་བརྒྱང་སྟེ།།བདེ་

55 བར་འགྲོད་ཙོང་།།སྐྱིད་པའྀ་བཀའ་དྲིན་

56 ནི་རབས་ཁྲིའི་བར་དུ་ཐོབ།།སྙན་པའྀ་

57 སྒྲ་སྐད་ནི་གཉི་ཟླས་སྙེབས་སོ་ཆོག་དུ་

58 ཁྱབ་སྟེ།།བོད་བོད་ཡུལ་ན་སྐྱིད།།

59 རྒྱ་རྒྱ་ཡུལ་ན་སྐྱིད་པའྀ་སྲིད་ཆེན་པོ་

60 སྦྱར་ནས་གཙིགས་བཅས་པ་འདི།།

61 ནམ་ཞར་གྱི་འགྱུར་བར།།དཀོན་མཆོག་

Translation

Tibetan territory is met, the Tibetans shall provide all facilities. According to the close and friendly relationship between Nephew and Uncle the customary courtesy and respect shall be observed. Between the two countries no smoke or dust shall appear. Not even a word of sudden alarm or of enmity shall be spoken and from those who guard the frontier upwards all shall live at ease without suspicion or fear both on their lands and in their beds[1]. Dwelling in peace they shall win the blessing of happiness for ten thousand generations. The sound of praise shall extend to every place reached by the sun and moon. And in order that this agreement establishing a great era when Tibetans shall be happy in Tibet and Chinese shall be happy in China shall

Note to Translation

1. *sa sa mal mal na* is echoed in and clarified by Pell T. 16 (34b) *'gro ba mang po so so gnas gnas mal mal du bde skyid chen po mdzad de* and I have amended my earlier translation.

West Inscription

62 གསུམ་དང༌། །འཕགས་པའི་རྣམས་དང་

63 གཉི་ཟླ་དང་གཟའ་སྐར་ལ་ཡང་དཔང་དུ་

64 གསོལ་ཏེ། །ཐ་ཚིག་གི་རྣམས་པས་ཀྱང་

65 བཤད། །སྲོག་ཆགས་བསད་དེ་མནའ་

66 ཡང་བོར་ནས། །གཙིགས་བཅས་སོ།།

67 གཙིགས་འདི་བཞིན་དུ་མ་བྱས་སམ།།

68 བཤིག་ན། །བོད་རྒྱ་གཉིས་གང་གིས་སྔར་ཉེས

69 པ་ལ་སྡིག་ཅིང༌། །ལན་དུ་དཀུ་སྒྲུ་ཚོ་བྱུས་ཀྱང་

70 གཙིགས་བཤིག་པ་ལ་མ་གཏོགས་སོ།།

71 འདི་ལྟར་བོད་རྒྱ་གཉིས་ཀྱི་རྗེ་བློན་གྱིས་ཞལ་

72 གྱིས་བཞགས་མནའ་བོར་ཏེ། །གཙིགས

73 ཀྱི་ཡི་གེ་ཞིབ་མར་བྲིས་ནས། །རྒྱལ་པོ་ཆེན་

74 པོ་གཉིས་ཀྱི་ནི་ཕྱག་རྒྱས་བཏབ། །བློན་པོ་

75 གཙིགས་འཛིན་པ་ལ་གཏོགས་པ་རྣམས་

76 ཀྱི་ནི་ལག་ཡིག་དུ་བྲིས་ཏེ། །གཙིགས་ཀྱི་

77 ཡི་གེ་ཡང་སོ་སོའི་ཕྱག་ཚལ་དུ་བཞག་གོ།།

Translation

never be changed, the Three Jewels, the body of saints, the sun and moon, planets and stars have been invoked as witnesses; its purport has been expounded in solemn words; the oath has been sworn with the sacrifice of animals; and the agreement has been solemnized.

If the parties do not act in accordance with this agreement or if it is violated, whether it be Tibet or China that is first guilty of an offence against it, whatever stratagem or deceit is used in retaliation shall not be considered a breach of the agreement.

Thus the rulers and ministers of both Tibet and China declared, and swore the oath; and the text having been written in detail it was sealed with the seals of both great kings. It was inscribed with the signatures of those ministers who took part in the agreement and the text of the agreement was deposited in the archives of each party.

North Inscription
(words in square brackets are reconstructions)

1 ༄། །བོད་ཆེན་པོའི་བློན་པོ་ཆེ་ཞྲ་མཇལ་

2 དུམ་གྱི་གཙིགས་འཛིན་པ་ལ་གཏོགས་

3 པའི་ཐབས་དང་སྨིང་ཏུས་ལ། །

4 ༄། །བོད་ཆེན་པོའི་ཆབ་སྲིད་ཀྱི་བློན་པོ་ཆེན་

5 པོ་བཀའ་ལ་གཏོགས་པའི་ཐབས་དང་སྨིང་

6 ཏུས། །

7 ༄། །བཀའ་ཆེན་པོ་ལ་གཏོགས་ཏེ་ཕྱི་ནང་

8 གཉིས་ལ་དབང་ཞིང་ཆབ་སྲིད་འཛིན[པ་]

9 [བན]དེ་ཆེན་པོ་དཔལ་ཆེན་པོ་ཡོན[ཏན། །]

10 [༄། ། · · · དམ]ག་གོ་ཚོག་གི་བླ་ཁང་ཁྲི་སུམ་རྗེ་

11 · · · · · · · ·

12 [༄། །] · · · · བློན་ཆེན་པོ་བློན་[ཁྲི་བཞེར་]

THE TREATY OF 821/822 A.D.

Translation

North Inscription

The rank, names and lineage of the ministers of Great Tibet, greater and lesser, taking part in the solemnization of the treaty.

The rank, names and lineage of the Great Ministers of the kingdom of Great Tibet taking part in the Council of State.

The Great Monk-minister Dpal-chen-po yon-tan, taking part in the highest Council of State, carrying out the administration with power over both outer and inner affairs.

Commander-in-chief of the army, Zhang Khri-sum rje.

The Great Minister, Blon (Lo-bzher).

North Inscription

13 [༄། །]བློན་པོ་[ད]པོན་དམག་ . . . . .

14 . . . བཟང . . . .

15 ༄། །ཆབ་སྲིད་ཀྱི་བློན་པོ་ཆེན་པོ་བློན་[རྒྱལ་]

16 . . . .

17 ༄། །ཆབ་སྲིད་ཀྱི་བློན་པོ་ཆེན་པོ་བློན་ཁྲི་

18 བཙན་… བཞེར།།

19 ༄། །ཆབ་སྲིད་ཀྱི་བློན་པོ་ཆེན་པོ་ཞང་ཁྲི་བཙན་

20 ཁོད་ནེ་སྟང།།

21 ༄། །ཆབ་སྲིད་ཀྱི་བློན་པོ་ཆེན་པོ་ཞང་ཁྲི་བཞེར་

22 ལྷ་མཐོང།།

23 ༄། །ཆབ་སྲིད་ཀྱི་བློན་པོ་ཆེན་པོ་བློན་རྒྱལ་བཟང་

24 འདུས་ཀོང།།

Translation

The Minister, Deputy Commander-in-chief . . . . . Bzang.
The Great Minister of the kingdom, Blon Rgyal . . . .
The Great Minister of the kingdom, Blon Khri-btsan . . bzher.
The Great Minister of the kingdom, Zhang Khri-btsan khod ne-stang.
The Great Minister of the kingdom, Zhang Khri-bzher lha-mthong.
The Great Minister of the kingdom, Blon Rgyal-bzang 'dus-kong.

North Inscription

25 ༄། །བོད་ཆེན་པོའི་བློན་པོ་ཞལ་ལ་གྱི་ཐབས་དང་

26 སྤྱིང་རྡུས།།

27 ༄། །ནང་བློན་མཆིམས་ཞང་རྒྱལ་བཞེར་ཁོད་ནེ

28 བརྩན།།

29 ༄། །ཕྱི་བློན་བཀའ་ལ་གཏོགས་པ་ཅོག་རོ་

30 བློན་བརྩན་བཞེར་ལྷོ་གོང།།

31 ༄།།སྣམ་ཕྱི་པ་མཆིམས་ཞང་བརྟན་བཞེར་སྟག་

32 ཙབ།།

33 ༄།།མངན་པོན་ཁབ་སོ་འོ་ཆོག་གི་བླ་འབལ་བློན་

34 ཀླུ་བཟང་མྱེས་རྨ།།

35 ༄། །བཀའི་ཕྲིན་བློན་བྲན་ཀ་བློན་སྟག་བཞེར་ཧབ་

36 ཀེན།།

THE TREATY OF 821/822 A.D.

Translation

The rank, names and lineage of the ordinary ministers of Great Tibet.

The Minister of the Interior, Mchims Zhang Rgyal-bzher khod ne-brtsan.

The Minister of the Exterior taking part in the Council of State, Cog-ro Blon Btsan-bzher lho-gong.

The Snam-phyi-pa, Mchims Zhang Brtan-bzher stag-tsab.

The Mngan-pon, head of the district officials, 'Bal Blon Klu-bzang myes-rma.

The Secretary General, Bran-ka Blon Stag-bzher hab-ken.

North Inscription

37 ༄། །རྗེས་པ་ཆེན་པོ་རྟེགས་བློན་སྟག་

38 ཟིགས་ཅན་ཀོལ།།

39 ༄། །ཞེ་བློན་འབྲོ་ཁང་སྐྱུ་བཟང་ལྷ་པོ་བརྟན་

40 ༄། །ཞལ་ཅེ་པ་ཆེན་པོ་ཞེལ་ཅེའོ་ཆོག་གི་

41 ༄། །སྦྱང་བློན་རྒྱལ་ཉེན་ལེགས་ཙན།།

Translation

The Accountant-General, Rngegs Blon Stag-zigs rgan-kol.
The Exterior Minister, 'Bro Zhang Klu-bzang lha-bo-brtsan.
The Chief Judge, head of the justiciary, Myang Blon Rgyal-nyen legs-tsan.

South Inscription

1 ༄། །རྒྱ་ཆེན་པོའི་བློན་པོ་ཆེ་ཞྲ། །མཇལ་དུམ་གྱི་

2 གཙིགས་འཛིན་པ་ལ་གཙིགས་པའི་ཐབས་

3 དང་སྦྱིང་ རུས་ལ །།

4 ༄། །རྒྱ་ ཆེན་པོའི་ཆབ་སྲིད་ཀྱི་བློན་པོ་ཆེན་པོ་

5 བཀའ་ལ་གཙིགས་པའི་ཐབས་དང་སྦྱིང་ རུས།།

6 ༄། །ཧེང་འགི་ དའེ་ཕུ་ཞི་ལུ་སུན་ཀ་ ཞི་ཡང་གི་ཐབས་

7 ཡོད་པ་ བཀའ་ཆེན་པོ་ལ་གཙིགས་པ་ · · · · · · · ·

8 ༄། ། · · · དའ་ཕུ་ཞི་ལུ་ཏུང་ ཀྱུ་ཞི་ཡང་གི་ཐབས་

9 ཡོད་པ་བཀའ་ཆེན་པོ་ལ་གཙིགས་པ་ · · · · ·

10 ༄། །ཐའི་རྟུང་དལེ་ཕུ་ཞི་ལུ་ཏུང་ ཀྱུ་གི་ཡང་གི་ཐབས་

11 ཡོད་པ་བཀའ་ཆེན་པོ་ལ་གཙིགས་པ་ལྡང་བ།།

THE TREATY OF 821/822 A.D.

Translation

South Inscription

The rank, names, and lineage of the ministers of Great China, greater and lesser, taking part in the solemnization of the treaty.

The rank, names, and lineage of the Great Ministers of the kingdom of Great China, taking part in the Council of State.

With the rank of Chen I Ta Fu and provisionally Vice-President of the Imperial Chancellery, taking part in the Great Council of State . . . .

With the rank of . . . Ta Fu and Provisionally Vice-President of the Imperial Secretariat, taking part in the Great Council of State, Ts'ui Chih.

With the rank of T'ai Chung Ta Fu and provisionally Vice-President of the Imperial Secretariat, taking part in the Great Council of State, 'Wang Pha (i.e. Wang Po).

South Inscription

12 ༄།།རྒྱང་དའེ་སྣུ་ཞིའུ་ཁང་ཕུ་རྗེ་རྡོ་ཞོ་ཡང་གི་ཐབས་

13 ཡོད་པ་བཀའ་ཆེན་པོ་ལ་གཏོགས་པ་དྲོ་ འགྱུན་

14 ལྡེང།།

15 ༄།།ཟིང་འགི་དའི་སྦུ་པེང་དྲོ་ཁང་ཕུ་ཐབས་ཡོད་

16 པ་བཀའ་ཆེན་པོ་ལ་གཏོགས་པ་སེའུ་འབྲེན།།

17 ༄།།རྒྱ་ཆེན་པོའི་བློན་པོ་ཕལ་གྱི་ཐབས་དང་སྦྱིང་

18 རྟུས།།

19 ༄།།ཀིམ་རྡོ་ཀྱང་ལེག་དའེ་སྦུ་ཁང་ཕུ་ཛེ་དྲོག་ཡའེ་

20 ཐབས་ཡོད་པ་ཧན་ཀའུ།།

21 ༄།།ཛེ་དུ་འགི་ལང་འགྱུ་ཤི་རྒུང་ཤིང་གི་ཐབས་ཡོད་ པ་

22 འགིའུ་སེང་ཞུ།།

23 ༄།།ཐ་འི་རྒུང་དའི་སྦུ་ཀུམ་ཀའུ་ཁང་ཕུ་ཙི་བོག་ཡ་ ལེ་

24 བོ་ ཁང་ཕུ་ཐབས་ཡོད་པ་ལེ་ཀྲང།།

Translation

With the rank of Chung Ta Fu and provisionally Vice-President of the Board of Finance in the Department of Government Affairs, taking part in the Great Council of State, D'o 'Gwan Yweng (i.e. Tu Yuan-ying).

With the rank of Cheng I Ta Fu and the office of President of the Board of War, taking part in the Great Council of State, Se'u 'B'en (i.e. Hsiao Mien).

The rank, names and lineage of the ordinary ministers of Great China.

With the rank of Chin Tzu Kuang Lu Ta Fu and the office of Left Vice-President of the Department of Government Affairs, Han Ka'u (i.e. Han Kao).

With the rank of Ch'ao I Lang and the office of Vice-President of the Tribunal of Censors, 'Gi'u Sing Zhu (i.e. Niu Seng-ju).

With the rank of T'ai Chung Ta Fu and the office of Acting Right Vice-President of the Department of Government Affairs and President of the Board of Civil Office, Li K'ang (i.e. Li Chiang).

South Inscription

25 ༄། །འགིན་ཚེང་ཀྭང་ལོག་དའི་ཕྱུ་ཏོ་པོ་ཞང་ཤུ

26 ཐབས་ཡོད་པ་ཡང་ཀྱུ་ལིང།།

27 ༄། །སྟོང་གྱི་དའི་ཕྱུ་ཤྲཱུ་ལྭེའི་པོ་ཞང་ཤུ་ཐབས

28 ཡོད་པ་ཐྭུའི་ཞིའུ།།

29 ༄། །འགིན་ཙེང་ཀྭག་ལོག་དའི་ཕུ་ཀེམ་ཀེའུ་ཞང

30 ཤུ་ཙི་པོག་ཡ་ཀྱིམ་ཐའི་ཧང་ཀེང་གི་ཐབས་ཡོད་པ

31 ཙའུ་རྫོང་ཞུ།།

32 ༄། །ཐའི་ཙུང་དའི་ཕུ་ལེའི་པོ་ཞང་ཤུ་ཀྱིམ་···

33 ཐབས་ཡོད་པ། །ཏྭེའི་ཤུ།།

34 ༄། །རྗིང་གི་དའི་ཕུ་ཞིའུ་ཀེང་ཙིའུ་ཡུན་ཀྱིམ་འཀྱུ་ཤི

35 དའི་ཕུ་ཐབས་ཡོད་པ་ལིའུ་གོང་ཙག།

36 ༄། །འབེན་ཆེང་ཀྭང་ལོག་དའི་ཕུ་ཀེམ་ཀྭའུ་གོང་ཏོ་ཞང

THE TREATY OF 821/822 A.D.

Translation

With the rank of Yin Ch'ing Kuang Lo Ta Fu and the office of President of the Board of Finance, Yang U Ling (i.e. Yang Yu-ling).

With the rank of T'ung I Ta Fu and provisionally President of the Board of Rites, 'Wu'i Zhi'u (i.e. Wei Shou).

With the rank of Yin Ch'ing Kuang Lu Ta Fu and the office of Acting Right Vice-President of the Department of Government Affairs and concurrently President of the Court of Imperial Sacrifices, Ca'u Tsong Zhu (i.e. Chao Tsung-ju).

With the rank of T'ai Chung Ta Fu and the office of President of the Board of Rites and concurrently President of the Court of Agricultural Administration, Be'i Bu (i.e. Pe'i Wu).

With the rank of Cheng I Ta Fu and provisionally Prefect of the Capital and concurrently President of the Tribunal of Censors, Li'u Kong Cag (i.e. Liu Kung-ch'o).

South Inscription

37 སྐུ་ཀྲུམ་ཚ་ཀིམ་འགོ་ལྡེའི་དའི་ཚ་ཀུན་གྱི་ཐབས་ཡོད

38 པ་ཀྭག་ཅྫིང།།

39 ༄།།ཇེའུ་འགི་ཡང་ · · · དའི་ཕྱུ་ · · ཀྲུམ་འགུ་ཤི་དའེ་

40 ཕྱུ་ཐབས་ཡོད་པ།།ཡིའུ་འགན་ཏེང།།

41 ༄།།ཇེ་འུ་འགི་ཡང་ཞིའུ་ཞང་ཕྱུ་ཛེ་སྲུ་ཡང་ཙུང་ཀྲུམ་ འགུ་

42 ཤི་ཙུང་ཤིང་གི་ཐབས་ཡོད་པ་ཡིའུ་ཤི་ཡའུ།།

43 ༄།།ཅིང་ཞི་ · · · · · · · · ཞང་ཕྱུ་

44 · · · · · · · · · · · · · · · ·

45 ཡོད་པ་ཡི་ · ·

46 ༄།།ཇེའུ་སན་ · ཀེང

47 · · · · ཀོ་

Translation

With the rank of Yin Ch'ing Kuang Lu Ta Fu and the office of Acting President of the Board of Public Works and concurrently Grand general of the Right Guard of Chin Wu, Kwag Tshung (i.e. Kuo Ts'ung).

With the rank of . . . . Ta Fu and the office of President of the Court of Supreme Justice and concurrently President of the Tribunal of Censors, Li'u 'Gwan Teng (i.e. Liu Yuan-ting).

With the rank of Ch'ao I Lang provisionally Director of the Left Bureau in the Department of Government Affairs and concurrently Vice-President of the Tribunal of Censors, Li'u Shi La'u (i.e. Liu Shih-lao) . . . .

With the rank of Ch'ao San Lang and the office of Ching Chao . . . .[1]

Note to Translation

1. The final entry is completely effaced.

The Bell at Yer-pa

Brag Yer-pa, some fifteen miles from Lhasa, is a group of small temples, shrines and hermitages scattered up and down a shrub-covered hillside at the head of a secluded valley north of the Skyid-chu. In the sheer rock face in which the valley ends, are several cave hermitages which can be reached only by ladders. According to later histories both Srong-brtsan sgam-po and Khri Srong-lde-brtsan founded temples at Yer-pa; and at the time of the *Phyi-dar* in the 11th century Klu-mes established one of the earliest foundations there (Ferrari, Mkhyen-brtse's Guide pp. 103, 104).

The bell, of which a photograph can be seen in Harrer's *Meine Tibet-bilder* p. 65, hangs in a small shelter apart from the other buildings. It is known locally as the *cong* and is very like the great Chinese-type bells at Bsam-yas and Khra-'brug. There are four lines of inscription round the upper part. The first three are in Tibetan letters similar to those of the Bsam-yas bell and containing several instances of the reversed *ki-gu.* They are in four panels all except the last having three lines of text, one above the other; the last panel, with which the inscription ends, has one line only. Unlike the Bsam-yas and Khra-'brug bells, the panels run from right to left so that going round the bell right-handed one reads the inscription continuously; but for convenience I have rearranged it to read from left to right. There is slight damage to the first line but the reconstruction is obvious for I am informed that the text is a well-known *sloka* from the *'Phags-pa bzang-po spyod-pa'i smon-lam rgyal-po* (*Arya-bhadracaryāpraṇidhāna rāja*) of Surendrabodhi, popularly known as the *Bzang-spyod.* The numerous fragments, and a few complete copies, with slight variations in the title, in the *mss* from Tun-huang show that it was popular in Tibet in the 8th and 9th centuries.

The lowest line is in a north Indian script appearing in various slightly differing forms in inscriptions of the 9th to 11th centuries. It records the dictum: *Ye dharmā hetuprabhavā hetum teṣām tathāgato hyavadat teṣām ca yo nirodha evemvādı mahāśramaṇaḥ* and ends with five mystic syllables *Om Hum Tram Hri* and one illegible.

That text is found in Tibet on images and clay *tsa tsa* sometimes in letters similar to those on the bell and sometimes in Tibetan, see for example the illustrations of *tsa-tsa* in plates 90 to 108 in Tucci's *Archaeologia Mundi, Transhimalaya.*

Although there is no direct evidence to associate the Yer-pa bell with any of the Tibetan kings, its design and the lettering on it suggest a 9th century date. Moreover, it is improbable that at the time of the *Phyi-dar* there would have been either a patron with the means to have so large a casting made or craftsmen with the skill to carry out the work.

THE BELL AT YER-PA

Tibetan Inscription

རྒྱལ་བ་རྣམས	ཆུབ་སྤྱོད་པ་ཀུན	རྣམ་པར་སྦྱང་བ	སྤྱོད་པར་བགྱི
ཀྱི་དམ་པའི་ཆོས	ཏུ་སྣང་བར་བྱེད།	ཡང་། །མ་འོངས	
འཛིན་ཅིང་། །བྱང	བཟང་པོ་སྤྱོད་པ	བསྐལ་པ་ཀུན་ཏུ	

Translation

Let us hold fast to the holy religion of the Buddhas and act in such a way as to display everywhere deeds of enlightenment; and let us perfectly practice good deeds and so act for all time to come.

REIGN OF KHRI GTSUG-LDE-BRTSAN 815–836 A.D.

These drawings of the Sanskrit inscription are based on rubbings from the bell which have unfortunately been lost. The letters are of different sizes but the proportions in the drawing are not quite accurate.

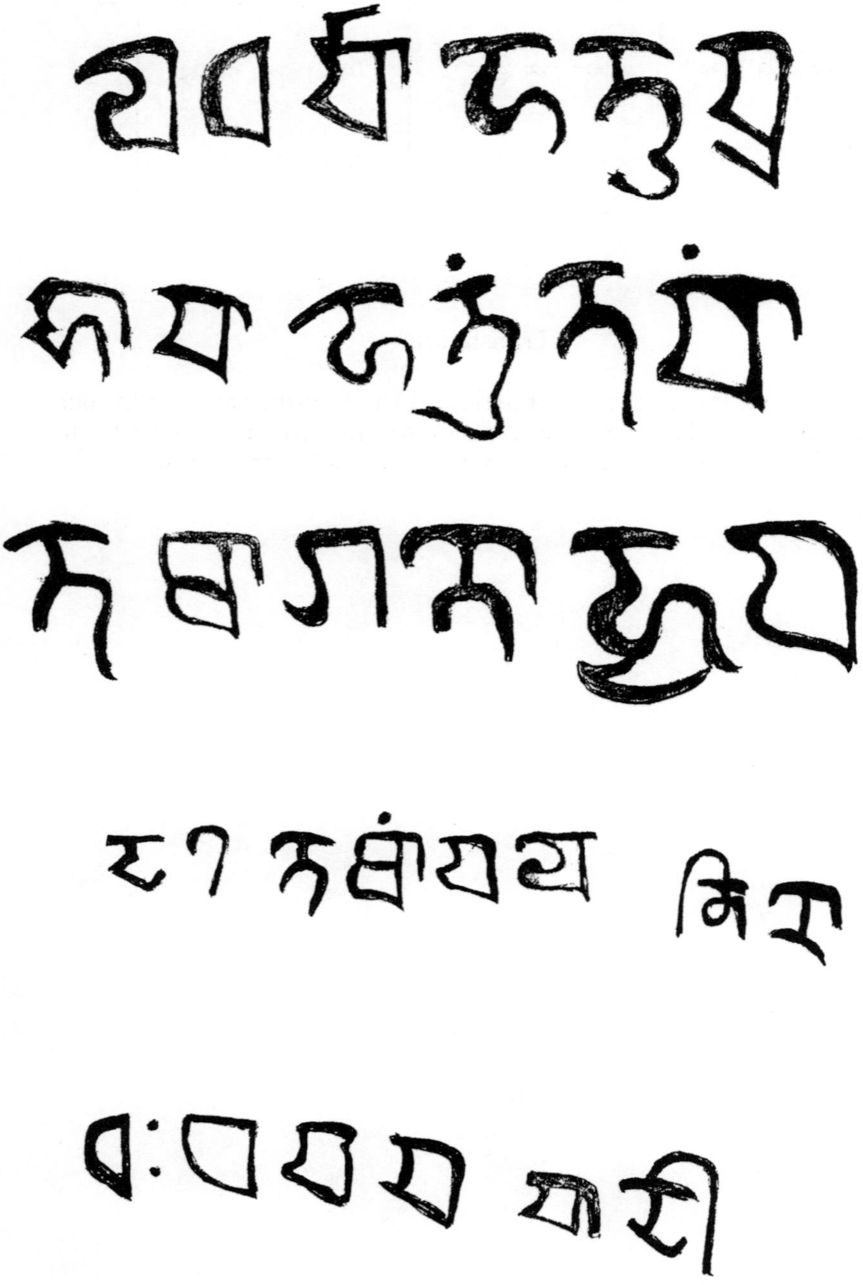

THE BELL AT YER-PA

Note to Text
1. fragment of letter

ADDENDUM

Rdo-rings at Rgyal Lha-khang

With the end of the kingdom the practice of erecting impressive stone pillars to record acts of state fell into abeyance; but there are a few small pillars of uncertain date and one which can be ascribed to the 11th century. It is at Rgyal Lha-khang in 'Phan-po which was founded in 1012 A.D. by Sna-nam Rdo-rje dbang-phyug a descendant of one of the great noble families connected by matrimony with the Tibetan kings. Khri Srong-lde-brtsan's mother was the Sna-nam queen of Khri Lde-gtsug-brtsan; and one of Khri Gtsug-lde-brtsan's wives also came from the Sna-nam clan as did Glang Darma's junior queen according to PT. Rdo-rje dbang-phyug was an important figure at the time of the *Phyi-dar* and his monastery at Rgyal was reputed to be very wealthy so it is probable that the pillar was set up in his time. In 1240 Rgyal was looted and burnt by a raiding Mongol force under Dorda and damage suffered by the pillar may have been caused at that time.

The inscriptions which I have published in *JRAS* 1957 are given below. The first line of each is obscured by an iron band. In the centre of the pillar is carved a large *rdo-rje;* the text continues on either side of it. The lower part of the pillar is so badly damaged that only a few words can be read: *bsam myi khyab pa . . . . rnam pa kun tu sgrib sbyang . . . . kyi dge-ba.*

The inscription on the south side is illegible except for the second line. There is no example of the reversed *ki-gu* but the *ya-btags* in *myi* has survived. Unlike earlier inscriptions letters preceding a *shad* are regularly followed by a *tsheg*

ADDENDUM

East Inscription

1 × × × × × × × × × × × ／ × ×

2 བརྩུགས་པ་ལ །སྤྱི་དེང་སང་གི་དུས་སུ་ནི་

3 དགེ་བ་ལ་ཕྱོགས་གཅིག་ལ་དང་།ལེགས་

4 པ་ལ་གྲོས་འཐུན་པ་ནི་ཅུང་ན་།འོ་ན་ཡང་དཀོན་

5 མཆོག་གསུམ་ལ་སྐྱབས་སུ་གསོལ་བའི་སྤྱི་

6 རྣམས་ཀྱི་ནི་།ལྟར་སངས་རྒྱས་གཟུང་།གྲོས་

7 ཕྱུགས་ཆོས་ལ་།གཏད།གཏོར་ལྟ་བ་སྤྱང་།ཚིག

8 སྤྱོད་རྒྱལ་དུ་དབབ་།འཚོ་བ་གཙང་མར་བསྐྱབ།

9 བྱེད་དགུ་ཆོས་དང་སྦྱར་།སྤྱི་གྲོས་གཅིག་དུ

10 བསྒྲུམ་།སྐོ་གཉེར་སོ་སོར་བླང་།ངན་གྲོས་དགོག

11 དུ་དབྱུང་།བདེན་གཏམ་དང་དུ་བླང་།འདི་ལྟར

12 བྱས་ན་ཚེ་འདི་དང་ཕྱི་མ་གཉི་གར་བདེ་བར

13 འགྱུར་བས་།ཚིག བཅུ་པོ་འདི་ཡལ་

14 བར་མ་བོར་ ཞིང་གཟུངས་

15 སུ་བཟུང་ན ལེགས་སོ་།།

RDO-RINGS AT RGYAL LHA-KHANG

Translation

East Inscription

. . . . . . was founded. Generally nowadays while there is little whole-hearted pursuit of virtue and little devotion to the good, still, men who in their prayers seek refuge in the Three Jewels should again cling to the Lord Buddha. They should direct all their thoughts towards religion; they should above all study correct views; they should subdue their way of speech to calmness; they should perfect their lives in purity, make all their actions conformable to religion, gather together the highest counsel, take upon each one the guardianship of the door of religion, cast out utterly evil counsels and earnestly accept the word of truth. If they act in this way they shall win happiness both in this existence and the next; and if they do not leave this tenfold commandment to wither away but hold it firmly, it shall be well.

ADDENDUM

South Inscription

འཕན། ཡུལ་ཀླུང་སྐྱེས་ངོ་མཚར་ཆེ།

RDO-RINGS AT RGYAL LHA-KHANG

Translation

South Inscription

. . . .

'Phan a country wonderful as the source of rivers . . . . .

ADDENDUM

Gtsang Grong Inscription

བདག་རོག་བཙུ་

ན་ལྱེ་[×]བཟོས་རྐོའི་

མཆོག་སྨྲེ་ཞུབ་

པའི་རྗེན་དུ་ཁར་

ཞུབ་གཉིས་སྲུ་ག་

× ལྱྟེ་ ?

Rdo-rings at Gtsang Grong

[Plates 15–16]

Two stone pillars which I have not myself seen are recorded in photographs by the late Sir Charles Bell in the India Office Library which are reproduced here with the permission of the Librarian. They are situated near a small village called Gtsang Grong described as being on the south bank of the Gtsang-po some five miles downstream from Grwa-nang towards Rnam-sras-gling (which is nearly opposite Bsam-yas). It is perhaps the Drongdre of the Indian Survey maps for Bell states that a *lha-tho* near the pillars is the residence of an irritable deity—perhaps a *'dre.* Unfortunately, Bell who visited the place in 1935, does not appear to have taken copies of the inscriptions which there are on one of the pillars or to have given a detailed description of their surroundings. The photographs show that one of them is of whiteish stone without any coping stone or finial. Its base is buried in the ground to an undetermined depth leaving about five feet of the upper part visible. The north face is decorated with the image in low relief of a Bodhisattva in the attitude of meditation wearing a simple three-pointed headdress. The inscription below the image reads:

bdag rog bcu
na l bzos rkon*
mchog myi nub
pa'i rten du shar
nub gnyis su g.

*this letter is damaged and may be *lta*.

The remaining lines of the inscription are buried below ground. The fragment may mean something to the effect that the image is dedicated "as a symbol that by fixing one's views on the ten saving virtues the most excellent (trinity) will not be eclipsed. In the east and the west . . . . ."

On the west side is inscribed the dictum *Ye dharmāhetu* . . etc. in Tibetan letters. It is almost complete; probably only two lines are below the ground.

The other pillar, apparently uninscribed, seems to be of darker stone and about six feet high. It stands on the worn stone figure of tortoise and is surmounted by a stone canopy and the remains of a finial representing a *mchod-rten* of which the stepped base survives. Apart from its rather clumsy proportions it resembles those of the early kingdom and it is interesting that Bell was told that the place was nearly chosen by the kings as the site of their capital. The tortoise base, which from the severe weathering looks to be of considerable antiquity, resembles those surviving, but without the stele which once surmounted them, near the site of the palace of the Mongol Khagans at Karakoram on the Orkhon; the place had earlier been the capital of the Eastern Turks from about the 5th century.

The two pillars may not be of the same date. Although no archaisms such as the *da drag* or the reversed *ki-gu* appear on the inscribed pillar, the lettering shows the boldness and clarity of the early inscriptions. But the orthographical lapses—*rog* for *rogs* and *rkon* for *dkon*—suggest a time when supervision was not very strict. Also, I have not seen in early *mss* any instance of the *Ye dharma hetuprabhavā* dictum in Tibetan letters; and although the image is of an early type, it cannot be dated accurately.

ADDENDUM

Pillars at Nyabzo

Another group showing signs of some antiquity in occasional reversed *ki-gu* and in the phrase *las stsogs-pa* consists of two roughly dressed short pillars of stone at either end of a *mani* wall on the north bank of the Gtsang-po not far from the *ko-sa* (ferry) of Nyabzo. Each pillar is inscribed on all four sides but the texts are badly damaged and although disjointed words and phrases can be read, it is not possible to make continuous sense of the inscriptions.

That on the south face of the west pillar is in some 26 lines beginning:

rdo ling las
las stsogs pa .
chen po rnams
'phags pa . .
. 'phags pa
spyan ras gzigs
dang phyag . .
rdo rje la stsogs
byang chub sems
dpa' . . . . dang
. . . rdo . . . .
. . . . . ched
med pa dang

The following lines are indecipherable; but in l. 16 *phyogs la* and in l. 26 *mdo rdo ring* can be read. On two of the other inscriptions the word *phyogs* appears.

No one in the neighbourhood or at Lhasa knew anything about the pillars. They may ante-date the *mani* wall because one face of each pillar is virtually obscured by being placed close up against the end of the wall.

Inscriptions at Ka-ru Ko-sa

Although the erection of *rdo-rings* may have become rare, the inscription of prayers and invocations on roadside boulders and rock faces was widespread. Few of these can be dated or have any historic interest but two groups are worth mention. One on the south bank of the Skyid Chu at Ka-ru Ko-sa, a ferry station just up-river from Lhasa, includes a large image of the Buddha in low relief and a lightly carved drawing of a *mchod-rten.* On either side are inscriptions which are mostly too badly damaged or too heavily shaded by overhanging rock to be read or photographed. One is the *Ye dharmā hetuprabhavā* dictum in Tibetan. Another begins with the invocation of the Three Refuges and later names Ami-ta-ba and Arya-pa-lo. It shows lingering traces of archaism in the use of the *ya-btags* in *myi.* Another inscription, next to the picture of the *mchod-rten,* has more archaisms including instances of the reversed *ki-gu.* It is unfortunately indecipherable except for a few phrases—*dge-ba . sems can kyi don . chos sbyang ba'i . mdzad pa rnams.*

The elongated form of the *mchod-rten* and its position near a river crossing, used for centuries by people travelling between Lhasa and Bsam-yas and the east, recalls the rock pictures of *mchod-rten* at Chitral and Chilas illustrated by Sir Aurel Stein in Serindia and in *JRAS* 1944 respectively. In particular, those at Chilas are near a crossing over the Indus. The carvings there are attributed to the 5th to 7th centuries and could perhaps have influenced the Tibetans during their occupation of the region from about 737 A.D. to the early years of the 9th century.

Inscriptions near Ger

At the point where the 'Phan-po Chu joins the Skyid Chu near the village of Ger (Sger?) some twenty miles N.E. of Lhasa (Gyarketso of the Survey of India map) there are four *mchod-rten* reputedly built to avert bad influences from the site of Dga'-ldan before the monastery could be founded. Not far from there are two slabs of stone by the side of the road. On one is the *Ye dharmā hetuprabhavā* dictum in rather decorative Tibetan lettering. The other is inscribed as follows:

. . . rin po che'i sbyin bdag chos rgyal
rin chen lhun-po'i . . .[1] *bzhed*
sems can thams cad kyi don du
khar sa pa na sku dang ma ṇi . . .[2]
. . .[3] *. pa 'dis 'gro kun sangs rgyas thob par shog*

Notes to Text
1. *thugs* (?)
2. *mdzad* (?)
3. *gzigs* (?)

It may be translated:

"This image of Khar-sa-pa-na and the *ma-ṇi* were made for the sake of all sentient beings as the fulfilment of a vow of Chos-rgyal Rin-chen lhun-po the patron of the (Rje?) Rin-po-che. By seeing it may all creatures attain Buddhahood".

According to the account of the Brag-dkar family in the Fifth Dalai Lama's Chronicle Rin-chen Lhun-po was a son of Rin-chen-dpal, the Rdzong-dpon of Brag-dkar, who was one of the principal patrons of the Rje Rin-po-che Tsong kha-pa and contributed to the building of Dga'-ldan. He married a lady of 'Phyong-rgyas and their son Rin-chen lhun-po, also, was a generous benefactor of Dga'-ldan.

The district of Brag-dkar is not far up river from Lhasa on the left bank of the Skyid Chu with its headquarters at what is now Bde-chen Rdzong. The Brag-dkar family descended from one of the Phag-mo-gru-pa's ministers who was of the lineage of Myang Ting-nge-'dzin bzang-po the founder of Zhwa'i Lha-khang.

BIBLIOGRAPHY

J. BACOT, F. W. THOMAS and C. TOUSSAINT, *Documents de Touen-houang relatifs à l'histoire du Tibet*, Paris 1940.

F. M. BAILEY, *No Passport to Tibet,* London 1957.

V. A. BOGOSLOVSKIJ, *Essai sur l'histoire du peuple Tibétain,* translated from the Russian, Paris 1972.

S. W. BUSHELL, *Early History of Tibet from Chinese Sources,* Journal of the Royal Asiatic Society, London 1880.

CHOIX DE DOCUMENTS TIBÉTAINS CONSERVÉS À LA BIBLIOTHÈQUE NATIONALE, edited by A Macdonald and Y. Imaeda, Vol. I, Paris 1978, Vol. II Paris 1979.

SARAT CHANDRA DAS, *Tibetan English Dictionary,* Calcutta, 1902.

P. DEMIÉVILLE, *Le Concile de Lhasa,* Paris 1952.

R. E. EMMERICK, *Tibetan Texts Concerning Khotan,* London 1967.

A. FERRARI and L. PETECH, *mKhyen-brtse's Guide to the Holy Places of Central Tibet,* Rome 1958.

E. HAARH, *The Yarlung Dynasty,* Copenhagen, 1969. *The identity of Tsu-chih-chien, the Tibetan "King" who died in 804 A.D.* Acta Orientalia Copenhagen 1961.

H. HARRER, *Meine Tibet-Bilder,* Chiemsee, 1953.

H. A. JAESCHKE, *Tibetan-English Dictionary,* London 1934.

J. KOLMAŠ, *Four Letters of Po Chü-i to the Tibetan authorities (802-810)* Archív Orientální, Prague 1966.

M. LALOU, *Inventaire des manuscrits tibétains de Touen-houang conservés à la Bibliothèque Nationale (Fonds Pelliot Tibétain),* Paris 1947 1960. *Revendications des fonctionnaires du Grand Tibet au VIIIe siècle,* Journal Asiatique, 1955.

B. LAUFER, *Loan Words in Tibetan,* T'oung Pao, Leiden 1916.

F-K LI, *The Inscription of the Sino-Tibetan Treaty of 821-822* T'oung Pao, Leiden 1956.

A. MACDONALD (*née* SPANIEN), *Une Lecture des Pelliot Tibétain, 1286, 1287, 1038, 1047 et 1290* Études Tibétaines, Paris 1971.

V. MINORSKY, *Ḥudūd al-'Ālam,* translation, 2nd Ed. London 1970.

P. PELLIOT, *Histoire Ancienne du Tibet,* Paris 1961. *Le "Cha Tcheou Tou fou T'ou king" et la colonie sogdienne de la region du Lob nor,* Journal Asiatique, Paris, 1916.

E. G. PULLEYBLANK, *A Sogdian Colony in Inner Mongolia,* T'oung Pao, 1952.

E. REISCHAUER, *Ennin's Travels in T'ang China* New York 1955.

H. E. RICHARDSON, *Three Ancient Inscriptions from Tibet,* Journal of the Royal Asiatic Society, Bengal, 1949. *Ancient Historical Edicts at Lhasa* Royal Asiatic Society, London 1952. *Tibetan Inscriptions at Zva-hi Lha Khang*, Journal of the Royal Asiatic Society, London (*JRAS*) 1952, 1953. *A Ninth Century Inscription from Rkong-po,* ibid. 1954. *A Tibetan Inscription from Rgyal Lha-khang,* ibid. 1957. *Early Burial Grounds in Tibet,* Central Asiatic Journal, 1963. *A New Inscription of Khri Srong Lde Brtsan, JRAS* 1964. *Names and Titles in Early Tibetan Records,* Bulletin of Tibetology, Sikkim, 1967 (1). *A Tibetan Antiquarian of the XVIIIth Century,* ibid. 1967 (3). *The Inscription at the Tomb of Khri Lde Srong Brtsan, JRAS* 1969. *Tibetan Chis and Tshis* Asia Major. 1969. *The Rkong-po Inscription, JRAS* 1972. *The Skar-cung Inscription,* ibid. 1973. *The Sino-Tibetan Treaty Inscription of 821/823 at Lhasa,* ibid. 1978. *The First Tibetan Chos-byung*. Tibet Journal. 1980.

G. N. ROERICH, *The Blue Annals,* (translation), Calcutta, 1949, 1953.

A. RÓNA TAS, *Social terms in the list of grants of the Tibetan Tun-huang Chronicle,* Acta Orientalia Hungarica, 1955.

E. SCHAFER, *The Golden Peaches of Samarkand.* Berkeley and Los Angeles, 1963.

N. SIMONSSON, *Indo-tibetische Studien,* Uppsala 1957.

SIR M. AUREL STEIN, *Serindia,* Oxford 1921. *Archaeological Notes from the Hindukush Region, JRAS* 1944.

R. A. STEIN, *Recherches sur l'épopée et le barde du Tibet*, Paris 1959. *Les tribus anciennes des marches sino-tibétaines*, Paris 1961. *"Saint et Divin"*. Journal Asiatique, CCLXIX, 1981.

F. W. THOMAS, *Tibetan Literary Texts and Documents concerning Chinese Turkestan* vols. II and III London 1951, 1955.

G. TUCCI, *The Tombs of the Tibetan Kings* Rome 1950. *Minor Buddhist Texts II,* Rome 1958. *Transhimalaya,* Archaeologia Mundi, Geneva, Paris, Munich, 1973.

G. URAY, *Prolegomena to the sources on the history of pre-Islamic Central Asia,* Budapest 1979.

L. A. WADDELL, *Ancient Historical Edicts at Lhasa, JRAS* 1909, 1920, 1911.

Tibetan Works

Chos grags (Dge-bzhes), Tibetan Dictionary, Lhasa 1948, Peking 1957.

Chos-byung mkhas-pa'i dga'-ston by Dpa'-bo Gtsug-lag phreng-ba, composed between 1545 and 1564.

Dagyab (Brag-g-yab blo-ldan shes-rab) Tibetan Dictionary, Dharamsala 1966.

Deb-ther sngon-po by 'Gos Gzhon-nu-dpal, 1576. see Roerich, *Blue Annals.*

Fonds Pelliot Tibétain, see *Choix de Documents de Touen-houang* etc.

Li-yul chos-kyi lo-rgyus, see *Tibetan Texts concerning Khotan,* R. E. Emmerick.

Padma bka'-thang yig 1352. Lhasa zhol edition.

Rgya-bod yig-tshang 1434, *ms* copy

Rgyal-po bka'-thang-yig 1347, Lhasa Zhol edition.

Rgyal-rabs gsal-ba'i me-long 14th century, Lhasa edition of Sde-srid 'Phrin-las rgya-mtsho.

Rgyal-po bka'-thang-yig 1347. Lhasa Zhol edition.

Rdzogs-ldan gzhon-nu'i dga'-ston, Chronicle of the Fifth Dalai Lama, 1643.

Sumatiratna, Tibetan Mongolian Dictionary ed. Prof Rinchen, Ulanbator 1959.

Sngon-gyi gtam me-tog phreng-ba by Ne'u Pandita Grags-pa smon-lam blo-gros (13th/14th century?). Rare Tibetan Historical and Literary Texts from the Library of Tsepon W. D. Shakabpa compiled and published by T. Tsepal Taikhang, First series. New Delhi 1974.

ABBREVIATIONS

AFL. *Ancient Folk Literature*, F. W. Thomas, see bibliography.

CAJ Central Asiatic Journal.

Chos Grags, Tibetan Dictionary, see Tibetan bibliography.

Dagyab Tibetan Dictionary, see Tibetan bibliography.

Das S.C.Das, Tibetan English Dictionary.

DTH *Documents de Touen-houang* etc. Bacot, Thomas and Toussaint.

JA Journal Asiatique.

JRAS Journal of the Royal Asiatic Society.

JRASB. Journal of the Royal Asiatic Society, Bengal.

KHO. *Tibetan Texts Concerning Khotan,* Emmerick.

Macdonald ET *Une Lecture des Pelliot Tibétain 1286* etc. A. Macdonald, Études Tibétaines.

Pell T. Fonds Pelliot Tibétain in Lalou *Inventaire:* and *Choix de documents de Touen Houang*. Bibliothèque Nationale, Paris, 1978, 1979.

PT Dpa'-bo Gtsug-lag phreng-ba, *Chos-byung mkhas pa'i dga' ston.*

RT Rig-'dzin Tshe-dbang nor-bu of Ka-thog.

T'ang Annals, S. W. Bushell, *JRAS* 1880; and P. Pelliot, *Histoire ancienne du Tibet.*

TLTD *Tibetan Literary Texts and Documents etc.* F. W. Thomas.

TTK *The Tombs of the Tibetan Kings,* Tucci.

VSP *Vaidūrya ser-po.*

Waddell, *Ancient Historical Edicts at Lhasa. JRAS* 1909-1912.

VOCABULARY

Entries are followed by inscription references (for abbreviations, see key below) and line numbers.
Inscriptions in the addendum are not included.

Abbreviations:
CANG Lcang-bu Inscriptions (p. 92). KDS Khri Lde-srong-brtsan's tomb (p. 84). KHRA Khra-'brug Bell (p. 82). KONG Rkong-po Inscription (p. 64). KSD Khri Srong-lde-brtsan's tomb (p. 36). LT Lhasa treaty inscriptions (p. 106). SAM Bsam-yas *rdo-rings* (p. 26). SAMB Bsam-yas bell (p. 32). SKAR Skar-cung Inscription (p. 72). Y Yer-pa Bell(p. 144). ZHWA Zhwa'i Lha-khang inscriptions (p. 43). ZHWA (F) fragmentary inscription at Zhwa'i Lha-khang (p. 62). ZHOL Zhol *rdo-rings* inscriptions (p. 1).
See also p. 159 for other abbreviations.

KA final particle, *chad-ka,* fine, CANG (1) 29. *glan-ka,* blame, ZHOL N. 60.
KUN all, KSD 29. ZHWA W 16, 25, 49. SKAR 27, 55. LT W 8, 19. Y.
KOL subject, *gnam kol,* KONG 8. cf. KHOL, *bkol,* TLTD II p. 279.
KONG CO princess (Chinese) ZHOL S 67/68. LT E 24, 28. See NAMES Index.
KOR round, *nang-kor,* ZHOL N 15. retinue, cf. 'KHOR.
KYUR for *Rgyur,* or *khur? chang kyur* ZHWA W 41, to hold. cf. Pell T.131 (330 *chang khyur.* TLTD II p. 25.
KLAS = *yas,* beyond; *mthas klas,* KSD 23.
DKA' difficult, *dka' ba dgu,* ZHOL E 7. *sems dka' ba,* ZHOL S 41, 73.
DKAR white, *dkar cag,* catalogue, register, CANG (1) 40.
DKU side, party, *dku rgyal,* promotion, ZHOL N 2, 32. cf. DTH 106. *dku la gthogs ste,* DTH 106. *dku dar nas,* KHO 75 b 2.
DKU', DKU trickery, ruse, ZHWA E. 29, 30. LT W 69, *dku sgyu,* cf. DTH 101, *dku' gang.* and *dku' ched po, dku' che,* DTH 101, 102; *dku' 'gel,* DTH 103. *dku' bel,* DTH 106, *dku 'pel,* TLTD II p. 53.
DKON rare, *dkon mchog,* ZHWA W 26. *dkon mchog gsum,* the Triratna, SAM 3. SAMB. SKAR 6, 9, 12, 17, 23, 29, 45, 47, 49. CANG (1) 16. LT W 61.
DKOR wealth, CANG (1) 28. *dkor nor,* LT E 44.
DKYIL centre, *dkyil 'khor* altar, LT E 60, 63.
DKYEL wide-ranging intellect (?) *sgam dkyel,* profound intellect, KSD 18. LT E 35. cf. TLTD II 95, 96.
BKA' (BK) order, command, *bka' la btags ste* adhering to the order, SKAR 42. See also *bka' la gtogs. bka'-khon* disagreement, grudge, KDS 24, 40. LT E 40, 43. *bka' gyod* charge, accusation, ZHOL N 24, 25, 63. ZHWA W 44. E 31. cf. DTH p. 24 I 1. *bka' gros* counsel, ZHOL S 23, 39, 43, 55. ZHWA W 8, 13. E 13. cf. TLTD II 53, 56 etc. *bka' brtan* firm order, KDS 14. *bka' drin* kindness, favour, KSD 30, 31. ZHWA W 21, 23, 57. E 7, 8, 10, 16, 19, 22. CANG (1) 12, 13, LT E 10, 36. W 18, 55. *bka' nard (mnar)* harsh, ZHWA W 39. *bka' non* a suppressing order, ZHOL N 57. ZHWA W 35. cf. TLTD II 94 *bka' nan;* and DTH 27(12). *bka' phrin(d)* message, LT E 44. W 38. N. 34. cf. TLTD II 165 *bka' spring. bka' stsal(d)* order, appoint, ZHOL E 3. S 28, 58. LT E 17. *bka' brtsan* firm command, KDS 8, 23. *bka' zhal* command, CANG (1) 24. *bka' lung* command, ZHOL E 6. KDS 9, 21. CANG 7. *bka' la gtogs pa,* member of council (adhering to the order) ZHOL S 24. LT N 5, 7, 28. S 5, 7, 10, 12, 14, 17. *bka'i sa* council hall, CANG (2) 13. *bka's* by order, ZHOL N 19. ZHWA W 2, 23, 57, E 2, 24, KONG 13, 20, 21. CANG (1) 27, 31, 34, 39, 46. (2) 20.
BKUR honour, ZHOL N 20. ZHWA W 34. LT W 48.
BKYON blame, reprimand, ZHOL N 34, 60. S 20.
RKANG foot, *rkang 'gros* animal CANG (1) 20. CANG (1) 38.

VOCABULARY

RKYEN means of support ZHWA E 6, 10. *rkyen bcad pa* allot a means of support (an estate); SKAR 49. CANG (1) 40. *rkyen ris* an estate, CANG (1) 32.

SKAD voice, sound, SAMB. SKAR 32. LT W 57.

SKABS occasion, ZHWA W 11.

SKAR star, LT W 63.

SKU body, person, ZHOL S 9, 12. ZHWA W 6, 37. E 12. *sku chu ngu* young, ZHWA W 5. SKAR 34. *sku don* purpose LT E 48. *sku bla* patron spirit, personal deity, KONG 6, cf. TLTD II 9, 10, 93 etc. *sku tse* lifetime ZHOL N 12; *sku tshe* LT W 43. *sku yon* donation SAMB. CANG (1) 14, 22, *sku yon tan,* merit. *sku ring la* in the time of, ZHWA E 12. KONG 13, 20. KSD 8. CANG (1) 5. *sku rim* personal service, KONG 7. *sku srungs* bodyguard, ZHOL N 45.

SKUN = *sku, skun mkhar,* castle, CANG (2) 6. cf. TLTD II 47, 133. etc.; DTH p. 25 (89); also KHO 80a 6, 80b 7 etc. for *sku-mkhar.*

SKYID happiness, KSD 26. KDS 18, 19. LT W 55, 58, 59. note p. 125. *bde-skyid* KONG 9. LT W 20. E 56. *skyid rtag,* "continuous happiness"; regnal era of Khri Gtsug-lde-brtsan, LT E 58, 62, 65.

SKYES *skye ba,* grow, KSD 13.

SKYES a present, KONG 18.

SKRAG fear, ZHOL S 47.

BRKYANG stretch out, LT W 54. See BAG.

BSKAR restrict?, SKAR 45.

BSKUL summon, KHRA 2.

BSKO appoint, ZHWA W 61. KONG 16. SKAR 36, 40, 43.

BSKYUNG diminish, ZHOL N 26. SAM 9. ZHWA W 40. KDS 16. cf. DTH p. 110.

BSKYED increase, ZHWA W 58. E 18, 24, 34, 38.

KHA mouth, speech, *Kha chems,* will, testament, KONG 16. *kha thabs* power of speech, ZHWA(F).

KHA part, some, *mnga' kha dbud pa,* detract from, SAM 13. SKAR 52. *kha cig,* some ZHWA W 11.

KHWA tax, CANG (1) 29. Das Dictionary p. 137, *khwa-ba = dpya-ba.*

KHAB palace, residence, *khab du blangs,* married, took to wife, LT E 25, 28. TLTD II p. 8, 10. *khab so,* government revenue officials, ZHOL E 10. KONG 10. LT N 32, and see note p. 5.

KHAMS country, territory, ZHOL S 30, 44. SKAR 47. TLTD II pp. 56, 92, etc.

KHAR towards, in presence of, ZHWA E 30. See note (p. 59) and see DTH p. 122 l. 2, and p. 191.

KHU paternal uncle, ZHWA W 55.

KHO NA exactly, LT W 33.

KHONG inside, KSD 24. the mind, KDS 14.

KHONG TA he, they, ZHOL S 19. N 53. TLTD II p. 162 etc.

KHONGS inside, KDS 18. cf. KHONG.

KHON grudge, disagreement, *bka' khon,* KDS 24, 40. LT E 40, 43. *Sha khon* ZHOL N 56. cf. KHO 85 b. 3 *khon dran pa.*

KHOL servant, *khol yul,* service tenure lands, ZHOL N 29. CANG (1) 36. cf. DTH pp. 103 and 116 *khol po;* and TLTD II p. 65.

KHYAB cover, extend over, KSD 32. LT W 58. E 36.

KHYIM house, *khyim tshes* neighbour, LT W 23, E 38. *khyim yig* household register, SKAR 50.

KHRAG KHRUG disturbance, violence, ZHWA W 13. Pell T 1091(3) see 'KHRUGS cf. DTH 109(4) *khra-khrugs.*

KHRAL tax, KONG 10, 18, CANG 29.

KHRI "The Enthroned". See NAMES index.

KHRI 10,000, ZHOL S 48. LT W 56.

KHRIN = *khrims* ? judgment, legal proceedings, ZHOL N 64. cf. TLTD II 8.

VOCABULARY

KHRIMS law LT E 9.

MKHAR fort ZHOL S 45, 62. *mkhar bu* small house, ZHWA W 27, 53, 58. E 48 see SKUN MKHAR.

MKHAS wise, ZHOL S 29. LT E 35.

MKHEN = MKHAN, *mkhen-pho,* abbot KHRA.

MKHYEN knowledge, LT E 51.

'KHOD establish, LT W 55.

'KHOR to go round, *chos 'khor,* the wheel of the Law, preaching the Dharma, SKAR 41, 42. cf. KHO 72b *chos kyi 'khor lo.*

'KHRAS be attached to? ZHOL S 68.

'KHRUG(S) be disturbed, ZHOL S 13, 37. ZHWA W 16. KDS 17. See KHRAG.

GANG who, which, what, ZHOL N 36, 44, 62. S 66. ZHWA W 19, 38, KONG 16, 17, 19. SKAR 49. W 69.

GANG full, *chab gang,* quality, LT E 30.

GAR whither, in whatever direction, ZHOL S 48.

GU = GUD apart, *gu du* SKAR 46. *gudu* ZHOL S 49.

GUD *gud na* SAM 21. KSD 14. cf. KHO 18 *gu du* and TLTD II 352 *gud na.*

GUN = KUN, all, SAM 19.

GUS respect, LT E 17.

GO place, ZHWA W 5,6.

GONG upper? *thugs gong* ZHOL N 68.

GYANG = KYANG, also, ZHOL N 48. SAM 13, 17. CANG 38.

GYIS do! (imp) ZHWA W 31. See BGYID.

GYUR(D) become, ZHOL S 19. N 62. KSD 25. ZHWA E 11, 32. SKAR 21. LT E 28, 48, 50.

GYES originate, ZHWA(F). KONG 9.

GYOD law suit, charge, ZHWA W 39, 40. See bka-gyod of Pell T 956(22).

GRAG sound, KHRA. LT W 51.

GRANGS number, SKAR 21.

GRU square, *yig gru* ZHOL N 3.

GRUB accomplished, SAMB. LT E 46.

GRO *'gro*? go, *rim gro,* service, allegiance. KONG 7.

GRONGS die, ZHOL 50.

GROS counsel, ZHOL S29. See *bka' gros.*

GLANG ox, *glang lo,* ox year, LT E 59.

GLAN retribution, blame, *glan ka,* ZHOL N 60.

GLO = BLO, mind. *glo ba nye,* loyal, ZHOL S 20, 22, 73. *glo ba rings* disloyal, ZHOL S 7, 15, 18. N 22, 59, 62.

GLO ? *glo-bur du,* suddenly, LT W 50.

DGA' be pleased, ZHOL N 54.

DGU many, ZHOL E 8, 16. cf. TLTD II 53, 121.

DGUNG sky, ZHOL S 10 *dgung du gshegs,* die.

DGUN winter, LT E 59.

DGONGS thought, ZHWA W 21. E 17. KDS 22. LT W 20 E 39, 55.

DGOS necessary, ZHWA W 59. KDS 16.

DGE virtue, KHRA. *dge-ba'i bshes-nyen,* religious teacher, SKAR 35, 36, 43. *dge-slong,* monk, priest, ZHWA W 22. SKAR 35. CANG 17.

DGYES be happy, take pleasure in, ZHWA W 7. LT E 17, 32, 39, 43. W 24, 38.

DGRA, DGRA' enemy, ZHOL S 37. KDS 20. LT W 51. *dgra chos,* LT E 49, Pell T 16 (26a), 986 (23). *dgra' thabs,* military skill, strategy, ZHOL S 28. KDS 20. *dgra zun,* neither war nor peace, LT E 50. *dgrar,* as an enemy, KDS 25. LT W 31.

BGAG obstruct, SKAR 38.

BGYI do, SAM 9, 14. SKAR 46, 53. Y. *bgyid* KONG 7. *bgyis,* KONG 7. KHRA.

MGO head, source, LT E 7. *mgo chen-po,* leading part, ZHOL S 55. *mgo nag,* black-headed (Tibetans), ZHOL E 14. S 13. *mgo nan,* strict instruction? SKAR 50.

VOCABULARY

MGON lord, ZHWA(F).
'GA' some, KDS 28. LT E 28.
'GYUR to be changed, KDS 3. LT E 6, 12. W 7, 61.
'GRENG erect, standing up, (man) KSD 30. KDS 15. TLTD II 93.
RGYA extent, KDS 22. CANG 13.
RGYA seal, *phyag-rgya,* ZHWA W 61. *phyag-rgyas,* ZHWA W 28. E 39. LT W 74.
RGYA China, *rgya-rje,* ruler of China, see NAMES Index.
RGYAL conquer, rule, *rgyal po,* king, ZHOL S 51, 70. KSD 17. ZHWA W 1, E 1. KONG 14, 15. KDS 24, 29, 45. LT W 1, 3, 73. E 1, 6, 13, 15, 19, 37. *rgyal phran,* tributary king, ZHWA W 49, E 36. *rgyal ba,* the Buddha, Y. *rgyal mo,* queen, SAMB. See also *dku rgyal;* and *chos rgyal.*
RGYUD line, family, ZHOL N 8, 13, 17, 21, 32, 36, 39, 44, 48, 59, 67, ZHWA W 32, 33, 43, 46, 55. KONG 14, 15, 16. SKAR 18, 25, 29. KDS 19. CANG(l) 35. *la-rgyud* range of mountain passes KSD 21.
RGYUN continuity, flow, *rgyun du,* continually, CANG (1) 22. LT E 45.
SGAM profound, *sgam-dkyel* KSD 18. LT E 35. *thugs-sgam* profound mind, ZHOL 42. KDS 9, 14.
SGO door, SKAR 37, 38.
SGOR private, personal, ZHOL N 63. ZHWA E 27. cf. TLTD II 23 (11) 24 (33). DTH 110 (l. 12); and KHO 87b *sgo sgo* private. Pell T. 1085. *Sgo Sgor.*
SGRA sound, SAMB. KHRA. LT W 57.
SGROM box, *sgrom-bu,* small box, casket, KONG 11. CANG (2) 16.
BSGAGS bind, constrain, ZHWA W 50. E 37.
BSGYUR change, ZHOL N 50. SAM 14. ZHWA W 31, 47. E 44. SKAR 53.
NGA I, ZHWA W 4, 10, *nga'i* ZHWA 14, 15, 23, 48, 57. E4, 11, 12, 17, 24, 33.
NGAG speech, KDS 20.
NGAN bad, ZHOL N 54.
NGU *chu-ngu,* small ZHWA W 5. SKAR 34.
NGED I, we, SKAR 44.
NGO face, *ngo-khar* ZHWA E 30.
NGOGS river bank, ZHOL S 59.
DNGUL silver, ZHOL N 9, 34, 37.
MNGAN official, CANG (1) 44. LT N 32. (note p. 101).
MNGA' authority, power, ZHWA W 29, 59. E 41. LT E 27. *mnga'-thang,* power, KDS 3, 7. *mnga' bdag,* ruler KDS 27. SKAR 35 *mnga' ba,* possess, KSD 28.
MNGON evident, ZHWA E 38. W 28.
RNGA drum, KHRA.
RNGUL stir up; agitate LT E 30, 49. See note, p. 115.
RNGO be able, *rngo-thog,* capable, ZHOL N 18, 19, 44.
SNGA before, KSD 6, ZHWA W 19. LT W 41. See also *zha-snga. snga-ma,* former, ZHWA E 33, 44, 47. KONG 13. *sngar,* formerly, ZHWA E 20, 25. LT W 68.
SNGON before, ZHWA W 20, 56. KDS 21.
BSNGO dedicate, ZHWA E 31. CANG (1) 32, 34, 41.
CAG = *chag, dkar-cag,* catalogue, register, CANG (1) 41. cf. TLTD II 41(3), 43(2) etc.
CAG enclitic plural, *bdag-cag,* we, KONG 9.
CAD ? *thams-cad,* all, SAM 17. ZHWA E 37. KHRA. SKAR 54. LT W 28, 30.
CAD see also CHAD, of time or place to or from, *phan cad,* ZHWA W 44/45. *phyin cad,* hereafter SAM 9/10. *man cad,* downwards, ZHWA W 49. SKAR 38. LT W 44. *tshun cad,* thereafter, KDS 27, 41, 43. LT E 32. *yan cad,* up to, ZHOL N 15. KSD 21. ZHWA W 60. SKAR 34. LT W 46, 52.
CAN possessing, *yi-ge-can,* possessing a letter, ZHWA E 27/28. *sems-can,* living creature, sentient being, KHRA.
CI what, whatsoever, ZHOL N 23, 25. KSD 11. ZHWA W 40, 45, 51. E 32 (*cir*). KONG 8, 10. SKAR 30, 32, 36, 48. LT W 17. E 3, 35.

VOCABULARY

CIG one, some, ZHOL S 47. ZHWA W 11. *cig cing,* each one, ZHOL S 47.
CUB = *chub,* perfected, *pyang-cub (byang-chub)* Y.
CES thus, SKAR 33.
COG plural sign. *'o cog,* all, whatever there may be, ZHOL S 44. N 52. SKAR 42. CANG(1) 37. cf. CHOG.
GCAD judge, punish, ZHWA W 36, *stams las myi gcad pa,* cut off, SKAR 37.
GCAL(D) impose a tax, ZHOL S 36.
GCIG one, ZHOL N 9, 14, 36. SAM 21. KSD 14. ZHWA W 52, 53. E 47, 49. LT E 22, 42, 71. W 20. *gcig gis,* on one occasion? ZHOL N 26. ZHWA W 40. *gcig cing,* being united, LT W 36. *gcig ste* being united, LT E 55. *gcig du* unite, LT E 2, 24, 27, 39, W 5.
GCUGS implant LT E 43.
GCUGS = *gcug* enmity, LT E 47.
GCUNG younger brother, ZHWA W 7. KONG 5.
GCEN elder brother, ZHWA W 7, 10, 48. KONG 5, 6, 15.
GCES dear, precious, SKAR 30. LT E 44.
BCAD cut off, ZHOL S 32. separate, apportion, *rkyen bcad pa,* SKAR 49. CANG (1) 21, 40.
BCA, BCA' to make a vow, SAM 12. SKAR 25, 52. *yi dam bca'.* LT E 46. *gtsigs bca.*
BCAS pf. of BCA' LT W 6, 60, 66.
BCUG appoint, allow, ZHOL S 25, 49. ZHWA W 54.
BCOM conquer, ZHOL S 46. *bcom-ldan-'da's* epithet of the Buddha, SKAR 40, 41. CANG (1) 41.
BCOS adulterate, modify, ZHWA W 31, 47. E 44.
MCOG = *mchog.* SAM 3.
LCAGS iron, LT E 59.
LCIGS = *theg-pa, chud-pa* (Sumatiratna) *nus pa* (Dagyab) *phyi lcigs,* postponement LT E 48.
CHA part, *sa cha,* place, ZHOL S 32.
CHA thing, things, *sde cha* district troops? ZHOL N 49. *lha cha,* sacred objects, CANG (1) 19.
CHAGS to be produced, *tshul chags,* LT E 52. *srog chags,* LT E 65.
CHAGS sway, authority KONG 8. Pell T. 16 (26a): 986 (112, 133) cf. CHAB.
CHANG hold, ZHWA W 41, TLTD II p. 24). See 'CHANG.
CHAD be cut off, ZHOL N 28, 32. ZHWA W 43. KONG 15, 16. LT E 32. *chad-ka,* fine, CANG (1) 29. punish, ZHWA W 35, 36.
CHAD time or place to or from, see CAD. *phan chad,* up to, KONG 4. *phyin chad,* hereafter SKAR 51. *man chad,* downwards, KSD 20. *tshun chad,* thereafter, KONG 4, 9. LT E 5. *slan chad,* henceforth, KONG 18.
CHAB power, authority, KSD 21. cf. Pell T 986 (109) *chab 'og. chab srid,* dominion, kingdom, ZHOL E 10. S 38, 40, 43, 73. KSD 13. ZHWA W 5, 10, 14, 15, 17, 29, 37, 49, 59. E 4, 11, 36. KONG 7. KDS 4, 10, 19, 25, 27, 28, 40, 44, 46. SKAR 34. LT E 2, 11, 23, 27, 38, 55. W 4, 36. N 4, 8, 14, 18, 20, 22. S 4.
CHAB = water essence, *chab gang* LT E 30 = *chu gang.*
CHIS administration, management, SKAR 51. CANG (1) 27. LT E 10. See "Tibetan *Chis* and *Tshis*". H. E. Richardson, Asia Major 1969 (2).
CHU water, LT E 63, 66. *chu-bo* river LT E 7.
CHU = CHUNG small, *chu-ngu,* young, ZHWA W 5. SKAR 34.
CHU = CHAB *chu-srid,* KONG 9.
CHUNG small, ZHOL E 12. S 70. SKAR 33.
CHUNGS to be small, ZHWA W 57. E 10.
CHUD enter, SKAR 36.
CHUB perfected, *byang chub* KSD 27, 33. See CUB.

VOCABULARY

CHE great, KSD 28. LT E 11, 30. *che chung* great and small, ZHOL E 11, 6, 70. SKAR 33. *che phra,* great and ordinary, ZHWA W 49. LT N 1. S 1. *che-ba,* be great, ZHOL S 23. KSD 4, 23, 24. KDS 4, 7, 10, 15, 23. LT E 11, 20.

CHEN great, *chen-po (pho),* ZHOL E 4. S 6, 39, 55. N 9, 37. KSD 11, 19, 32, 34. ZHWA W 17, 20, 41. E 14, 19, 22. KDS 3, 5, 24. LT E 6, 7, 9, 13, 18, 35, 45, 48, 54, 56, 57, 58, 61, 62, 65, 66. W 1, 3, 6, 17, 21, 25, 30, 37, 59, 73. N 1, 4, 7, 9, 11, 24, 36. S 1, 4, 7, 10, 12, 14, 17, 18.

CHEMS *bka'-chems,* will, KONG 16.

CHER greater, ZHWA E 16. KDS 22, 43. CHANG (1) 12, 15.

CHES be great, see CHE, *thugs ches pa,* reliable, ZHWA W 60, *yid ma ches pa,* unreliable, suspect, LT W 33.

CHO GA service, *cho-gar mdzad* KONG 7.

CHOG = COG all, ZHWA W 13. LT E 17, 32. W 57. N 10, 32, 39.

CHOS (I) custom, religious law. *bka'-drin sbyin pa'i chos,* ZHWA W 23; *dgra chos,* LT E 49. cf. Pell T 986 (64) (k): *gnam gyi chos,* KDS 8. (Pell T 986 (11); *gnam sa'i chos,* KSD 7/8.: *ma zhig pa'i chos,* SKAR 50. *chos gtsug lag,* KSD 2. *chos lugs,* KDS 2. *chos-srid,* LT E 35. (II) the religion of the Buddha, SKAR 36, 37. *chos rgyal,* dharma-raja, KSD 11. *chos 'khor,* the Buddha's preaching, SKAR 41, 42. *chos gtsigs,* edict about religion, CHANG (1) 8. *'jig-rten las 'da's-pa'i chos bzang-po,* the Buddha's excellent religion. *dam-pa'i chos,* the holy religion, SKAR 2. CHANG 6, 7, 10. KHRA. sangs-*rgyas kyi chos,* the religion of the Buddha, SAM 5. SKAR 5, 19, 30.

MCHIS to be, ZHOL N 16. SAM 21. KONG 8, 10.

MCHED brother, sister, ZHWA W 48, KONG 6, 9.

MCHOG excellent, see DKON.

MCHOD religious offering, SAMB. SKAR 46. *mchod gnas,* priest, SKAR 44, 46.

'CHANG hold, ZHOL N 33. ZHWA W 54. E 49. Pell T 1089. cf. *chang.*

'CHAD cut off, CANG (1) 22.

'CHOS to correct, *yo-gal 'chos-pa,* a judicial post. ZHOL E 3.

JI what, so, *ji ltar,* like that, ZHWA W 51. CANG (1) 33. *ji tsam,* so much as, ZHOL N 19. ZHWA W 34.

JO lord, *jo-mo,* lady, queen, SAMB. ZHWA W 48. E 35. KHRA.

MJAL meet, *mjal dum,* treaty, KDS 28, 44. LT E 2, 3, 40, 45, 56. W 5, 25, 36/37. N 1 S 1.

MJUG appendage, CANG (1) 26.

'JAL pay, ZHOL S 51.

'JIG RTEN the world, SAM 14, 16. KSD 28. SKAR 53, 53/54.

'JIGS fear, LT W 53.

RJE ruler, lord, ZHOL S 46, 49, 50, 54, 61, 63. KDS 6, 16. *rje blon,* king and ministers, ZHOL S 47. SAM 19. ZHWA E 20, 41. KONG 20. SKAR 26, 55. LT W 71. 9 Pell T. 1b (29b) *rgya-rje,* ruler of China, ZHOL S 53, 63. LT E 42. See NAMES *thugs-rje,* mercy, kindness (noble heart). LT W 17. *rjer,* to become king, KONG 4. KDS 2.

RJE change? *rje blas,* an official post or duty, ZHOL E 7. S 4. N 18. KONG 18. See note 2 p. 5. cf. TLTD II 23 (9) 59 (9) 120, 404 etc. Pell T. 1089 (18, 35) 986 (60). AFL VI (77, 93, etc.).

RJES after, ZHWA W 10. LT E 46. *rjes dbangs,* follower, subject, ZHWA W 21. cf. Das Dictionary p. 466 *rjes 'brang.*

BRJE(S) exchange, ZHOL N 54. LT W 43.

BRJOD speak, relate, KSD 9. ZHWA(F) 3. LT W 43.

NYA See PHO-*nya.*

NYAN hear, obey, LT E 18.

NYAM(S) mind, ZHOL E 8. CANG (1) 10. *nyam drod,* attention, interest, ZHOL S 25. ZHWA W 12.

NYAMS impair, KSD 7. KDS 4. LT E 13.

NYI sun, *nyi-ma.* See GNYI.

NYID self, ZHWA W 21. E 7. KDS 15.

NYE near, ZHOL N 30, 36, 54. S 12. KONG 16. LT W 47. E 33, 50. *glo-ba nye,* loyal, ZHOL S 20, 22, 40. *snying nye,* loyal, ZHWA W 4, 16, 20, 51, 56. E 16, 22.
NYES offence, ZHOL N 63. ZHWA W 36, 38, 39, 40. E 28. LT W 17, 68.
GNYAN strict, LT E 54.
GNYI sun, LT W 57, 63.
GNYEN relationship. LT E 27, 30, 38. W 22, 47.
RNYING old, LT E 40, 47. W 23, 41.
SNYAN ear, hearing, ZHOL S 17.
SNYAN(D) PA pleasant to hear, praise, ZHOL S 72. LT E 44. W 39, 56.
SNYING heart, *snying nye,* loyal, ZHWA W 4, 9, 15, 19, 38, 51, 56. E 15, 21.
SNYUNG ill, *thugs snyung,* be grieved ZHOL S 52.
SNYUNG to take an oath (put at risk?) *dbu snyung* ZHOL N 6. SAM 19. ZHWA W 48, 55. E 3, 36. SKAR 27, 55.
SNYOMS make equal, ZHOL E 13. LT E 53.
BRNYES find, KSD 29. CANG (1) 6.
TA see KHONG-*ta*.
TAN see YON-*tan*.
GTANG let go, SAM 6. SKAR 25. CANG (1) 7. LT W 35.
GTAN established, *gtan tshigs,* the facts, ZHOL S 15. LT E 4.
GTAM story, account, KSD 14. LT W 34.
GTOGS belong to, ZHOL S 24, 30, 33, 45, ZHWA E 30. *bka' la gtogs pa* member of council (see BKA'). ZHOL S 24. LT N 5, 7, 28. S 5, 7, 10, 12, 14, 17. *gtsigs 'dzin pa la gtogs,* among those who adhered to the treaty, LT W 76. *gtsigs bshig pa la ma gtogs,* not included in those destroying the treaty, LT W 70.
BTAGS attach to, SKAR 20, 21. CANG (1) 24.
BTANG let go, SKAR 20, 21. cf. GTANG.
BTAB put, *phyag-rgya(s) btab,* to seal, ZHWA W 28, 53, 54, 61. E 40. LT W 74.; *smon-lam btab,* pray, CANG (1) 15.
BTUNGS be killed, ZHOL S 61. cf. *ltung* ? *brdung* ?
BTUL subdue, LT E 11.
RTA horse, LT W 43.
RTAG perpetual, ZHOL S 47. N 16. SKAR 40. KDS 29. LT E 58, 62, 65.
RTEN support, shrine, image, SAM 4. ZHWA 26. SKAR 7, 9, 12, 15, 17, 24, 29, 45. *'jig-rten,* the world, SAM 16, 17. KSD 28, SKAR 53, 54.
RTOG consider, ZHOL S 26.
LTA look at, *de lta bas na*, so regarded; KDS 15. *lta zhig*, as for, regarding, KONG 9. LT E 37. *lta bu,* like, LT E 46. *ltar,* like, thus, KSD 23, 30. ZHWA W 19, 51. KONG 19. SKAR 19, 28, 33. CANG (1) 33. LT E 33. W 26, 37, 71.
LTAS omen, sign, SKAR 31.
STANGS accompanied by ?. *stangs dbyal,* consort, SAMB. see note p. 35.
STAMS harsh, strict, oppression, ZHWA W 35, 36. cf. TLTD II 75 B 12, 122 (4). Pell T 986 (36).
STI respect, *bkur-sti,* LT W 48.
STE'A early form of gerund affix *ste,* ZHOL S 62.
STENG on top of, ZHWA E 21, 33, 44.
STONG thousand, thousand district, ZHOL N 42, 46. ZHWA E 27.
STONGS help LT E 31.
STOBS strength, SAMB. KDS 15.
BRTAN(D) firm, ZHOL S 23. ZHWA E 38. W 25, 46. SKAR 2. KDS 14, 19. CANG (1) 44.
BRTUD succession, ZHWA W 10.
BSTUD succession, LT E 41.
BSTOD praise, honour, ZHOL N 20. ZHWA W 35. E 25.
THA final?, *tha tshig,* solemn words, LT W 64.
THAG nearness, *ma thag du,* as soon as, KDS 25.

VOCABULARY

THAG certain, *yang thag par,* certainly, LT W 30.
THANG extent, *mnga' thang,* power, KDS 3, 7.
THANG rank, ZHOL N 40. CANG (1) 31.
THAB fighting, ZHOL S 60.
THABS way, manner, ZHOL S 29. ZHWA W 45. SKAR 48. KDS 20. LT E 11, 49. Pell T 1091 (24). See DGRA. title, rank, LT E 68. N 3, 5, 24. S 2, 5, 12, 14, 16, 18, 22, 25.
THAMS CAD all, SAM 11. ZHWA E 37. SKAR 54. KHRA. LT W 28, 29.
THAR be freed, delivered, SKAR 38, 39.
THIL(d) centre, ZHOL S 53.
THUGS mind, ZHWA E 17. SKAR 36. *thugs gong* (dgongs?) ZHOL N 67. *thugs sgam,* profound mind, ZHOL S 42. *thugs ches,* reliable. *thugs rje,* compassion, LT W 17. *thugs snyung,* heartsick, grieved, ZHOL S 52. *thugs stobs,* strength of mind, KDS 15. *thugs brtand,* firmness of mind, ZHOL S 23. *thugs nongs,* disagreement, dissension, ZHWA W 10. LT E 32, 47. *thugs pag,* attention, care, KONG 10. cf. TLTD II 277 B 1. *thugs brel,* concern LT E 30. *thugs yi dam,* vow, LT E 33/34.
THUB be able, *zung thub,* power of comprehension? KDS 14.
THOG upper, top, KDS 26. *thog-ma,* first, ZHOL S 27. KONG 3, 6, 9.
THOG THAG, KDS 27. *mdzad ma thog la.*
THOG = THOGS? *rngo thog,* able, capable. ZHOL N 18, 19, 44.
THOGS to come up against, cf. GDAGS. ZHWA W 44. = 'dogs, be attached to? *phan thogs pa,* useful, LT E 31.
THOB get, LT W 56.
MTHA' limit, border, KSD 17. ZHWA W 28. E 39. KDS 22. LT E 37. *mthar,* to the end, ZHWA W 4. *dbung mthar* in the centre and on the borders, SKAR 14. *mthas* (*mtha' yas*?) KSD 23.
MTHUN agree, KDS 7. LT W 22. E 39, 52, 55.
MTHO high, KONG 8. LT E 7.
'THAB fight, LT E 32. See THAB.
'THUN agree, KSD 8. ZHWA W 7. See MTHUN.
DA now, LT W 36. *da ltar,* as it is now, KONG 19. LT W 26/27. *da phyin cad,* from now onwards, SAM 9. SKAR 51.
DAG plural, SAM 13. ZHWA W 11. SKAR 53. KDS 44. LT E 30, 31, 32, 49.
DAG certain, see THAG. *yang dag pa,* ZHOL N 62. ZHWA W 36.
DAG merely? *she dag,* LT E 48.
DANG PO first, KONG 9. KDS 25. LT E 21, 59.
DAD belief, faith, *dad-pa'i rnams,* believers, SKAR 39.
DAM vow, *thugs dam,* CANG (1) 25. *thugs yi dam,* LT E 33. *yi dam,* SAM 12. SKAR 25, 52.
DAM PA holy, SKAR 2. CANG (1) 2, 7, 10. KHRA.
DAR(D) harm, ZHOL S 9, 12.
DAR silk, ZHOL S 48.
DUD smoke, LT W 50.
DUD (to bend down,) respect? *phu dud* LT W 44, 46.
DUM be reconciled, ('DUM ?), see MJAL, *mjal dum* treaty.
DUS time, KHRA.
DENG today, *deng-sang,* nowadays, KONG 9.
DO a pair, LT E 31.
DOGS fear, LT W 53. E 48.
DOD emerge, LT E 3.
DON purpose, LT E 48. W 21.
DOR reject, ZHWA E 30. Pell T 1091 (12a).
DRANG(S) lead (an army), attack, ZHOL S 27, 54, 56, 59. KDS 26. LT W 32.
DRIN kindness, favour, see BKA'-*drin.*
DRIL bell, KHRA.

VOCABULARY

DRIS ask, LT E 34.
DRUNG ZHWA E 41. LT E 57.
DRUNG wise, *drung-po*, ZHWA W 6, and note 3, p. 47.
DRUNG see G-YUNG.
DROD see NYAM.
GDAGS implicate, ZHOL N 64. ZHWA W 39. ZHWA E 31) attach, CANG (1) 26.
GDAMS precept, KDS 20.
GDUNG lineage, *gdung-rabs,* generation, SAM 10. ZHWA 32. KONG 4. SKAR 18, 25, 29, 51. CANG (1) 6. LT E 6, 42.
GDOD the beginning, ZHWA W 4.
GDON evil spirit, ZHWA W 11.
BDAG self, KONG 7, 8, 10.
BDAG master, *mnga bdag,* SKAR 35, KDS 28. *gtsigs bdag,* holder of the edict, ZHWA W 60. *yon bdag,* donor, KHRA.
BDE peace, happiness, KSD 26. ZHWA W 25, 41, 46. E 15, 27. KONG 9, 10. KDS 17. LT E 56. W 19, 54. See SKYID.
BDEN true, ZHOL S 19.
MDO summary, account, ZHOL N 3. ZHWA W 27. E 15, 39. KDS 11, 29. LT E 45, 65. W 11. *mdor,* in short, ZHOL N 66. SKAR 47.
'DA'S pass beyond, *bcom-ldan-'da's,* the Buddha, SKAR 40, 41. *'jig-rten las 'da's pa,* passed from the world, SAM 15. KSD 28. SKAR 53.
'DIR here, ZHWA W 26, 51. E 48 ZHWA(F) 4.
'DUG exist, be, *'dug-pa,* KDG 24. LT E 18.
'DUN council, CANG (1) 42.
'DUM make a treaty, LT E 37.
'DONG proceed, LT W 40.
'DON(D) raise up, ZHWA W 15. E 4.
'DRA like, KSD 18. ZHWA 56, 57. KONG 8, 9. CANG (1) 45. (2) 10. LT E 3, 19.
'DRANG lead an army, attack, ZHOL N 45. ZHWA, bring, summon, ZHWA W 60.
'DRI = *'bri,* to write, LT E 68. cf. TLTD II 74 (19, 22).
'DRUL = *'grul,* to travel (as a messenger), LT E 45. W 39. cf. TLTD II 147 (8) etc.
RDUL dust, LT W 50.
RDO stone, ZHWA W 28. *rdo-rings,* stone pillar, ZHOL N 3. KSD 10. ZHWA W 27, 31. E 39, 43. SKAR 28. KDS 12. CANG (1) 3. LT W 11. E 4, 65, 67, 68, 70.
LDAN possessing, SAMB.
SDANG hatred, LT E 51.
SDIG sin, SKAR 21. LT W 69.
SDE district, ZHOL N 48. ZHWA W 42. ZHWA (F) 10. LT E 15.
BSDUS gather together, annex, ZHOL S 31, 46.
BSDO challenge, vie with, KDS 25, 28, 41.
NAG black, *mgo nag,* black-headed (Tibetans), the Tibetan populace, ZHOL E 14. S 13.
NANG inside, interior, ZHOL E 9, KSD 25. KDS 10, 17. LT E 10, 36, 53. W 19. N 7. *nang nas,* from among ZHOL N 61. KONG 16. SKAR 39. *nang kor,* inner attendants, ZHOL N 15. *nang blon, interior minister,* ZHOL E 2. S 24, 63/64. N 26.
NAN important, insistent, *mgo-nan,* SKAR 50.
NAM forever (with negative, "never"). *nam kyang,* KDS 3/4. *nam du yang,* SAM 6. KONG 10. SKAR 19, 37. KDS 11. *nam zhar,* ZHOL N 8, 48. KSD 25/26. ZHWA W 32, 43, 46. E 34, 42. SKAR 22. KDS 18. LT E 12. W 7, 61. *nam zhig,* permanent? KSD 10. ever, ZHWA W 58. CANG (1) 35. cf. DTH p. 110 *nam nam nam nam zha zha zha zha.*
NAMS see BSOD.
NAR *na,* age, *nar du,* come of age, KDS 28.
NAS barley, KONG 19.
NU younger brother, ZHWA W 39. *nu-po,* ZHOL N 30, 63.
NUB west, KSD 22. KDS 45. LT W 29. E 14, 57.

VOCABULARY

NUS able, ZHWA W 34. SKAR 40.
NONGS fault, ZHOL N 22. *thugs nongs,* disagreement, ZHWA 10. LT E 32, 47.
NOD receive, ZHWA W 22. E 8.
NON suppress, *bka' non,* a suppressing order, ZHOL N 57. ZHWA W 35.
NOR wealth, *nor pyugs,* wealth and cattle, or "wealth in cattle" ZHOL N 29. cf. TLTD II 81 (13) *phyugs nor;* and 141 (8) *nor phyugs: nor rdzas,* property, CANG (1) 19. *dkor nor* riches and wealth, LT E 44.
GNANG grant, ZHOL N. ZHWA W and E. KONG. SKAR, CANG. *passim.*
GNAM sky, heaven, KSD 7. ZHWA W 1. ZHWA (F) 3, 5. KONG 8. KDS 1, 8. LT E 8.
GNAS place, *gnas-brtan* (sthavira) elder, CANG (1) 44. *mchod gnas,* object of worship, chaplain, SKAR 44, 46.
GNAS dwell, KSD 26.
GNOD harm, ZHWA E 29. LT E 29.
MNANGS dominion, authority ZHOL S 31. KDS 42. cf. TLTD II 95 DTH 99 (33).(A3).
MNA' oath, SAM 13. ZHWA W 50. E 36. SKAR 52. LT E 66, 72. W 65.
MNAR oppress, torment, ZHWA W 35.
RNAM piece, part, (used with numbers) *rnam gnyis,* the two individual (pillars), ZHWA E 42. cf. TLTD II 21 (6) 24 (46).
RNAM PAR completely, Y.
RNAMS plural suffix, ZHWA W 29, 49. E 36. LT W 75. as a noun, after a genitive, ZHOL N 19, 39. ZHWA E 26. SKAR 44, 49. LT W 62, 64.
SNA leading, important, *sna chen-po,* ZHWA W 41. *dpon-sna,* KONG 10.
SNA different kinds, KONG 10.
SNANG appear, appearance, LT E 32. W 50.
SNANG brightness? *bar snang,* the heavens, empyrean.
SNAM to take, receive *snam-phyi-pa,* an official post LT N 30. cf. DTH 106 (35).
BRNAN(D) confirm, ZHWA W 58. SKAR 3, 55.
MRNAM = bsnam, ? to seize, LT W 33.
BSNAN add to, ZHWA W 38, 45. E 34. KHRA CANG (1) 39.
PAG measure, care, *thugs-pag,* KONG 10. cf. DPAG.
PU = *phu,* elder brother, *pu-nu -po,* elder and younger brothers, ZHOL N 30, 63. ZHWA W 39.
PELD increase, ZHOL N 27, 44, 59. cf. 'PHELD, PHELD.
PYUGS cattle, wealth, ZHOL N 29. = *phyugs.*
DPAG measure, *dpag du myed pa,* beyond measure, SKAR 20.
DPAGS proportionate, *dpags pa las,* ZHWA E 9.
DPANG witness, SKAR 54. LT W 8, 63. cf. DPHANG.
DPE copy, example, ZHWA W 52, 53. E 47, 48. KONG 11. CANG (1) 41, 43, 44. (2) 5, 15. *zla dpe,* precedent, ZHWA W 20. E 6. *dper,* as a copy, ZHWA W 54. E 49.
DPEN(D) benefit, ZHOL E 11. S 40, 73. ZHWA W 9, 12, 18, 51. E 14. cf. PHAN.
DPON chief, officer, ZHOL S 56. N 46. ZHWA W 42. KONG 10. LT N 12.
DPYA tax, ZHOL S 47, 48, 51. KONG 18.
DPYID spring, LT E 67.
DPROG take away, deprive, ZHOL N 53. ZHWA W 45.
'PELD increase, ZHOL N 14, 55. cf. PELD, PHELD.
SPA fear, ZHOL S 32. KDS 26.
SPANG abandon, SKAR 32, 46, 48.
SPUN brothers, kinsmen, ZHWA(F) 7.
SPUS quality, KONG 16.
SPO transfer, ZHOL N 49.
SPYAD act, behave, SKAR 37. CANG (1) 33, Y. cf. SPYOD.
SPYAN eye, inspection, LT E 68. *spyan ras,* watch over, ZHWA W 33.
SPYIR in general, ZHWA W 8, 14, 18. E 14.
SPYOD act, behave, KSD 27, Y. cf. SPYAD.

SPRAS regard, esteem, gces spras, SKAR 30. cf. KHO 72a 7.
PHA father, ZHOL N 39, 66. KONG 9.
PHAN benefit, ZHOL E 15. phan thogs par, LT E 31.
PHAN up to beyond, *phan cad,* ZHWA W 44/45. KONG 4. *phan tshun,* on either side, LT E 17, 29, 31, 39, 43. W 31, 40.
PHAN-PHUN trouble, faction, ZHWA W 11. cf. TLTD II 47 (7) *pan pun*. Pell T 986 (71).
PHAB *to bring down, cause to fall,* ZHOL S 20, 63.
PHABS = *'bebs,* to establish, lay down etc. (Das Dictionary p. 921) *thugs-yi-dam phabs-pa las* a firm resolve having been taken, LT E 35.
PHAM lose, fall short, ZHWA E 10. cf. 'PHAM.
PHAL general, ordinary, ZHOL S 31. LT N 24. S 18.
PHU respect? *phu dud,* to pay respect, LT W 44, 46.
PHUGS interior, ZHOL S 71.
PHUN see PHAN PHUN trouble, faction, ZHWA W 11.
PHUL offer, ZHOL S 48. ZHWA W 51, 56. E 16, 22.
PHUL ultimate? *mas ma phul* until the very last? ZHWA W 44.
PHE'U accuser,? *phe'u pa,* ZHWA E 30.
PHELD increase, ZHOL N 67. see PHELD, 'PHELD.
PHO NYA messenger, LT E 44, 68. W 40.
PHO BRANG palace, court, ZHOL S 54. ZHWA E 23. SKAR 45, 47. LT E 61.
PHONGS be sparing of, *srog phongs,* KONG 7. cf. DTH 105, 112. *srog spongs*.
PHYWA auspicious, good quality? KONG 19.
PHYAG hand, ZHWA W 44. KDS 25. *phyag rgya,* seal, signature, ZHWA W 28, 53, 54, 61. E 39. LT W 74. *phyag sbal,* treasury, archive, cf. Pell T 986 (146). ZHWA W 52. E 46. LT W 79.
PHYAD continue, LT E 44.
PHYI *phyi-nang,* outside and inside, outside, ZHOL E 9. KDS 10, 20. LT E 11, 36, 53. W 19. N 3. *phyi blon,* outer minister, LT E 28, 38. See also PHYIR.
PHYI after, ZHWA W 19. E 41. LTE 48. *phyi-ma,* subsequent, ZHWA W 29. E 33.
PHYI ? See SNAM.
PHYIN to go, proceed, LT E 46.
PHYIN after, *phyin cad(chad),* hereafter, SAM 9. SKAR 22, 51.
PHYIR outwards, KDS 4. LT E 11.
PHYIR back, LT W 35.
PHYIR on account of, ZHWA E 22. SKAR 32.
PHYIR in order to, ZHWA W 26. CANG (1) 13. KHRA.
PHYIR afterwards, LT E 13.
PHYUG wealthy, KSD 25. KDS 18.
PHYUNG addition, supplement, (*'byin-pa*?) *zur-phyung*, ZHWA W 58.
PHYE separate, KONG 9.
PHYOGS direction, ZHOL S 26, 34. SAMB. ZHWA W 16. E 14, 47. KDS 23, 26, 29, 39. LT E 13, 14, 18, 36, 57, 61. W 28, 29.
PHRA small, *phra-mo*, minor, ZHWA E37. *che phra*, great and small, ZHWA W 49. LT N 1. S 1.
PHRA slander, *phra-ma*, ZHOL N.59. See 'PHRA.
PHRAD meet, LT W 44, 45.
PHRAN small, lesser, *phran tshegs*, small matters, LT E 47. cf. TLTD II 186 (B6). *rgyal phran*, lesser kings, tributary kings, ZHWA W 49. E 36.
PHRI diminish, ZHWA E 9.
PHRIG doubt, *dogs phrig*, doubts, LT E 48.
PHRIN(D) message, *bka' phrin*, LT E 44. W 38. *bka'i phrin blon* LT N35. *phrin las*, deeds, KSD 11.
DPHANG = DPANG SAM 17.
'PHAGS holy, LT W 62.

VOCABULARY

'PHAM fall short, ZHWA E 19. cf. PHAM.

'PHEL(D) increase, ZHOL N 8, 18, 39, 48, 51, 61. ZHWA W 33, 37, 42, 46. E 26. KONG 14. cf. PELD, 'PELD, PHELD.

'PHRA slander, ZHWA W 36. cf. PHRA.

'PHRA ? = PHRA, 'jewel'. *'phra-men*, a precious stone. KONG 11. CANG(2) 15.

'PHRAL the present, now, *'phral-yun*, present and future, ZHWA 18. E.12.

'PHRUL supernatural wisdom or power. *'phrul gyi dgongs-ba*, supernaturally wise thought, LT E 55. *'phrul gyi tshul chags*, supernaturally wise nature, LT E 52. *'phrul gyi lha*, supernaturally wise divinity, KSD 16, 33. ZHWA W 1. E.1. SKAR 1, 4, 22. LT E 1, 5, 16, 22, 25, 34, 51. W 2, 12. *lha-'phrul*, divinely wise, KDS 13, 22. LT E 34.

BAG ? = 'BAG, pretext, ZHOL N 56.

BAG ? BAG CHAGS, habit, nature, *bag brkyang*, be at ease, LT W 54. cf. Chos-grags dictionary *bag-rkyong*.

BAN DE monk, ZHWA W and E *passim*. LT N 9.

BAB befall, ZHOL N 25. ZHWA E 29. amount to? ZHWA E 10.

BAR up to, until, ZHWA W 5. ZHWA (F) 10. KONG 4. LT E 18, 43. W 56. in between, in the interval, KDS 24, 40. LT E 29, 47. W 50.

BAR SNANG space, empyrean, KHRA.

BARD ? ZHWA(F) 4.

BAS ? = LAS, ZHWA E 25. KONG 13.

BU son, *bu tsha*, descendants, ZHWA W 39. CANG (2) 2. *bu tsha rgyud* line of descendants, CANG (1) 35. *bu tsha rgyud 'phel(d)* etc. increasing line of descendants. ZHOL N 7, 13, 17, 21, 27, 32, 36, 38, 44, 48, 50, 55, 58, 67. ZHWA W 33, 37, 42, 46. E.26. *bu tsha 'phel* Zhol N 61. *bu tsha 'phel rgyud*, KONG 14.

BUR see GLO BUR.

BOR to swear an oath, *dbu snyung dang bro bor ro*, swore an oath, SAM 20. SKAR 27, 55. cf. DTH 110 (34, 37) *bro bor ro.* and 104 (11) *mna' bor ro.*

BYA do, ZHWA 11, 25. E 32, 39. SKAR 19. LT E 30. W 20, 45, 46.

BYANG north, KSD 22. KDS 41. LT E 14.

BYANG CHUB SAMB. KSD 27, 33. KHRA. and see PYANG.

BYAD see YO BYAD.

BYAMS love, LT E 10, 36.

BYAS did, ZHOL E 16. S 4, 41, 60, 72, 74. ZHWA W 5, 6, 8, 15, 16, 17, 38. E14. SKAR 44. CANG (1) 49. LT E 30, 31. W 8, 67, 69.

BYIN glory, splendour, KSD 12, 18, 24. KDS 4, 20. LT E 12.

BYIN gave, KSD 30. ZHWA W 41.

BYUNG happen, ZHOL N 23. ZHWA W 10. SK KDS 24, 40. LT E 5?, 32, 43. *rab du byung ba*, become a monk, enter religion. SKAR 43.

BYUNG = *phyung* (*'byin-pa*), come out, proceed, ZHOL S 62, LT E 5?, W 41.

BYED do, ZHOL S 14. N 57. ZHWA W 9, 19. E 15, 29. SKAR 41, 43. CANG (1) 22. Y.

BRANG dwelling? PHO BRANG q.v.

BRAN bondsman, ZHOL N 51. ZHWA W 43. KONG 18. CANG (1) 19.

BRI write, CANG (1) 3.

BRIS written, ZHOL N 4. KSD 10. ZHWA W 31, 52. E 39, 43, 46. KONG 11. SKAR 28, 56. KDS 12. CANG (1) 4. LT E 4, 65, 67, 70. W 11, 73, 76.

BRO oath, SAM 20. SKAR 27, 55. cf. BOR; also DTH 104 (22). *bro len:* (2) *bro mna' gcod pa:* 105 (8, 14) *bro stsol to;* 108 (34) *bro khud par* 110 (1) *bro 'dor ba;* (13) *bro la ma thogs pa;* (21, 33) *bro stsald pa.*

BLA above, uppermost, ZHOL N 57. ZHWA W 35. CANG (1) 27, 41. (2) 4. LT N 10, 32, 40. *bla na myed pa*, the highest, SAMB. *bla 'og* high and low, ZHWA 7, 16. E 14, 32. See BLAR.

BLANGS receive, take. ZHOL E 8. CANG (1) 10. *khab du blangs*, take to wife, marry. LT E 25, 28.

VOCABULARY

BLAR to the superior, *blar bzhes pa*, resume (by the king), ZHOL N 35, 52. CANG (1) 37. but cf. *slar*, back.

BLAS by, or from, above? See RJE BLAS.

BLUGS cast, found, KHRA.

BLON minister (in compounds) ZHOL E 1, 2. S 24, 47. N 1, 7, 31, 35, 43, 66. SAM 19. ZHWA W 33, 46, 49. E 20, 25, 41. KONG 20. SKAR 27 55. LT W 71. N *passim*, and see RJE.

BLON PO minister, ZHOL S 6, 69. ZHWA W 17. E 36. KONG 3. LT E 29. W 74. N 1, 4, 14, 16 etc. S 1, 4, 17.

DBANG power, ZHOL N 52. ZHWA E 32. SKAR 43. CANG (1) 37. LT N 8.

DBAB make to fall, impose upon, ZHOL N 10, 24, 64. KONG 18. CANG (1) 29.

DBU head, *dbu snyung*, oath, ZHOL N 6. SAM 19. ZHWA W 48, 55. E 3, 35. SKAR 27, 55. See BOR. *dbu snyung dang bro bor ro.* cf. DTH 104(24) *dbu snyung bro mna' gcod pa.* 109 (15) *dbu snyung yang gnang.* 110 (5) *dbu snyung gnang.* (18) *dbu snyung la ma gthogs. dbu rmog*, helmet, KSD 3, 12, 19. KONG 8. KDS 4. LT E 12, 16, 33.

DBUNG centre, SKAR 14, cf. DBUS.

DBUD = *'bud*, to take away from, SAM 13. SKAR 53.

DBUS centre. LT E 7.

DBON nephew, grandson, (see note p. 79) *dbon sras*, SKAR 34, 48. KDS 18, *sras dbon*, ZHOL N 12. ZHWA W 29, 59. cf. DTH 110 (20, 23) *dbon zhang*, Nephew and Uncle, relationship between rulers of Tibet and China, LT E 28, 33, 42, 46, 54. W 4, 38, 47.

DBYANGS sound, SAMB.

DBYAR summer, LT E 63.

DBYAL consort, *stangs dbyal*, SAMB. See note p. 35.

DBYUNG take out, ZHWA W 61.

DBYE open, ZHWA W 61.

DBRI = *'bri*, diminish. ZHOL N 53. SAM 8. ZHWA W 31. E 43. KONG 18.

'BA' ZHIG only, ZHWA W 18.

'BANGS subject, ZHOL S 66 (?). ZHWA W 21. KDS 18, 19. SKAR 38. CANG (1) 28.

'BAB make to fall, KONG 7. cf. DBAB.

'BUL offer, ZHWA W 20. E 5. KONG 19.

'BYUNG arise, *zhes 'byung ba*, according to, SKAR 26. *las 'byung ba*, according to, ZHWA W 30. E 43. SKAR 51. CANG (1) 9.

'BRAS rice, KONG 19.

'BRING middle, LT E 63, 67.

'BRING follow? (*'brang*) *zham-'bring*, service. ZHOL N 14. ZHWA W 34. cf. TLTD II 8(12) *zham ring.*

'BRUG dragon, ZHWA E 22.

'BROG grazing ground, ZHOL N 51. ZHWA W 53. KONG 18. CANG (1) 19.

SBAL treasury, archive? *phyag sbal*, ZHWA E 46. W 52. LT W 79.

SBYANG practice, Y.

SBYAR(D) add to, adhere to, SAM 7. ZHWA W 8, 20, 56. KONG 17. CANG (1) 18. LT E 10, W 49, 60.

SBYIN bestow, ZHWA W 21, 23, 44. E 19. CANG (1) 38.

SBREL join together, ZHWA W 61.

MANG many, ZHOL S 45, 61. LT W 19.

MAN downwards, KSD 20. ZHWA W 49. SKAR 35, 38. LT W 44.

MAR below, KSD 20.

MAL bed, LT W 54. Pell T. 16 (34b) *gnas gnas mal mal.*

MAS from below, the last? ZHWA W 44.

MING PO brother, ZHOL S 68.

MU boundary, limit, KDS 16.

MEN see PHRA MEN.

MO divination, SKAR 31.

MOL consult, confer, ZHWA E 20. KONG 30. LT E 2, 24, 27, 40, 46. W 5, 25.
MYI man, KSD 2, 32. ZHWA(F) 2. KONG 4, 9. KDS 2, 6, 11. LT E 8, 34, 52.
MYI MA YIN spirit, SAM 16. SKAR 54.
MYING name, ZHWA W 41. KONG 15. LT E 58, 62, 65, 66. W 51. N 3, 5, 25. S 3, 5, 18.
MYED not being, KSD 32. ZHWA W 13, 16. SKAR 21, 47. KDS 17, 21. CANG (1) 36. LT E 17, 36. W 19, 53.
MYES grandfather, ancestor, ZHOL N 43. KSD 1, 6. ZHWA W 33. ZHWA(F) 9. SKAR 4, 7, 10, 29, 48. CANG (1) 5.
DMAG war, army, ZHOL S 27, 54, 56. N 40. KDS 26. LT E 31, 49. W 32. N 10, 12.
DMANGS common people, ZHOL N 45. ZHWA E 26.
DMA'S to lower, degrade, ZHOL N 57. SKAR 50.
RMA enquire, investigate, ZHOL N 63. ZHWA W 38, 39.
RMOG helmet, see DBU. *dbu-rmog*, KSD 3, 12, 19. KDS 4. KONG 8. LT E 12, 16, 53.
RMYI dream, SKAR 31.
SMAD depreciate, reduce, ZHWA E 9.
SMON(D) pray, SAMB. CANG (1) 14.
SMOS speak, tell, ZHWA(F).
TSA = TSHA grandchild, KONG 14.
TSAM about as much, somewhat, *tsam zhig*, merely, KONG 10. KDS 12. *ji-tsam*, as much as ZHOL N 19. ZHWA W 34. E 7.
TSE = TSHE, time, ZHOL N 12 *tse-rabs*.
GTSANG an official post. ZHWA E 26. See note p. 57.
GTSIGS edict, solemn declaration. agreement, ZHOL N 2. SAM 20. ZHWA W 3, 24, 26, 27, 50, 51, 52, 53, 55, 57, 58, 60, E 3, 5, 8, 16, 17, 20, 23, 38, 40, 42, 44, 45, 46, 47, 48, KONG 1, 10, 11, 12, 13. SKAR 2, 27, 55, 56. LT E 45, 60, 64, 70. W 6, 60, 66, 67, 70, 72, 76. N 2. S 2. Pell T. 986.
GTSIGS = TSHIGS *gtan gtsigs*, the (connected) facts, ZHOL S 16.
GTSUG the order of the world, KDS 3. See note p. 39.
GTSUG LAG *do.* KSD 2, 7. KDS 5. LT E 8, 20.
GTSUG LAG KHANG temple, SAM 2, ZHWA W 26. E 40. SKAR 5, 8, 11, 14, 16. CANG(1) 2, 16, 23, 25, 32, 38, 40, 43, 45. (2) 17.
GTSES injure, trouble, KONG 10.
BTSAN powerful, *btsan-po*, the ruler of Tibet, ZHOL S 1, 8, 11, 16, 41, 52, 65. N 5, 12, 21. SAM 11, 18. SAMB. KSD 1, 5, 16. KONG 1, 4, 5, 12. SKAR 1, 4, 23, 26, 33, 45, 47, 52, 54. KHRA. KDS 1, 6, 13. CANG (1) 3, 5, 10, 14, 21, 24. LT E 1, 5, 16, 22, 25, 28, 34, 42, 51. W 2.
BTSA' look at, look after, ZHWA W 34. *btsas* (pf.) ZHWA W 34.
BTSAL look for, ZHOL N 60.
BTSUGS establish, SAM 4. ZHWA W 27. SKAR 7, 9, 12, 15, 18, 24, 30, 45. CANG (1) 17. LT E 9.
BTSUD cause to enter, SKAR 39.
RTSAL *rtsol*? to strive, KDS 46.
RTSIS count, calculate, *rtsis-pa*, finance office, LT N 36.
RTSEG pile up, accumulate, *rtseg-ma*, accumulation, LT E 38.
STSANG grain, *stsang ra,* granary KONG 19.
STSAL(D) bestow, appoint, ZHOL E 4, S 28, 58. N 11, 30, 37. KONG 11, 14, 17. CANG (1) 8, 12, 44. See also BKA'.
STSOGS = *sogs* etcetera, *la stsogs-pa*, LT E 15. *las stsogs-pa*, ZHOL S 64. N 52. KSD 13. ZHWA W 9, 14, 30, 45. E 27, 33. ZHWA(F) 7. SKAR 6, 8, 13, 17, 18, 26, 32. CANG (1) 20, 30, 36.
STSON = *rtsod*? contend, ZHWA W 11.
BRTSAN firm, KSD 5, 12, 19. ZHWA W 24. E 35. KONG 8. KDS 5, 8, 23. CANG (1) 34. LT E 12, 16, 49, 53.
BRTSAL incite? LT E 47.

BRTSIGS build, SKAR 6, 9, 11, 14, 18. CANG (1) 2, 16.
BRTSEG pile up. accumulate, cf. RTSEG *brtseg-mar*, accumulation, LT W 24.
GSTSAN(D) = *gsan*, hear, ZHOL N 59. ZHWA W 36.
TSHA = *tsha-bo*, grandchild, see BU TSHA.
TSHAD measure, *tshad kha*, measure, LT W 24.
TSHAB in place of, LT E 30.
TSHAR complete, finish, LT E 46.
TSHAL woodland, ZHOL N 52. ZHWA W 43. LT E 61. (KHRA?).
TSHAL ? food, ZHOL N 16. but see note 6, p. 19.
TSHIG word, *tha tshig*, solemn words, oath, LT W 64.
TSHIGS connection, ZHOL N 25. *gtan tshigs*, the facts, ZHOL S 15. LT E 4. *sa tshigs*, a transport stage, KONG 19.
TSHUN hither, *tshun cad* (*chad*), thereafter, KONG 4, 9. KDS 27, 41, 43. LT E 5. *phan tshun*, hither and thither, on either side, LT E 17, 29, 31, 39, 43. W 31, 40.
TSHUL manner, ZHWA W 22. LT E 3, 33, 50, 52. W 47.
TSHE time, ZHOL S 52. KONG 6. LT E31. lifetime, ZHWA(F) 5. *sku tshe*, LT E 42. *tshe tshe rabs rabs* LT W 9.
TSHEGS trouble, *phran tshegs*, small matters, cf. KHO 83 a. *tshegs,* and word index p. 148 *tshegs chen pos.* TLTD II 236 (87).
TSHES date, LT E 59, 63, 67.
TSHES see *khyim tshes*, neighbour (*khyim -mtshes,* Das Dictionary).
MTSHAN name, KSD 33. CANG (1) 23.
MTSHAMS frontier, boundary, KSD 20. LT W 27. *sa mtshams* LT W 52.
MTSHUNGS like, KDS 8.
MTSHO ocean, LT E 18.
'TSHAMS suitable, KONG 16.
'TSHAL ask, ZHWA E 18. KONG 10.
MDZAD do, ZHOL S 44. N 58, 68. SAM 5. KSD 8, 12. ZHWA W 29, 35, 40, 59. E 1, 41. KONG 7, 10. SKAR 5, 19, 24, 28, 33, 35, 48, 51. KDS 7, 16, 27. CANG (1) 7, 27. LT E 2, 3, 6, 37, 52, 56. W 6, 26, 37.
MDZOD treasury, CANG (2) 18.
'DZIN hold, ZHWA W 22. LT W 75. N 2. S 2. Y.
'DZEGS ascend, LT E 60, 64.
RDZAS things, *nor rdzas*, wealth, CANG (1) 19.
BRDZANGS despatch. LT W 35.
ZHA ever, *nam nam zha zhar*, forever, ZHOL N 8. ZHWA W 30, 32, 46, 47. E 42. SKAR 22.
ZHA = *zhal*? face, presence, *zha snga nas*, by (high honorific) ZHOL N 6. KSD 5, 13. ZHWA W 48. E 35. KDS 14, 22. LT E 34, 51. *zha-sngar*, to the presence, ZHOL N 22, 62. ZHWA W1 15. E 11.
ZHANG maternal uncle; ZHWA W 6. title of families related to *btsan-po* by marriage, ZHOL S 57. CANG (1) 1, 9, 12, 33, 35. (2) 1. LT N 10, 18, 20, 26, 30, 38. *dbon zhang*, Nephew and Uncle, relationship between *btsan-po* and Emperor of China, LT E 28, 33, 42, 46, 54. W 4, 38, 47.
ZHANG perhaps equivalent to the Chinese title *shang. zhang lon,* ministers in general, ZHOL N 40, ZHWA W 49, E 36/37 part of Chinese title, LT S *passim.* See note 12 (p. 53).
ZHAM = *zhabs*? *zham-'bring*, service ZHOL N 14. ZHWA W 34. See 'BRING.
ZHAR forever, see ZHA. nam zhar, ZHOL N 48. KSD 26. ZHWA E 34. KONG 14. KSD 18. LT E 12. W 7, 61. *nam nam zha zhar* ZHOL N 8. ZHWA W 30, 32, 46, 47. E 42. SKAR 22.
ZHAL face, mouth, *bka' zhal*, command, CANG (1) 24. *zhal gyis bshags*, made a declaration, LT W 71. *zhal-ce-pa*, a judicial officer, LT N 39.
ZHAL BU ? ZHWA (F) 10.

ZHIG one, some, ZHOL N 33, 57. ZHWA W 38. E 29. LT W 33. *nam zhig*, ever, ZHWA W 58. CANG (1) 35. *nam zhig*, permanent, KSD 10. *tsam zhig*, merely, KONG 10. KDS 12. *la la zhig*, some, ZHOL N 28, 56, 61. ZHWA W 37.
ZHIG imperative sign, *lta zhig*, just consider! as regards, ZHWA 4. KONG 9. LT E 37.
ZHIG destroy, SAM 6. SKAR 20, 21, 25, 50. CANG (1) 36.
ZHING field, ZHOL N 51. ZHWA W 43. KONG 18. CANG (1) 19.
ZHING extent, KDS 4. LT E 11, 12.
ZHING participle, *re re zhing*, each, SAM 10. SKAR 51.
ZHIB fine, precise. *zhib-tu*, in detail, ZHWA E 45. *zhib mo*, detailed, SAM 20. KSD 14. ZHWA W 52. SKAR 56. *zhib mor*, in detail LT W 73.
ZHU offer, *sri zhu*, respect, LT W 23, 48. E 43.
ZHUGS enter, ZHOL S 51. LT E 21.
ZHEN desire, ZHWA W 6.
ZHES so saying, KONG 10. SKAR 31. LT E 8. *zhes 'byung ba* SKAR 26.
ZHO milk, *zho sha*, milk and meat, offerings, ZHWA W 20, 23, 51, 56. E 5, 6, 9, 16, 19, 22. Pell T. 1091 (22). See note 4 (p. 49).
GZHAG put (fut.) ZHWA W 34, 62. CANG (1) 46. (2) 19. See BZHAG.
GZHAN other, another, ZHOL N 23, 42, 53, 63. KSD 18. ZHWA W 35, 38, 39, 44. E 32. CANG (2) 8, 12. LT E 19.
GZHAR ever, cf. ZHAR. KDS 3.
GZHIG destroy, be destroyed, SKAR 32.
GZHUG be appointed, ZHOL N 15, 42. KONG 14. SKAR 57.
BZHAG put (pf.) ZHWA W 28, 52. E 41, 47, 48. CANG (1) 42. (2) 9, 13. LT W 77.
BZHI four, KSD 17. CANG 18.
BZHIN like, according to, KSD 6. ZHWA W 61. E 6, 21. CANG (1) 9, 34. LT W 41 *bzhin du*, ZHWA E 34. KONG 11, 20. SKAR 28, 44, 51, 52, KDS 6. LT W 47, 67.
BZHUD go away, ZHWA (F) 3.
BZHUGS dwell, ZHWA E 23. KONG 5, 6. SKAR 34. KHRA.
BZHES receive, take, ZHOL N 30, 35, 52. ZHWA W 11, 44, 45. KDS 25. CANG (1) 30, 37.
ZAR to eat, ZHOL N 16. but see note 6 (p. 19) ? tassel.
ZIN hold, ZHWA W 12.
ZUNG = *zungs,* power, *zung thub*, KDS 14.
ZUR side, ZHWA W 57.
ZLA moon, LT W 63. *zlas*, by the moon, LT W 57.
ZLA companion, pair, SKAR 56. CANG (2) 9, 12. *zla dpe,* precedent, ZHWA W 20. E 6.
GZA planet, LT W 63.
GZUNGS = *gzung,* interest, ZHWA W 16.
GZUD to lead SKAR 38.
BZANG good, ZHOL N 54. KSD 3, 29. KDS 2, 9, 21. LT E 9, 16, 20, 45. Y.
BZUNG take hold of, ZHWA W 14. LT E 60, 64. W 34.
BZLOG rout, defeat, ZHOL S 61.
'OG below, after, ZHOL N 49. KDS 45? LT E 22. lower, *'og-dpe* lower copy, secondary copy, ZHWA W 54 CANG (1) 43. (2) 15. *chabs 'og*, beneath the sway of, KONG 8. *bla 'og*, high and low, ZHWA W 7, 16. E 14, 32.
'ONG come, SKAR 22.
'ONGS come (pf.) *ma 'ongs*, the future, Y.
'OS suitable, ZHWA W 34. E 7. KONG 17.
YA upper, *ya rabs*, upper class, SKAR 38.
YANG *yang thag par*, certainly, LT W 30. *yan dag pa*, certain ZHWA W 36. *yang dag par*, certainly, ZHOL N 62.
YANGS wide, KDS 14.
YAN above, beyond, *yan cad*, ZHOL N 15. KSD 21. ZHWA W 60. SKAR 34. LT W 46, 52.
YAB father, ZHOL S 8, 49. SAM 20. SAMB. ZHWA W 5, 7, 9. KONG 1, 20. SKAR 12, 23, 26, 28, 44, 52, 56. CANG (1) 5. See MYES, YUM, SRAS.

YAR upwards, KSD 19.
YAS from above, KONG 6. cf. YA.
YI GE letter, ZHOL N 9, 32, 34, 37. SAM 20. KSD 9, 14. ZHWA W 30, 40, 52. E 24, 42, 46. SKAR 27, 56. LT E 67. W 73, 77. cf. YIG *yi-ge-pa*, holding a letter, ZHOL N 40. *yi-ge-can*, ZHWA E, 27/28.
YI = *yid*? *yi dam*, vow, SAM 12. SKAR 50. *thugs yi dam*. LT E 33/34.
YIG letter, ZHOL N 3. SKAR 50. CANG (1) 41. LT W 76.
YID mind, *yid ma ches-pa*, untrustworthy, LT W 33.
YUG a length, piece (of silk etc.) ZHOL S 48.
YUN a period of time, enduring, LTE 9 *yun-gyi legs-pa*, good for (all) time. *yun-tu*, for (all) time, ZHWA W 25, 41. E 38. SKAR 2. KDS 5. *yun ring-po*, a long time, LT W 21. *'phral-yun*, now and for all time. ZHWA W 18.
YUM mother, *yab yum* father and mother, ZHWA W 5. *yum sras* mother and son. SAMB. ZHWA W 71.
YUL country, lands, ZHOL S 53. N 41, 46. KSD 24. KONG 4, 6. KDS 18, 26, 43. LT E 5, 7, 38, 57, 61. W 27, 31, 33, 49, 58, 59. *khol-yul*, service-tenure lands. ZHOL N 29. CANG (1) 36.
YO GAL an official post, ZHOL E 3. Pell T. 1091, l. 26.
YO BYAD furnishings, SAM 7.
YONG certain, *yong yang*, furthermore, KONG 8. LT E 50. cf. TLTD II 93 A 1 and 3.
YONGS all, the whole, KSD 9, 24, 32. SKAR 37. KDS 11, 17.
YON gift, offering, *yon bdag*, donor, KHRA. *sku yon*, offering donation, CANG (1) 14, 22.
YON TAN good qualities, KSD 9. cf. KHO 171b 7. 172a 1.
YOS BU hare (year), LT E 66.
G-YA right (direction), LT E 15 see G-YO.
G-YUNG DRUNG unchanging, enduring, like the swastika, ZHWA E 24. KONG 9. KDS 5. LT E 13. *g-yung-drung-du,* in perpetuity, ZHOL N 10, 37, 46. ZHWA W 3, 24, 50.
G-YUL battle, *g-yul bzlog*, win a battle.
G-YO left (direction) LT E 15.
RA enclosure, *stsang -ra*, granary, KONG 19.
RA BA first month of a season, *dgun sla ra-ba*, first month of winter, LT E 59.
RANG self, *rang nyid*, KDS 15.
RAN proper, suitable, ZHWA E 9.
RAB excellent, the best, *rab tu*, excellently, KDS 47. *rab tu byung ba*, become a monk, enter religion, SKAR 43.
RAB ford, ZHOL S 59.
RABS lineage, ZHOL N 28, 33. ZHWA W 43. *rgyud rabs* KONG 15, 16: *ya rabs*, upper classes, SKAR 38: generation, *tshe tshe rabs rabs*, LT E 22. *gdung rabs,* SAM 10. ZHWA W 32. KONG 4. SKAR 18, 25, 29, 51, CANG (1) 6. *phyi rabs*, ZHWA E 41. *tse-rabs*, ZHOL N. 12.
RAS *spyan ras*, watch over, regard, ZHWA W 33.
RING life-time, ZHOL S 2. KONG 1, 12, 20. SKAR 1, 5, 8, 10, 13, 16, 23, 49. *sku ring la*, ZHWA E 12. KONG 13. CANG (1) 6.
RING(S) long, *yun ring-po*, a long time, LT W 21. *glo-ba rings*, distant, disloyal, ZHOL S 7, 15, 18. N 22, 59, 62. and see RDO.
RING LUGS established tradition, juridical or religious; also one who carries on that tradition; registrar, abbot. ZHWA W 59, 62. SKAR 40, 42, CANG (1) 42. See note p. 53.
RIM due order, *rim gro*, service, respect, KONG 7.
RIS a portion, *rkyen ris*, estate provided for support, CANG (1) 32. *lha ris*, monastic estate, ZHWA E 31. SKAR 50. CANG (1) 28, 30.

RUNG right, proper, *ma rung* ZHOL S 52. LT E 50: *yang-rung* whatever, ZHOL N 23. ZHWA E 29. KONG 19. SKAR 32, 49.
RUS bone, lineage, LT N 3, 8, 25. S 3, 5.
RE each, ZHOL N 13. SAM 10. SKAR 51.
RLAG destroy, ZHWA 41. KONG 15.
RLABS wave, abundance, overflow, KSD 27. KDS 9.
LA see STSOGS, *la stsogs-pa* etcetera, LT E 15.
LA mountain pass, KSD 21.
LA LA some, *la la zhig*, someone, ZHOL N 28, 56, 61. ZHWA W 37.
LAG hand, ZHOL N 33, 51, LT W 76. See also GTSUG LAG.
LAN requital, ZHWA W 23. E 19. retribution, LT W 69.
LAM road, way, LT W. *smon-lam*, prayer, CANG (1) 14.
LAS work, actions, ZHWA W 8, 15, 17, 35, 36, 41. E 14. KONG 19? SKAR 42. KDS 16. *'phrin las*, KSD 11.
LAS from, *las 'byung ba*, arising from, ZHWA W 30. E 42/43. SKAR 51. CANG (1) 9. *las stsogs-pa* etcetera, see STSOGS.
LUGS custom, manner, KSD 6. ZHWA W 22. KDS 2, 7, 10. LT E 10, 16. W 41, 48. and see RING LUGS.
LUNG command, order, *bka'-lung*, ZHOL E 6. KDS 9, 21. CANG (1) 7.
LEGS good, ZHOL E 15. S 44. ZHWA W 6, 8, 13, 14, 18. E 13. SKAR 20, 31. KDS 10, 21. LT E 48. W 16.
LO year, ZHOL S 47. ZHWA E 22. LT E 21, 24, 27, 58, 59, 62, 63, 65, 66, 67. *lo rgyus*, history, CANG (1) 3.
LOGS direction, LT E 19.
LON pass (of time) LT E 22.
LON minister, cf. BLON. *zhang lon*, official, ZHOL 40. ZHWA W 49. E 27, 37. See Richardson. "Names and Titles".
SHA meat, *zho sha*, milk and meat offerings, ZHWA W 20, 23, 51. E 5, 6, 10, 16, 19, 22. See note 4 (p. 49).
SHA KON resentment, grudge, ZHOL N 56.
SHAR rise (of the sun) LT E 19.
SHAR east, KSD 22. KDS 23, LT E 18, 61. W 28.
SHIG imperative, *gyis shig*, act! ZHWA W 31.
SHE DAG merely, LT E 48.
SHES know, ZHWA W 25. KDS 11. LT W 8.
GSHEGS go, ZHOL S 10. KSD 2. KONG 4, 6. LT E 8.
BSHAGS avow, declare, LT W 72.
BSHAD explain, LT W 65.
BSHIG destroy, violate, LT W 68, 70.
BSHES know, be friends with, *dge-ba'i bshes nyen*, friend of virtue, religious adviser, SKAR 36, 43.
BSHOS beget, KONG 6.
SA earth, place, KSD 8. ZHWA (F) 2. LT E 5. W 54. *sa mtsham*, frontier, LT W 52. *sa tshigs*, staging post, KONG 19. *bka' sa*, council office, CANG (2) 13. *rgyal sa*, capital, LT E 21. *'dun sa*, assembly place, CANG (1) 42.
SANG tomorrow, *deng sang*, nowadays, KONG 9.
SU who, *su la*, ZHWA E 29. *sus*, SKAR 33.
SUM three, ZHOL N 40.
SEMS mind, ZHOL S 41, 73. *sems can*, KHRA.
SO frontier, LT E 29.
SO guard, *khab so*, revenue officers, ZHOL E 10. KONG 10. LT N 32.
SOG fallow land, ZHOL N 51. ZHWA W 43.
SOD prosper, ZHOL S 29. = *bsod*? See note (p. 11).
SOL request, KHRA. cf. *gsol*.

SRAS son, ZHOL S 11, 16, 50. ZHWA (F) 5. KONG 3, 5, *sras dbon*, descendants, ZHOL N 12. ZHWA W 29, 59. *yab sras*, father and son(s), SAM 11, 18. SAMB. ZHWA W 7. KONG 1. SKAR 26, 44, 48, 52. *yum sras* SAMB. ZHWA W 7. *lha sras*, son of god, prince, KONG 5, 7, 8, 12, 13, 19, 20. KDS 1, 6, 13. CANG (1) 5, 11. *dbon sras*, SKAR 34, 48. KDS 18/19.

SRI ZHU respect, LT W 23, 48. E 43.

SRID position, status, state, ZHOL S 13, 25, N 67. ZHWA W 24, 46. LT E 9, 19, 21. W 59. *srog srid*, life and position, ZHOL N 23, 64. ZHWA E 28. *chab-srid*, dominion, kingdom, see CHAB. *chos-srid*, religion and the state, LT E 35.

SRUNG(S) guard, protect, LT W 27, 52. *sku srungs*, ZHOL N 41, 45, 49.

SROG life, ZHOL N 67. *srog srid* see SRID, ZHOL N 23, 64. ZHWA E 28. *srog phongs*, sparing of one's life, KONG 7. cf. DTH 105 (2) T.986 (59), Pell. *srog spongs 'tshal re. srog la 'bab pa man cad*, from risking one's life downwards, KONG 7. cf. Pell T. 134 (16/17), *srog srid la phab pa man cad. srog chags*, animal LT W 65.

SLA = *zla*, month, LT E 59, 63, 67. cf. TLTD II 43, 5.

SLAD after, ZHWA E 3. for the sake of, SAMB.

SLAN after, *slan chad*, hereafter, KONG 18.

SLAR again LT E 12.

SLOB teach, SKAR 37.

SLEBS come, LT W 57.

GSAR new, ZHWA E 24. LT E 41.

GSAL clear, LT E 35.

GSUNG voice, speech, SAMB.

GSOL(D) request offer, ZHOL S 17, 39, 55. SAM 18. KSD 34. ZHWA W 8, 13, 22. E 12, 13, 18. KONG 3, 6, 11, 16. SKAR 33, 54. KDS 29, 44. LT W 64.

BSAD kill, LT W 65.

BSAB repay, CANG (1) 13.

BSALD clear up, LT E 41.

BSOD good, *bsod nams*, merit, good fortune, SAMB.

BSRING extend, KONG 19.

BSRIS be sparing, take care, LT E 31.

BSLAS = to weave a rope or basket. Sumatiratna p. 1290. LTE 41. conjoin.

LHA god, SAM 16. KSD 2. KONG 9. SKAR 54. LT W 8. lha'i KSD 7. ZHWA(F) 5. KHRA. *lhas* ZHWA E 1. *lha bdag*, divine master, KONG 7. *lha 'phrul* divine manifestation, KDS 13, 22, 33. LTE 34. *lha btsan-po*, the divine *btsan-po*, SAMB. KONG 1, 5. SKAR 15. *'phrul gyi lha btsan-po*, KSD 16. ZHWA W 1. E 1. SKAR 1, 4, 22. KDS 13, 22. LT E 1, 5, 16, 22, 25, 51. W 2, 12. *lha ris*, monastic estate, ZHWA E 31. SKAR 50. CANG 28, 30. *lha sras*, divine son, prince, KONG 5, 7, 8, 12, 13, 19, 20. KDS 1, 6, 13, CANG (1) 5, 11.

LHAG exceedingly, ZHWA W 19. LT E 38.

LHAB = *lhabs*, middle, ZHWA W 1. See note 1 (p. 47).

LHO south, KSD 22. KDS 29, 44. LT E 13.

LHO BAL barbarians, LT E 19. See note 3 (p. 111).

NAMES IN THE INSCRIPTIONS

Chinese names in italic; identifications by Li Fang-kuei marked L; those by Hisashi Sato marked S.

KWA CHU in Brag-mar SKAR 11.
KWAG TSHUNG, Kuo ts'ung (L) LT S 38.
KWANG PENG WANG ZHOL S 61/62.
KAR PO KONG 6, 12, 15. cf. RKONG DKAR PO.
KAR PO RGYALBRTSAN KONG 15.
KAR PO MANG PO RJE KONG 3, 14, 15.
KIM SHANG LT E 28.
KIM SHENG ZHOL S 67.
KENG LUNG, Ching lung (L) LT E 27
KENG SHI, Ching shih (L) ZHOL S 56, 59, 62, 63. LT E 57, 71.
KLU KHONG ZHOL S 14, 20, 72. See NGAN LAM STAG SGRA KLU KHONG.
KLU BZANG RMYES RMA (*'Bal blon*) LT N 34.
KLU BZANG LHA BO BRTSAN (*'Bro zhang*) LT N 39.
RKONG KAR PO KONG 18.
RKONG DKAR PO KONG 2.
RKONG YUL KONG 6.
SKAR CUNG SKAR 16.

KHAR TSAN ZHOL S 265.
KHRI 'DUS SRONG SKAR 7.
KHRI LDE GTSUG RTSAN (BRTSAN) ZHOL S 1/2, 8/9. SKAR 10. LT E 25.
KHRI LDE SRONG BRTSAN ZHWA W 1/2. E 2. KHRA. SKAR 1, 15/16. KDS 6, 13. LT E 34.
KHRI GTSUG LDE BRTSAN CANG (1) 11, 21. LT E 1, 51. W 12/13.
KHRI BTSAN KHOD NE STANG (*zhang*) LT N 19/20.
KHRI BTSAN x x x BZHER (*blon*) LT N 17/18.
KHRI BZHER LHA MTHONG (*zhang*) LT N 21/22.
KHRI RTSE of Gling (SKAR 8).
KHRI SUM RJE (*zhang*) LT N 10.
KHRI SRONG LDE BRTSAN ZHOL S 11, 16/17, 21, 42. N 5. SAMB. KSD 5, 16/17. KONG 1, 12. SKAR 12/13, 23.
KHRI SRONG BRTSAN SKAR 3. LT E 23.

GYIM PO ZHWA (F) 7.
GLING KHRI RTSE SKAR 8.
'G'IU SING ZHU, Niu seng-ju (L) LT S 22.
RGYA China ZHOL S 31, 48, 60. KDS 24, 26. LT E 3, 18, 56, 58, 62, 66. W 26, 29, 42, 44, 59, 68, 71. S 1, 4, 17. Rgya'i ZHOL S 25, 30, 32, 44. KHRA. KDS 26. LT E 68. W 3. RGYAS, KDS 28. LT E 60. W 44.
RGYA GAR India, KDS 29. LT E 14.
RGYA RJE The Chinese Emperor, ZHOL S 54, 63. LT E 42.
RGYA RJE *KWANG PENG WANG (Taitsung)* ZHOLS 61. See *WANG PENG WANG.*
RGY RJE THE'E TSONG B'UN BU SHING HWANG TE, (T'ai tsung) LT E 23.
RGYA RJE *B'UN B'U HE'U TIG HWANG TE* (*Mu tsung*) LT E 1/2, 54. W 13/14.
RGYA RJE *WANG PENG WANG* (*Tai tsung*) ZHOL S 50. See KWANG PENG WANG.
RGYA RJE *ZHENG SHIN B'UN B'U HWANG TE* (*Tse tsung*) LT E 39/40.
RGYA RJE *LI* (*Li yuan: Kao tsung*) LT E 21.

NAMES IN THE INSCRIPTIONS

RGYA RJE *SAM LANG KHA'E 'GWAN SHENG B'UN B'U HWANG TE* (*Hsuan tsung*) LT E 26
RGYA RJE *HE'U 'KI WANG TE* (*Su tsung*) ZHOL S 46/47, 49/50.
RGYA YUL ZHOL S 53. KDS 26.
RGYAL NYEN LEGS TSAN (*Myang blon*) LT N 41.
RGYAL MO BRTSAN (*Jo-mo*) SAMB.
RGYAL BRTSAN (*Kar-po*) KONG 15, 16.
RGYAL BZHER KHOD NE BRTSAN (*Mchims zhang*) LT N 27/28.
RGYAL BZANG 'DUS KONG (*blon*) LT N 23/24.

NGAN LAM KLU KHONG ZHOL S 3, 22, 53. See KLU KHONG: STAG SGRA KLU KHONG.
NGAN LAM GSAS SLEBS ZHOL N 47. (43).
RNGEGS BLON STAG ZIGS RGAN KOL LT N 33.

CANG KENG (*Ch'ang k'ing*) LT E 59, 62, 66.
CA'U TSONG SHU, Chao Tsung-ju (L) LT S 31.
CI'U CIR, Chou chih (S) ZHOL S 59.
CENG KWAN, Cheng kuan (L) LT E 24.
COG RO BLON BTSAN BZHER LHO GONG LT N 29/30.
BCOM LDAN 'DA'S SKAR 40, 41. CANG (1) 41/42.
LCANG BU CANG (1) 2, 15.

CHO PHYI ZHWA(F) 5.
MCHING PHU SKAR 11.
MCHIMS RGYAL RGYAL ZIGS SHU THENG (*zhang*) ZHOL S 57.
MCHIMS ZHANG RGYAL BZHER KHO NE BRTSAN LY N 27/28.
MCHIMS ZHANG BRTAN BZHER STAG TSAB LT N 31.

NYA KHYI KONG 5.
NYA KHRI KONG 4.
NYA STO (*zhang*) CANG 12, 33, 35. See ZHANG TSHES PONG NYA STO: ZHANG TSHES PONG STAG BZANG NYA STO.
GNYAN PO (*sku bla*) KONG 6.
TA ZHIG KSD 20. LT E 14.
TANG LT E 21.
TING NGE 'DZIN (*Ban-de Myang*). ZHWA W 2/2, 4, 12, 32, 50, 54, 56. E 3, 4, 11, 21.
STAG SGRA KLU KHONG (*blon*) ZHOL E 1. S 58, N 1, 7, 31, 35, 38, 43, 66. See NGAN LAM.
STAG BZHER HAB KEN (*Bran-ka*) LT N 35/36.
STAG ZIGS RGAN KOL (*Rngegs blon*) LT N 37/38.
STAG BZANG NYA STO (*Zhang Tshes pong*) CANG (1) 1.
STOD CANG (1) 2.
STOD LUNG CANG (1) 15.
BRTAN BZHER STAG TSAB (*Mchims zhang*) LT N 31/32.
THE'E TSONG B'UN BU SHING HWANG TE (*Rgya-rje*) LT E 23.

DE MO (*sku bla*) KONG 6.
D'O 'GWAN YWENG (*Tu yuan-ying*) LT S 13/14.
DO TSE'E (*Tu tsai*) LT E 69.
DONG KWAN ZHOL S 64.
DRI GUM BTSAN PO KONG 5.
DRU GU LT E 14.
MDA' MI ZHWA(F) 6.

NAMES IN THE INSCRIPTIONS

'DUS SRONG (*Khri*) SKAR 7.
LDE SRONG KONG 13, 20. See KHRI LDE SRONG BRTSAN.
LDONG TSAB (*'Bal*) ZHOL S 5.

NO SMAL LT E 15.
SNANG BZANG 'DUS KONG *blon* (*of Myang*) ZHWA W 33, 37, 42, 46, E 25/26.
PO LDONG TSE MYAG ZHWA(F) 9.
DPAL CHEN PO YON TAN (*Ban-de chen-po*) LT N 9.

PHYWA YA BLA BDAG DRUG KONG 3.
PHYING BA STAG RTSE KONG 4/5.
PHYING BA'I SKUN MKHAR CANG (2) 5.
'PHAN YUL ZHOL N 41, 45/46.

BAL LT E 19.
BE'I BU, Pe'i wu (L) LT S 33.
BO KEN YA ZHOL S 65.
BOD Tibet ZHOL E 13. S 51, 54, 57, 60, 61. KSD 24. SKAR 36, 37, 48, 47. LT E 3, 6, 20, 56, 57, 61, 64, 65. W 1, 26, 30, 42, 45, 58, 68, 71. N 1, 4, 25.
BRAG MAR SAM 1. SKAR 10, 13.
BRAN KA BLON STAG BZHER HAB KEN LT N 35.
DBA'S ZHWA W 56.
DBYAR MO THANG ZHOL S 33.
DBYI GONG ZHWA W 55.
'BAL ZHOL S 5, 14, 18. LT N 33. 'BAL BLON KLU BZANG RMYES RMA.
'BYE'U TSIN KENG, Miao tsin keng (S) ZHOL S 64.
'BRO ZHANG KLU BZANG LHA BO BRTSAN LY N 39.
SBRA STOD TSHAL LT W 61. See LHA SA.
MANG PO RJE (*Kar-po*) KONG 3, 14.
MU RUG BTSAN ZHWA W 48.
MUN SHENG KONG CO LT E 24.
MON RGYA GAR LT E 14.
MYANG ZHWA W 56, 57.
MYANG TING NGE 'DZIN (*Ban-de*) ZHWA W 2/3. E 3. See TING NGE 'DZIN.
MYANG BLON RGYAL NYEN LEGS TSAN LT N 40.
MYES ZIGS (of *Lang*) ZHOL S 6.

TSANG KUN YOG, Chiang-chun ku (L) LY W 42/43.
TSENG SHU HYWAN, Ch'ing-shui hsien (L) LT W 45.
TSONG KA ZHOL S 34.
BTSAN BZHER LHO GONG (*Cog-ro blon*) LT N 29.
STSE ZHUNG CHEG, Sui-jung cha (L) LT W 43.
TSHAL KHRA.
TSHES PONG NYA STO CANG (1) 9. See NYA STO.
TSHES PONG STAG BZANG NYA STO (*zhang*) CANG (1) 1. See above.
TSHES PONG GSAS STO (*zhang*) CANG (2) 1/2.
WANG PHA, Wang po (L) LT S 11.
WANG PENG WANG ZHOL S 50.
WU'I ZHI'U, Wei shou (L) LT S 29.
ZHENG SHIN B'UN BU HWANG TE (*Rgya-rje*) LT E 39/40.
ZLA GONG (of *Ngan-lam*) ZHOL N 13, 17, 21, 27, 36, 39, 50, 55, 58.

'A ZHA ZHOL S 30.
'ON CANG DO ZHWA E 23. CANG (1) 25.

NAMES IN THE INSCRIPTIONS

YA BLA BDAG DRUG KONG 3.
YANG U LING, Yang yü-ling LT S 27.

RA SA SAM 1. SKAR 5.
RIN CAN KHRA
RIN CHEN LHUN PO (p. 157).
LANG ZHOL S 15, 18.
LANG MYES ZIGS ZHOL S 5.
LI rgya-rje LT E 21.
LI K'ANG Li Chiang (L) LT S 24.
LI KRI BU LT E 70.
LI'U KONG CAG, Liu Kung-ch'o (L) LT S 35.
LI'U 'GWAN TENG, Liu Yüan-ting (L) LT S 40.
LI'U SHI LA'U, Liu Shih-lao LT S 43.
LONG SHAN KSD 20/21.

SHA KHYI KONG 5.
SHEG SANG SI'I LT E 57.
SSHEM CI'U, *Hsien-chou* (S) ZHOL S 63.

SANGS RGYAS SAM 4/5. SKAR 5, 19, 24, 30.
SAM LANG KHA'E 'GWAN SHENG BU'N B'U HWANG TE, rgya-rje LT E 26.
S'EU B'EN, Hsiao mien (L) LT S 16.
GSAS STO *Tshes-pong* CANG (2) 2.
GSAS SLEBS (*Ngan-lam*) ZHOL N 43, 47.
BSAM YAS SKAR 13.

HAN KA'U, Han Kao (L) LT S 21.
HE'U 'KI WANG TE, Hsiao Kan Huang ti: Su-tsung, (S) ZHOL S 46/47, 49.

LHA RI GYANG DO KONG 4.
LHA SA LT E 61.
LHA'I ZUNG (*blon-po*) KONG 3.
LHO BAL LT E 19 See note 3 (p. 111) also Pell T 1091 l. 22.

GENERAL INDEX

For texts and translations see Vocabulary and index of names.

GENERAL INDEX

GENERAL INDEX

PLATE 1

The Lhasa Zhol pillar (See p. 1)

PLATE 2

The Lhasa Zhol pillar: east inscription (See p. 4)

PLATE 3

The Lhasa Zhol pillar: south inscription (See p. 6)

PLATE 4

The Bsam-yas pillar (See p. 26)

PLATE 5

Pillar at 'Phyong-rgyas (See p. 36)

PLATE 6

Zhwa'i Lha-Khang. The east pillar (See p. 43)

PLATE 7

Pillar at Zhwa'i Lha-Khang. Detail of east inscription (See pp. 54 and 56)

PLATE 8

Pillar at Zhwa'i Lha-Khang. Detail of east inscription (See p. 56)

PLATE 9

The Skar-cung pillar (See p. 72)

PLATE 10

The Skar-cung inscription. Detail (See pp. 76 and 78).

PLATE 11

Pillar at tomb of Khri Lde-srong-brtsan (See p. 84)

PLATE 12

The Lcang-bu pillar (See p. 92)

PLATE 13

The Lhasa Treaty pillar (See p. 106)

PLATE 14

The Lhasa Treaty pillar: east face, lines 24-49 and south face, lines 17-32
(See pp. 110, 112, 114, 138, 140)

PLATE 15

Pillar at Gtsang-grong
(See p. 155; from collection in the India Office Library and Archives)

PLATE 16

Pillar at Gtsang-grong
(See p. 155; from collection in the India Office Library and Archives)